Move Over, Santa—
Ruby's Doin' Christmas!

Move Over, Santa— Ruby's Doin' Christmas!

RUBY ANN BOXCAR

CITADEL PRESS
Kensington Publishing Corp.
www.kensingtonbooks.com

CITADEL PRESS books are published by

Kensington Publishing Corp.
850 Third Avenue
New York, NY 10022

All Kensington titles, imprints, and distributed lines are available at special quantity discounts for bulk purchases for sales promotions, premiums, fund-raising, educational, or institutional use. Special book excerpts or customized printings can also be created to fit specific needs. For details, write or phone the office of the Kensington special sales manager: Kensington Publishing Corp., 850 Third Avenue, New York, NY 10022, attn: Special Sales Department; phone 1-800-221-2647.

Photos by Ruby Ann's husband, Dew

The following are trademarks of their respective owners, who do not endorse this book: Amaretto DiSaronno, Amway, Aqua Net, Avon, Bailey's Irish Cream, BeDazzler, Bisquick, Chambord, Colby, Cool Whip, Crisco, Crock-Pot, Curaçao, Diet Coke, Ding Dong, Dr Pepper, Frito-Lay, Fry Daddy, Fun-Foam, Hawaiian Punch, Heinz, Jean Nate, Jell-O, Kahlua, Kellogg's, Kool-Aid, Lipton, Love My Carpet, M&M's Minis, Mary Kay, Merle Norman, Midori, Miracle Whip, Oreo, Oxi Clean, Pepto-Bismol, RC Cola, Red Hots, 7-UP, Shaklee, Spam, Splenda, SpongeBob SquarePants, Sprite, Target, Teflon, Tums, Tupperware, Velveeta, Wheaties, Worcestershire Sauce.

First printing: October 2004

10 9 8 7 6 5 4 3 2 1

Printed in the United States of America

Library of Congress Control Number: 2004109740

ISBN 0-8065-2665-3

I can only imagine that Christmas at the High Chaparral Trailer Park without the love of my family, my husband, Dew, my neighbors, or all my wonderful fans across the world would be somethin' similar to Ground Hog Day in the Antarctic. This book goes out to all y'all.

Contents

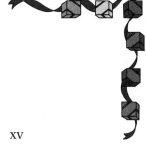

Preface   ix

An Inspirational Holiday Thought by Pastor Ida
    May Bee of the Holier Than Most Baptist Church   xv

Preparin' Yer Trailer Inside and Out for the
    Holiday Season   1

1   The First Day of Christmas   21

2   The Second Day of Christmas   49

3   The Third Day of Christmas   71

4   The Fourth Day of Christmas   91

5   The Fifth Day of Christmas   109

6   The Sixth Day of Christmas   131

7   The Seventh Day of Christmas   149

8   The Eighth Day of Christmas   171

9   The Ninth Day of Christmas   191

10   The Tenth Day of Christmas   207

11   The Eleventh Day of Christmas   229

12   The Twelfth Day of Christmas   249

13   Christmas Day Itself   275

Acknowledgments   289

Index   291

A snowy trailer park tribute to Ruby Ann, her husband, Dew, and her drunken sister, Donna Sue.

Preface

If I asked y'all to guess what our favorite time of the year is over at the High Chaparral Trailer Park, some of y'all, who obviously didn't read the title of this here book, would most likely guess the weekend in February when they hold the Daytona 500. Well, you'd be about as wrong as me in a two-piece swimsuit. The Daytona 500 comes in a close second among my fellow trailer dwellers and me only to what has been called the most wonderful time of the year, the Christmas season. Boy do we love Christmas! Sure it's colder than my late brother's ex-wife's heart, and busier than my drunken stripper sister at last call on a Saturday night, but we just can't wait for December to get here. The only problem we ever had was that Christmas Day was like a bad trailer park date. Before you knew it, it was on top of you. We'd start bakin' cookies, candy, pies, and other delightful trailer foods of the season right after Thanksgivin', send out our sure-to-be-late Christmas cards, and start our shoppin', only to find Christmas was just a day away. Naturally the blessed day would arrive in all its joyous glory. We'd rush to the livin' room to open the presents that Santa and his helpers had left for us, join our loved ones for a Christmas feast, and then before you could say, "I hope you kept the receipt for this," it was all over. Talk about your letdown! It was almost as disappointin' as the show over at the nearby Blue Whale Strip Club where my fifty-eight-year-old sister Donna Sue and our 350-pound neighbor Little Linda dance. And bein' the good Baptists that most of us are in the trailer park, we kind of felt bad that we were so dissatisfied on Christmas Day since the reason for the season, other than hopefully gettin' a tool set or some cookware from the local hardware store, was the celebration of our savior's birth. Even I, who happened to be a little girl at the time when all this first came up at the trailer park, felt bad for bein' so unhappy by Christmas afternoon. Of course, a little girl's corncob Christmas doll from Santa with a marshmallow head and licorice arms and legs can only last so long when you've got a pig in the house, but that's another story altogether—that even some fifty years later as an adult is still vividly burnt into my mind. Anyways, gettin' back to what I was sayin', we all had a trailer park residents meetin' in February of 1954 to try and see what we could do as a community to fix this. Nobody seems to recall who came up with the idea, but after a few openin' Christmas carols to get us in the holiday mood, which naturally were led by the then elementary school music teacher and trailer Lot #4 resident Nellie Tinkle, the adults took a vote, and they all agreed to follow the lead of our English friends, by celebratin' the twelve days of Christmas. It wasn't until later that we found out that the traditional celebration of Christmas in the Anglican and Catholic churches included these twelve days. Naturally upon hearin' this information, the president of the local chapter of the Baptist Association of Baptized Women (BABL) Gladys Bluemoker of Lot #12, mother of our very own Sister Bertha, demanded to change her vote. She wanted nothin' to do with some kind of "Roman holiday." Luckily Pastor Pickle of the local Baptist church, which all of us folks attended, was at the second meetin' that Gladys had called in order to change her vote. He'd been asked to act as a spiritual leader at this meetin' by many of those who lived in the trailer park. Pastor Pickle pointed out to Gladys that most of the good Baptists over in England celebrate the twelve days of

Christmas as well, which kind of nipped the whole thing in the bud. But it was my momma who tied the rock to the dilemma and threw it into the river when she suggested that instead of celebratin' the twelve days of Christmas beginnin' on December 25 like it's normally done, we could celebrate 'em before December 25. It'd be more like a buildup to Christmas rather than an afterthought. As you can imagine, everybody in the park agreed to this proposal. And now, fifty some odd years later, we still agree that addin' them twelve days to our Christmas celebration was the best thing we've ever done. Why, now the holiday season at the High Chaparral Trailer Park is as fun and excitin' as one of them Target commercials. I tell you, the warmth of the Yuletide bein' shared and marked as a countdown to Christmas Day is somethin' that's so special it's almost a sin not to share it, which is why I decided to take pen to paper and write this here book. But even if you and your family decide that you ain't got time for more celebratin', which really is too bad, you can still use these down-home ideas, crafts, recipes, and even my personal memories of this special time that comes only once a year to make your Christmas celebration better than it's ever been.

There are a lot of Christmas books out there that folks either give as gifts or use to plan their holiday season, but personally when I started readin' some of 'em, I was completely appalled. They was either givin' you recipes that would've required you to hire a chef just to prepare, or some kind of pie that your kids would've spit in the trash and your dog would've even passed on. And the decoratin' tips would've taken you and a team of twelve all year long to make and put up. They took a simple holiday like Christmas and turned it into manual labor that no one everyday person like you or me could've ever completed. Instead, after tryin' our hand at their crafts, recipes, or even decoratin' ideas, they'd have left us feelin' like complete failures. Why, even the gift books of memories past were so full of garbage that I had to keep a paper sack near me while I was readin' 'em. I'm tellin' you, the stories they were sharin' were so sugary sweet that they would've made the Waltons nauseous. Well, that ain't the way it is in this one. As you read through this here book, you're gonna find that I've divided it up into thirteen chapters, one for each of our trailer park twelve days of Christmas and one for Christmas Day. In the first twelve chapters you'll find crafts, decoratin' ideas, recipes, dinner menus, holiday hints, cocktails, some Christmas facts that you can share with your friends so you look smart, and just about anything else you might need to make each of these days special. Why, I even share a Christmas memory or two in each chapter that me and the other folks around the High Chaparral Trailer Park hold dear. Chapter 13, "Christmas Day Itself," offers a full day's recipes to keep everybody satisfied.

I also hope that this here book will help y'all to see just how important Christmas is to all of us at the trailer park. I wanted to share the joy that Christmas and them twelve days hold for people like me. I wanted to show the world what a real-life Christmas is like, warts and all. I wanted to set a goal when it comes to decoratin' that everyone can achieve. But most of all, I wanted y'all to rediscover the excitement that y'all use to feel way back when y'all was kids in a classroom, countin' down the days till Santa would arrive. I want y'all to recall the smells of the holidays, of home-baked desserts that were not only Christmastime-honored traditions, but items that everyone would actually eat. I want y'all to recall the thrill of throwin' things into Uncle Bob's mouth after Christmas dinner when he'd fallen asleep on the couch watchin' TV. I want y'all to remember how you use to peek from the hallways at all your parents' friends durin' the evenin' Christmas party, thinkin' that you couldn't wait till you was grown up and could join in on the fun. These are things that made our Christmases of the past so very special, and unfortunately things that we've lost as we celebrate the holiday today. But thanks to this book that you're readin' right now, you can reclaim the Christmas that you once loved.

You know, I'd have to agree with a friend of mine who once made the comment that Christmas is actually the end of the Thanksgivin' season in America. By this she meant that durin' Thanksgivin' we're thankful for what we have, and with Christmas we share that thanks with the good family and friends that are around us. I think that this might be one of the reasons that folks all over the world enjoy the Christmas season. I also know that some folks hate Christmas. They say it's too commercial, and that people should treat other people the same all year long and not just at Christmas time. To them folks I simply say, "Bah, humbug!" In the trailer park our celebrations ain't commercial, which of course is simply 'cause our checkin' accounts won't allow us to be commercial, and we always treat people the same way regardless of the time of year. If I didn't like you in September, I ain't gonna pretend I like you in December. We just ain't that way. Plus we celebrate Christmas longer than anyone else. You see, our outside lights stay up all year round, and we keep our Christmas lights burnin' all the way up to Good Friday, which for you non-Baptists is the Friday before Easter. We unplug the tree and our outside lights on Good Friday, and then plug 'em back in on Easter mornin'. Then at bedtime we unplug everythin', throw a trash bag over the Christmas tree, and roll it into the closet till next year. That is the official endin' of Christmas in the trailer park. Of course we'll still plug our outside lights in for special occasions like a party, or when the Razorbacks win, or for some other special event.

So set back, relax, and get ready to rediscover the joy that is Christmas at the High Chaparral Trailer Park.

One more thing, fans and friends, please do me a favor and send all your used Christmas cards (that you don't reuse for crafts) to the wonderful people at St. Jude's Ranch for Children. They take your old cards and make new ones, which they sell to support the ranch. You can get more information by goin' to their web page at www.stjudes ranch.org, and you can send your used Christmas card fronts to

St. Jude's Ranch for Children
100 St. Jude Street
Boulder City, NV 89005

And now to get you in that Christmas spirit, I'm proud to present a brief inspirational thought from my pastor over at the Holier Than Most Baptist Church, Pastor Ida May Bee.

> Love, Kisses, and Trailer Park Wishes,
> Ruby Ann Boxcar
> rubylot18@aol.com
> www.rubyannboxcar.com

An Inspirational Holiday Thought

by
Pastor Ida May Bee
of the
Holier Than Most Baptist Church

The divinely insired Pastor Ida May Bee of the
Holier Than Most Baptist Church.

FROM THE KITCHEN TABLE (WITH A MATCHBOOK UNDER ONE TABLE LEG SO IT DON'T ROCK) OF PASTOR IDA MAY BEE

Dear Brothers and Sisters,

Merry Christmas from me and all the folks at the Holier Than Most Baptist Church, and I hope that the celebration of the Twelve Days of Christmas touches you in ways that you've never been touched before. Being a pastor, I tend to pick up my Bible from time to time and actually read a passage or two, which is one of the reasons why I know that the good Lord above uses the scriptures to speak to us. I also know this to be a fact because that's what they taught all of us in the four-month theological seminary course at the Flatland Baptist Bible Academy in beautiful Kansas, where I got my preaching diploma. Yes, every little word, phrase, verse, and chapter contains a personal message to each of us from God. Some of these messages are easy to understand, like Genesis 20:12, which says, "And yet indeed she is my sister; she is the daughter of my father, but not the daughter of my mother; and she became my wife." Nobody in the trailer park has a problem grasping the meaning of that passage, I can tell you that. But then there are those other passages that you kind of have to study more to get any meaning from them at all. A fine example of this would be Ezekiel 23:20, "For she doted upon their paramours, whose flesh is as the flesh of asses, and whose issue is like the issue of horses." I'm still working on that one. Then you have those wonderful stories in the Holy Bible that are easy to understand and follow, but also have hidden messages in 'em that we sometimes have to reread to truly understand. A prime example of this is the beautiful story of the very first Christmas, which y'all will find in the second chapter of the Gospel of Saint

Luke. I've included the passages in this text so that you can refresh your memory on them and follow along. You'll also note that these scriptures are taken from the King James Version, which according to the Flatland Baptist Bible Academy is the language that the folks in the Bible days actually spoke.

1 And it came to pass in those days, that there went out a decree from Caesar Augustus that all the world should be taxed.

2 (And this taxing was first made when Cyrenius was governor of Syria.)

3 And all went to be taxed, every one into his own city.

4 And Joseph also went up from Galilee, out of the city of Nazareth, into Judaea, unto the city of David, which is called Bethlehem; (because he was of the house and lineage of David:)

5 To be taxed with Mary his espoused wife, being great with child.

6 And so it was, that, while they were there, the days were accomplished that she should be delivered.

7 And she brought forth her firstborn son, and wrapped him in swaddling clothes, and laid him in a manger; because there was no room for them in the inn.

Isn't that beautiful? We've all heard or read this story and have even seen it acted out each year during the Christmas pageant for as far back as we can remember. We also use this setting of the cold damp manger in our nativity sets when we decorate our trailers. The text seems to be plain, simple, and straightforward. Joseph and his pregnant wife Mary went back to Joseph's hometown so they could take part in this new tax, but when they got there no rooms were available, so they had to live in the manger, which is where Mary gave birth to our savior. But how does this pertain to us? We ain't got to go back home for a tax with our pregnant wife. And with the modern facilities in even the small towns, nobody has to give birth in a barn anymore. So what should the reader take from this passage other than our savior was born just like you and me? Well, if you take another look at these seven short passages, you can see the lesson that the Lord is trying to tell us. The two messages are as obvious as the nose on your face, but since I know that this is the first time for some of y'all to try and decipher the scriptures, I'll be more than happy to do it for you so you can see how it's done.

The first thing the good Lord is telling us is that if Joseph would have just taken the time to make reservations before setting out on this long holiday trip, they could have had a room to sleep in instead of some stinky old run-down barn when they arrived. I know that Expedia.com or even Hotels.com wasn't around in those days, but if I were a biblical man and my wife was with child, I would've made sure that the Inn 6 had left a doggone light on for us that's for sure. But oh no, you men don't heed this lesson even today. You think that once we get to where we're going, we can look for a room, and we usually end up in some hole in the wall with pillows that are as flat as a pancake or hard as a rock and nothing but backaches the next day. Or better yet, y'all are like Joseph and you expect your pregnant miserable worn-out wife to make the reservations. Or since it's your hometown, you think that all you have to do is show up on one of your relatives' doorsteps as if they got no plans for the holidays, and they'll put you up for the night. Shame on you men! Shame on y'all. But the Lord has another message to share.

Joseph is going back to the part of the country where his family is from, so he thinks he knows this region real good, which is why he arrives in the middle of the night after he travels for days with this pregnant woman ridin' on the back of a donkey. The Lord is saying in these verses that if Joseph would've only stopped and asked for directions, him and Mary would have arrived during the day when they could've found somebody that would let them stay the night or at least been able to locate the YWCA so Mary would have a place to rest. But oh no, Joseph had to be a hard-headed male and wander around, trying to find his way with his manliness just like the men of today. To heck with his wife's needs or condition, he had to prove that he was a man. I've got a feeling that in Mary's mind as she laid there in that itchy hay with the cold drafts whipping around her, the donkey she'd rode in on wasn't the only ass in that stable that blessed night.

In closing let me just add that clearly the Lord is talking to you men in these seven verses. His Christmas message, which he wants y'all to hear loud and clear when you think about holiday travel, is to call ahead to make reservations, and buy a doggone map and use it, for crying out loud. And if you're flying, get to the airport two hours before your flight, and for goodness sakes, take off your shoes and your belt before going through security. You only delay the rest of us because of your laziness. Okay? Thanks.

Happy Holidays,
Pastor Ida May Bee

Preparin' Yer Trailer Inside and Out for the Holiday Season

As RV owner Little Linda of Lot #20 (on the right) and her friend Flora Delight can attest, in some cases, smaller is better.

Here's a quick question for y'all. What is the one time of the year that the King has to step aside even though he's still in our hearts and minds throughout that period? If you answered the Christmas season, you'd be right. You see, it's durin' the end of November all the way up to January first that the Christmas tree actually replaces the velvet paintin' of Elvis that you got hangin' in your livin' room as the main focal point in any good trailer home. As a matter of fact, on account of a lack of space in the livin' room, some trailer residents actually have to take down the King's velvety likeness just so they can have a location to put their Christmas tree (if you happen to be one of these folks, make sure you follow trailer park protocol and rehang Elvis in the bathroom durin' the holiday season so all your guests can still enjoy his presence when they visit). So it's on account of this fact that your Christmas tree must look its best. As a matter of fact, your whole trailer, with the exception of your bedroom, which is almost always closed off to guests at all times of the year on account of how that's where you throw everythin' when you pick up the trailer before the guests arrive, should be a Christmas showplace. I've noticed that lots of people will go all out on decoratin' their yard for the season but neglect the inside of their trailer, which is really a shame. I always try to make sure that when folks stop by my place durin' the Christmas season, they're as wowed by the inside of my home as they are by the outside. Naturally, with my help, there's no reason you can't have a holiday showplace as well. You'll be surprised just how much more you'll enjoy Christmastime when you're spendin' it in a themed environment. So with that in mind, before we actually jump into the twelve-day celebration or the meat and potatoes, if you will, of this here Christmas guide, I've decided to give y'all a helpin' hand, a boost, or a yank if you will, so your trailer can be the talk of the town. Not only will you find that it helps put you in the mood, but you'll have strangers knockin' on your door just to get a look inside. So with that in mind, let's get started on the tree first.

More and more, I see that folks just don't know the proper way to decorate their trees. Why, you'd be surprised at what some folks have in their trailers that they call Christmas trees in the first place. Well, this is where me and my talents come in. I'm gonna tell you how to pick a tree, where to put it, and how to decorate it. Yes, I will give you all the professional help you'll ever need when it comes to the subject of Christmas trees. I personally promise that after readin' the following pages, none of y'all will ever have an ugly tree again in your abode. So grab a pencil and take notes, or simply open up that highlighter and mark the important parts in this here book.

PICKIN' OUT A TREE

I got to tell y'all that I still find myself surprised when folks come up to me and ask if they should get a real tree or a fake tree for Christmas. I tell 'em to weigh the pros and the cons. Sure I could just tell 'em, but I find that if they work it out themselves, it sticks with 'em a lot longer. So let's take my advice and look at the pros and cons about trees.

Real Tree

Pros: You get a fresh tree smell in your home while it's in the house.
Cons: You have to keep it watered; the needles fall off; bugs and spiders can live in your tree; it can catch fire and burn your trailer to the ground; it only comes in one color.

Fake Tree

Pros: You can use it over and over, you can spray it down with real tree smell in a can, no waterin', no needles to clean up, since it comes in a box you ain't got no bugs or spiders to worry about, most fake trees are made with fire-retardant materials, and it comes in every color under the rainbow.
Cons: Price.

So it's safe to say that the fake tree is your best bet unless you're poor or rich. If you're poor, then you'll definitely want to skip the fake trees 'cause even at the Salvation Army or Goodwill, they can be pricey, and you don't need to waste your money on somethin' like that. And if you're rich, heck, it don't matter, 'cause you can pay people to take care of a real tree. That's one good part about bein' rich.

So to recap . . .

Poor and Rich = Real Christmas Tree
Everybody Else = Fake Christmas Tree

Okay, so now that you know what kind of tree you need, the next step is to decide what size you need. We do this by first figurin' out where in the house we're gonna put it. Your normal trailer is broken down as follows: livin' room, kitchen, hallway, bathroom, washer and dryer area, and bedroom. Now, in some of the slightly bigger models, you might even find an additional bedroom, which also has a master bathroom in it. The question is where do you want to put your Christmas tree? If this question is still a problem for you, then you can easily select your tree's location by goin' through the above list and eliminatin' rooms that just won't work. Cross out the bathrooms, 'cause they're just too small for a tree. The bedroom or bedrooms might work, but nobody will see your tree. A Christmas tree in the hallway and washer/dryer area would just block your comin's and goin's. And even if you take out your kitchen table and somehow manage to get that hangin' lamp out of the way, the kitchen is a bad place for a tree. So this leaves one place and one place only—the livin' room. Not only will it be beautiful settin' there, but everybody and their dog will be forced to view it.

Now that you got your room, it's time to pick the best location. The first thing to remember is that regardless if your tree is real or fake, you'll never want to set it directly on a heat register unless you can close that register off. Of course, this means that there won't be any kind of heat in that part of the room, or if this happens to be your only heat register, there won't be any heat at all in your livin' room. So I suggest that you skip that part of the room altogether. The second rule of thumb is to do as little work as possible when it comes to findin' the right spot. This means that even though you want your tree in a nice area, you don't want to have to rearrange your entire livin' room either. If you have to move a chair, that's fine, but don't take it clean out of the livin' room—'cause you most likely ain't got no place to put it except outside, and with the winter weather you're sure to ruin it no matter how many old blankets you put on it. So basically, just squish everything in the livin' room together to make room. Don't worry about who can see the TV and who can't. Just as long as you and your family have good seats for TV watchin' then so be it. If your guests won't be able to see the TV from their seat, then they can just set there and listen to whatever's bein' broadcast while they take in the beauty of your Christmas tree. One last thing, it's good if you can set your tree close to a window so it can be seen from outside. You might as well show off your good taste and the fact that you celebrate Christmas.

Now that you have your tree located in the trailer, you'll need to grab a tape measure and get some figures. The first thing you're gonna measure is the tree topper that y'all have decided to use. Measure from the top of the topper to the area inside where it and the tree top will actually touch. So even if the topper is ten inches long from top to bottom, you will still need to look inside and see where the topper ends and measure from that point to the top of the topper. This means that even if your topper is ten inches long as I stated earlier, you will only need to remember the measurement of four inches. Now measure the height in your livin' room from the floor to the ceilin' and round that off to feet. So if it's eight feet five inches, we'd just call it eight feet. Now take the four inches that you got for your tree topper and add another six inches that the tree stand will take for a total of ten inches. Subtract ten inches from the eight feet that you got when you measured from the floor to the ceilin', which comes to seven feet two inches, and round that off to feet for a grand total of seven feet. Now you know that if you want it to fit in your trailer, seven feet is the tallest your Christmas tree can possibly be. Anythin' else won't work, so don't even waste your time tryin' it. And don't worry if you ain't any good at math, 'cause all you got to do is grab a measurin' tape and a calculator and fill in the blanks below. This shouldn't be any harder to do than the cross-word puzzle in the *TV Guide*—which means that some of y'all are still gonna mess this tree thing up real bad.

   A. Top of tree topper to the inside point = _____ inches

   B. Space for the Tree Stand = + __6__ inches

   C. Subtotal (combine the inches from lines A and B) _____ inches

   D. Height from floor to ceilin' = _____ feet

   E. Take line D _____ feet and multiply by 12 = _____ inches

   F. Subtract line C from inches total of line D = _____ inches

   G. And divide line F _____ inches by 12 = _____ feet

So your maximum tree height for your trailer is the total on line G. There, now wasn't that easy?

Our next measurement is gonna decide how wide your tree can be. This one is easier than my sister. Just go to the space and meas-ure the amount of space you have from, say, the chair to the TV where you want your tree to fit. That is the widest your tree can possibly be. I told you it was easy.

Now that you have both the height and width measurements, you can go get your tree. Of course, how you do this depends on if you're gettin' a real tree or a fake tree. If it's a fake tree, just go in and tell the clerk what your measurements are. They should be able to help you find the best tree for your needs. Just remember, if you get one of them real pretty aluminum trees, you're gonna have to figure a little more space for the color wheel. Unfortunately, gettin' a real tree ain't as easy. Y'all will want naturally to start your shoppin' in either a Christmas tree lot or in front of a local grocery or department store that sells trees. The first thing y'all will want to do is find the best kind of tree for your trailer, which would be one of them high needle-retention trees like a Nordman, Noble, or Fraser fir, or blue or white spruce. Once you locate it, measure it to see just how tall and wide it is. Sure you can just cut it down if it's too tall, but who wants to do all that manual labor? Don't be a lazy behind, just measure the tree. Once you've found the perfect tree for your trailer, ask a salesperson how much it is. Let me warn you, a high needle-retention tree ain't cheap. But that don't mean you need to be an idiot and say somethin' like, "Are you out of your mind?" or "For that price, the dang thing better decorate itself," or "I only want the tree, not the whole dang lot." Just 'cause you're poor don't mean you got to be stupid, and if you're rich and sayin' this kind of stuff then you need to get your head examined or buy a fake tree. In any case, don't embarrass your family durin' the holiday season, let them embarrass themselves. So, now you have three choices—you can either buy the tree, go somewhere else, or mark it by sprayin' a big spot of orange spray paint on one side so you can tell which one it is when you come back later that night to steal it. (If you choose the latter, just remember to put that side by the wall when you set it up.)

The Stand

For those of you who get a real tree, you got a couple of choices when it comes to stands. You can buy the regular old tree stand, but be warned that you'll need to add a little water every day to that one so your tree don't get dry and catch the trailer on fire. Another choice is one of them self-watering tree stands, but you still got to keep an eye on the water level. After all, the last thing you want is a naked decorated tree towerin' over a pile of dried-out pine needles.

For those of you who were smart enough to get a fake tree, all you got to do is put it in a simple little stand. Of course you're gonna want to go out and get four of them little tiny swivel caster wheels to put on the bottom of your stand so you can just throw a trash bag over your tree and push it into the closet till next December. If you ain't got room in your closet for your tree, go ahead and put it out in your shed. With everythin' taped on the tree, you should be able to grab hold of the metal trunk in the middle of the tree and carry it down the front steps like that without worryin' about breakage. Then just set it back up and roll it to the shed. Just make sure you put it behind the four-wheeler, 'cause you know you'll need to get to that so you can take your trash down to the dumpster.

BRACIN' THE TREE

If for some reason you feel like you've got to brace your tree by runnin' wire or fishin' string from the tree to the walls, make sure you incorporate 'em into your tree decoratin' as well. Hang ornaments from the wires or strings. Or you can also simply drape garlands on 'em. In any case, for the beauty of your tree and the safety of your loved ones, put somethin' on the bracin' wires. After all, the last thing you want to be doin' is rushin' your loved ones to the hospital 'cause they nearly decapitated themselves on them dang wires or strings.

THE LIGHTS

Now that you got your tree all standin' up and everythin', it's time to put on the lights. If you get one of these new fangled pre-lit trees, you don't have to mess with the light thing at all. If not, well, don't worry, I'm here to help. The first thing we want to do is plug the lights in. There ain't nothin' worse than hangin' up lights, only to find out that they don't work. So plug those lights in first and test 'em before you wrap 'em loosely around your tree. The glow will also help you to see just where you've put 'em and if they're balanced. The mistake that most folks make when puttin' up the lights is that they put 'em all along the outside of the tree. This is wrong. Your lights should be more of a backlight to your ornaments rather than the main show. So what you want to do is push back your lights toward the inside of the tree, about halfway from the trunk and the tip of the branches. It don't matter if your lights chase or blink or don't do nothin', just as long as you and your family like 'em. One thing to remember is that if they play music, you're gonna need to be able to reach that control, 'cause when you got company over and y'all get to talkin', some folks will have problems hearin' you over that doggone Christmas music your lights are puttin' out. In any case, once we know what lights we're gonna use, go to the first branch either at the top or at

the bottom, find the middle of that branch and wrap your lights around it. Next, grab some clear packin' tape and wrap it around the branch one time just to make sure that your lights ain't comin' off. Do this on each branch after you've done the lights. Just make sure you get the nonflammable kind of tape. It's okay if the heat from your lights, which should be very little if any, melts holes in the tape where it touches 'em, but you sure don't want a fire durin' the holidays. Them firemen want to be able to enjoy Christmas too.

Before we leave the lightin' section, I know that some of y'all are askin', "Ruby Ann, what do I do if my lights burn out on my tree?" Well, the first thing you don't want to do is take the time to cut off the clear tape from each branch and try to take the lights off. Instead, add new lights on top of the old ones. Since your lights are inside the tree so to speak, nobody is gonna see that the old ones don't work. Just don't plug the old ones back in. Also remember to tape the new set of lights to the tree with that clear packin' tape.

COLOR SCHEME

For some reason lots of folks think you should go with a color scheme when decoratin' your tree, but I personally believe that is wrong. Number one, the last thing you want to do is have to go out each year and buy a whole set of new ornaments for your tree just so you can keep up with the current color scheme. Oh yes, the so-called *in* color for Christmas trees changes every year, so if you want to keep up with the Joneses, so be it. But I'm happy bein' able to put my SpongeBob SquarePants ornament that my niece Lulu Bell gave me and my husband, Dew, right up next to my tribute Dale Earnhardt Christmas ball ornament without fear that the colors might not fit this year's scheme. But y'all do what you want.

GARLAND

After the lights are finished, it's time to add the garland. Now, I know some folks don't like garland, but to me it's like a man without pants. Sure it's nice, but after a while, it just don't seem right, and I mean that in a nice Baptist way. You need your garland to help tie everythin' like your lights and ornaments together. So use the doggone garland.

When you put the garland on your tree, you'll want to swagger it rather than just runnin' it around. Feel free to put several different types of garland on as well, just make sure that they're vivid. If you want to use ribbon, that's good, too, just make sure that it's wide and colorful. And also remember that when you put your garland on a branch, wrap it around the branch one time, and then put a piece of that clear packin' tape around it to make sure it stays on the branch.

Another thing about garland is that it don't have to be store bought neither. You can string together some popcorn if you like, although every time we tried that when I was growin' up, we never seemed to get much of it strung up. Maybe if Momma hadn't salted and buttered it, more might have ended up on the string and not in our bellies.

Another good item to use for garland is barbed wire. This is especially handy if you got cats that like to climb in trees or children who need to learn not to touch the Christmas tree. I'd even suggest electrical fence wire for this same reason, but you'll have a large enough electric bill from the lights alone, so forget that one.

The most frequently asked question that I get about garland is

How much should I buy? To this I always say, ten feet of garland for every foot of the tree should do it. In other words, if your tree is seven feet tall, you'd multiply that times ten feet of garland to come up with the amount you need to buy. So in this case, you'd need seventy feet of garland.

Height of tree _____ feet

Multiplied by 10 feet

= _____ feet of garland

ORNAMENTS

Ornaments are very personal things. Some may have special meanin' to you while others may just be somethin' that you saw on sale so you bought it. In any case, the more the merrier as I always say. Of course, if you can't see the glow comin' from the lights, you've got too many on your tree. The rule of thumb is fifteen ornaments for every two feet of tree, but you do as many as you want to do. Just make sure that you fill in all the holes with them ornaments, and of course, make sure—since you ain't got to see the hooks that hold the ornaments to the tree—that you just duct tape those babies on. Since ornaments are always the first thing to fall off your tree, duct tape is sure to hold better than the package tape on these little devils.

ANGEL HAIR AND TINSEL

Angel hair can really make a tree beautiful just as long as you don't put a ton on it. It's a Christmas tree that will be displayed in your trailer home, not a haunted mansion. So go gently. And now with all the different colors you can get it in, angel hair can really add that special somethin' to your tree.

Tinsel can be real pretty on a tree as well, just don't mix it with angel hair or you'll have one messy lookin' tree. Speakin' of tinsel, the way it's applied to Christmas trees is the number-two biggest mistake that I see every year. Folks, you can't just take a handful and toss it on the tree. That looks real bad. Instead, take a handful and lay it over your hand. Use your thumb to hold it in place. Next, turn on your hair dryer, aim it at your hand, which should be facin' the tree, and slowly ease up with your thumb, releasin' just a few strands of tinsel at a time. Keep doin' this at different parts of the tree, and you'll have that son of a gun tinseled in no time. Just remember to keep movin' your hand and the blow-dryer in a steady pace so as not to overtinsel any one area.

THE TREE SKIRT

The tree skirt is a must-have for any Christmas tree, regardless if it's fake or real. It helps to keep your pets and small children out of the water in your stand if you got a real tree. It also helps to catch any fallen needles. It hides your wheels if you go with the fake tree. And it also helps to finish off your decorative look. But before you go out and buy a fancy tree skirt, why not consider usin' somethin' around the trailer that you've already got. How about the blanket that your spouse or parent snuck out of jail when they finished servin' their time? I bet that ugly red blouse your mother-in-law got you last year would be perfect. Or maybe that dress that your granny willed you when she passed would look real good under that tree.

Regardless if you buy it or recycle it, complete your Christmas tree this year by coverin' its unsightly nether regions with a tree skirt. Your tree will thank you.

TAKIN' IT DOWN

This section only concerns those of you who used a real tree. You can easily take down the ornaments from the tree by usin' a pair of wire cutters. Once you've finished with the ornaments, simply set your tree outside and wait. By the end of summer, that thing should have dried out enough for you to easily break the branches apart and reclaim your garland and lights. If not, then wait and try breakin' the branches apart in November. That should have been plenty of time.

LAST BUT NOT LEAST

When you roll your tree out next year, make sure you get the vacuum out and give it a good suckin'. Some folks like to simply dust their tree, but I am all for the vacuum. Not only does it clean it real good, but if you clean the bag out first, you can reuse all that tinsel and angel hair that you just sucked up.

CHRISTMAS DECORATIN'

The most important things about decoratin' your trailer for Christmas are that you have a good time doin' it, and you don't stop until you've got everything that looks like Christmas set out in your livin' room. As you can imagine, we go all out, and not just with the store-bought items, but as you'll see in the followin' chapters, we also take Christmas crafts to another dimension. Why, it's not unusual for somebody to give you one of their handmade crafts for a Christmas present. And as you can guess, some of these crafts are outstandin' while others are, shall we say, pure unadulterated trash. And even though you'd rather shove a Christmas tree up your behind, you have to set these "crafty presents" out so they can be seen. Of course you can always pass 'em off to your guest just so they know your taste ain't that bad by tellin' 'em that it's somethin' that so-and-so gave you, which is usually followed by an "Oh, I see," or a "Hmmm." On occasion you do get a sympathy reply, which is when the person cocks his head to the side, peers over at you, and shakes his head as he lets out a sigh. In any case, you can't just not display an item regardless if it's the ugliest thing you've ever seen or not. The last thing you want to do is hurt somebody's feelin's durin' Christmas. And don't even think about not puttin' it out 'cause it accidentally got broken. Trust me, folks, that one don't work. No, all you can do is make sure that everythin' gets put out on display, try to overlook the bad ones, and pray for a trailer fire. At the High Chaparral, we also make an additional craft on each of the Twelve Days of Christmas. This helps us to remember that each of these extra days is special, and it keeps us in the Christmas spirit, even way into January. But I'll get to those a little later in this book.

When I decorate my trailer I like to do a couple of things first. Number one, I put on some of my favorite Christmas music to get me in the mood. Number two, I take out all my decorations and I decide what stays in the livin' room and what goes in the guest bathroom. Typically anythin' that was given to me by a friend or relative that lives more than 100 miles away will end up in the bathroom, unless, of course, I love it. Everythin' else goes in either the livin' room or the kitchen since it's almost as visible. I always put my favorite things on or around the TV since that's where most of my focus will be. I do hand-select a few of my all-time smaller items to go in my bathroom, bedroom, or office by my computer. This way I got a little bit of Christmas everywhere in my home.

Some of y'all don't understand how important the placement of mistletoe is in a trailer. Typically folks put it in the doorway, which is the biggest mistake in the world if you live in a trailer park. With people like my sister Donna Sue or her other trampy little cowork- ers from the Blue Whale Strip Club comin' over to my trailer, all I end up with is them blockin' the doorways waitin' for somebody to kiss 'em. I can't tell you how many times I've had to tell my sister to get out of the way 'cause she was blockin' the entrance into the kitchen. And I almost had a whole Christmas party go wrong when I caught an invited guest, dog-ugly Opal Lamb, standin' in the front door with the mistletoe hangin' over her head. I'd peeked out the window and wondered what all my guests were doin' standin' in my yard. Nobody wanted to go first with that old dog-face cow hoggin' the door. Needless to say, I've learned from my mistakes and now when I throw a party durin' the holiday season I hang the mistletoe over the kitchen sink. If my drunken sister or one of her friends wants to wait somewhere for a kiss, they can do it in my kitchen while they wash my dishes.

Now we need to talk about decoratin' outside. When it comes to plastic snowmen, nativity scenes, or lit-up Santas, I can tell you that I could care less what you put in your yard just as long as you ain't runnin' your little parade of lights off my electric line. I'm serious. If you want to light up the night with your Christmas yard display, go for it. My bedroom windows already have foil over 'em so there ain't any kind of light comin' in there regardless of what your wattage is. As a matter of fact, I think all the light is wonderful 'cause it keeps criminals and them little high school punks away from my trailer. So plug 'em in and enjoy yourself when layin' out your yard display. Of course, your Christmas lights that you string up on your trailer is a different story altogether.

If you find yourself out drivin' in a trailer park community, you'll most likely notice the Christmas lights that are strung up on the trailers. Naturally we never take any of our outside lights down, but simply continue to pile 'em on top of each other. Well, this is how you can tell who has the most money in the park. The more strands of workin' lights means the most money. Don't confuse that with the most strands of light with some workin' 'cause that is a sign of elderly folks who've been addin' more each year, but didn't have the money or the get-up-and-go to perform any kind of maintenance on them older strands of lights. As for those other trailers that y'all will see that just have a few strings of Christmas lights hangin' on 'em, they most likely are either new to the trailer park, young people in their first trailer, newlyweds, or Jewish.

CHAPTER 1

The First Day of Christmas

DECEMBER 13

Sometimes it takes more than just a Christmas card in order
to share your true feelin's with your neighbors.

Traditional Gift on This Day
   A partridge in a pear tree.

Trailer Park Gift on This Day
   A Partridge Family album (on eight-track tape)

ABOUT THIS DAY

The first day of Christmas for us at the High Chaparral Trailer Park actually starts on December 13, even if it falls on a Friday. After all, we got lots of stuff to do from here on out. This is also the time of year when we kick off our Christmas parties. If y'all are anything like us folks at the High Chaparral Trailer Park, you'll find that your schedules can get pretty busy on account of all the holiday gatherin's. Well, I suggest that y'all think about tryin' what we folks did way back when. We came up with the idea of throwin' everybody's name who wanted to throw a party that year in a hat and then draw out twelve names. Those folks will be the twelve party throwers for that year's holiday shindigs. Naturally you'd want to get someone unbiased to draw the names. We usually use my sister Donna Sue since she's typically too drunk to cheat even if she wanted to. Y'all can also have folks cosponsor the parties if you like just as long as you keep 'em down to twelve parties only. Mind you, church parties, work parties, visitin'-out-of-town-relatives parties, club parties, fund-raisers, and other non-neighbor Christmas gatherin's don't count as one of these twelve parties.

A CHRISTMASTIME TREASURE
FROM THE HIGH CHAPARRAL TRAILER PARK

For some reason over this past year, it seems like everybody and their dog has tried to take me to one of these fondue restaurants or invited me over to their places for a fondue gatherin', and I just have to tell 'em, "Thanks, but no thanks." Even though I just love the taste of most fondues and even think the idea of plungin' into a shared pot of warmed sauces is a wonderful way of gettin' to know the folks around you at a dinner party, you couldn't pay me to dip a meat stick or bread chunk into one of them little pots. I know this sounds strange comin' from a gal who'd happily attack just about any buffet she can find, but I simply refuse to have anythin' to do with anything that pertains to fondue. I tried it once back when it was the deal in the 1970s, and I will never even try it again. Of course I blame my feelin's regardin' this matter on the folks who used to live in Lot #19, Jeannie Janssen and her husband, Jimmy. They put me and everyone else at the trailer park off on the fun pleasures that fonduin' can bring, back in 1971 when they had a little Christmas get-together for those of us who belonged to the trailer park's canasta club, and even though Jimmy is dead and Jeannie has moved away, after that night's party, I still ain't been able to forgive 'em. But no, that couldn't have happened could it? Sure we all had fun playin' cards while Elvis's renditions of Christmas songs played in the background on their new stereophonic hi-fi. They'd gone all out and decorated their trailer to the point that you'd have swore you was only minutes away from the jolly old elf's place. And we even enjoyed the wonderful assortments of fondue sauces that Jeannie had prepared for us to sample. And who wouldn't enjoy the feelin' of bein' so doggone fancy and all that we was gettin' as we stab up a piece of meat or bread and dipped it into the fondue pot? If only Jeannie and Jimmy had been better parents, then all of us in attendance could have enjoyed the early seventies craze like everybody else from that era did. But instead, our new love for fondue fun would end later that night. You see, just before the party ended, Jeannie brought out dessert, a chocolate fondue sauce along with an entire tray of banana chunks, strawberries, apples, and marshmallows. And since it was already late with all the card playin' and such, we just tore into that stuff, shovin' it into our faces as fast as we could so not to keep our guests up past their bedtime. When it was all gone, we wished the Janssens a very Merry Christmas, and we all headed home to what would end up bein' a night of pure hell on earth. I'd be willin' to bet that never in recorded history did so many people at one time in a trailer park pray to the Lord above for help and holy intervention. Most of us thought we was gonna die. We'd find out the next day, after the sheriff had finished his investigation, that those doggone Janssen twins had put an entire box of chocolate laxative in the dessert fondue when their parents weren't watchin' 'em. Needless to say, we were all livid and fit to be tied. I can promise y'all that if any of us had been able to actually walk that next day, them boys wouldn't have made it out of that trailer park alive. Luckily we was all fine and out of the hospital a few days later, and we were able to enjoy Christmas in our own trailers. But that Christmas season was the first time I ever had fondue as well as the last. Just the thought of it makes me have to grab a chair and set down. Coincidently that Christmas season was also the first time someone or some ones tipped over the Janssens' trailer home in the middle of the night. As you can imagine though, with them Janssen twins around, it wasn't the last time.

Christmas Crafts from the Heart

Durin' the Twelve Days of Christmas, makin' a new craft to proudly display in your trailer livin' room will not only help keep you in that holiday mood, but it will also help to make your trailer even more beautiful than it already is. So put on an apron, an old shirt of your husband's, or that ugly, cheap-o top your mother-in-law gave you last Christmas and lets get to craftin'.

Wooden Spoon Reindeer

I just love my wooden spoon reindeer. Not only is it creative, but every mornin' when I see his little face, I just smile. That little spoondeer, which is what I like to call him, always puts me in a good mood. If you want, you can even make a whole herd of 'em with different-sized spoons. Hey, it's your trailer, do as many of these fun little reindeer friends as you want.

SUPPLIES

5 large wooden spoons
Black craft paint
Hot glue gun and glue sticks
10- × 4-inch red felt
3- × 5-inch brown felt
8$\frac{1}{2}$- × 11-inch brown
   Fun-Foam
20 inches of holiday rick rack

4 large tan pom-poms
1 small white pom-pom
2 googly eyes
1 medium white pom-pom
1 small red pom-pom
30 inches of red yarn
1 miniature ornament

1. Take 4 of the spoons and paint $\frac{1}{4}$ inch of the end of each handle black. These are the hooves. These 4 spoons will make the legs and the body.

2. Take your fifth spoon and cut 4 inches off the bottom. The inside of this spoon is gonna end up bein' the face while the remainin' handle will be its neck.

3. Take one of the leg spoons, hoof down, and hot glue the back of that spoon to the end side of the 4-inch handle piece you cut off. Make sure you glue it so the leg spoon is at an angle. We want the reindeer to be able to stand up on its own. Let the glue dry and then go ahead and glue another leg spoon to the opposite side of the discarded 4-inch handle. This will be the front quarter of the deer. Let the glue dry before movin' on to step 4.

4. Take the 2 remainin' spoons and do the same thing you did in step 3, but this time do it to the other end of the discarded handle. This will be the hindquarters. Just make sure that all spoons are glued at an angle so that when all four hooves are standin' on the table, the spoons resemble a tent.

5. Next you will want to cut out the ears, antler, and blanket. The ears are cut from the brown felt. The antlers are cut from the Fun-Foam. And you use the red felt for the blanket. Turn for the patterns to cut by.

6. Take the fifth shorter spoon that will be the head and hot-glue it to the front quarter section. Just make sure that you turn the spoon so it is facin' to the side. If you look at the reindeer from the side you will be able to see his face and all four legs.

7. Take the red felt blanket, and glue the holiday rick rack around the edges. You can be as creative with this part as you like. Once it is dry, drape it over the reindeer's body so the long portion is hangin'. Glue the top of the back only.

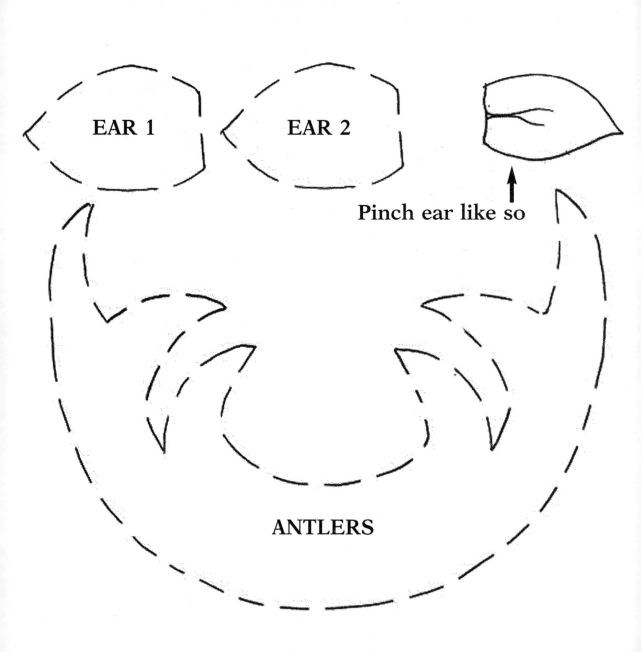

EAR 1

EAR 2

Pinch ear like so

ANTLERS

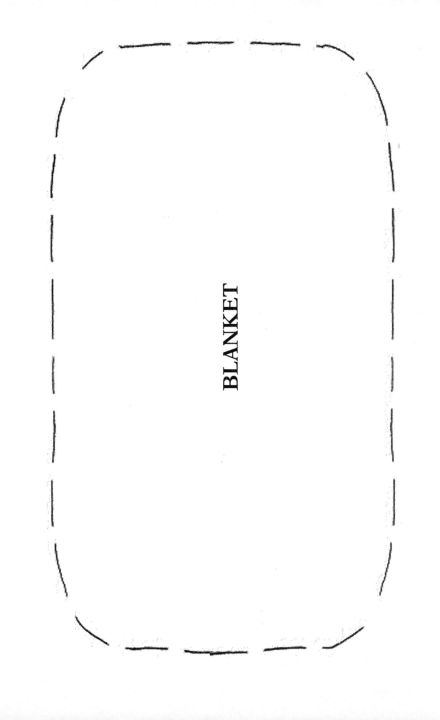

BLANKET

8. Take one of your tan pom-poms and glue it on the back of the hindquarter to give the reindeer a behind. Glue the second pom-pom on the front of the neck and head spoon so the reindeer has a chest. And finally, glue the third and fourth pom-poms on the underside of the reindeer's midsection to give him a body. Glue the small white pom-pom on the back tan pom-pom to make a fluffy tail.

9. Glue the blanket down on the sides of the third and fourth pom-poms.

10. Now pinch ear 1 and hot glue it to the top back section of the head spoon. Do the same with ear 2. Now hot-glue the antler on, right behind the ears.

11. Glue on the googly eyes about a quarter down from the top of the spoon. Take a black marker and draw on top eyelashes. Just below the eyes, but not so that it blocks them, glue on the medium white pom-pom. Then hot glue the little red pom-pom on this ball to make the red nose.

12. And finally, tie the red yarn around the little fella's neck and into a bow.

Tip for the Holiday Hostess

The holiday season is known as the most social party-givin' time of the year, unless of course you happen to be a Jehovah's Witness. If you're like me, you find you got more people comin' in and out of your trailer durin' the holiday season than Little Linda's RV on a good Saturday night. It just seems like it's party after party after party, which is fine by me. I'm always a good hostess, even when it seems like I'm doin' one or two of these shindigs a week. I think I got that gene from my daddy. Why, back when he worked as a greeter at Lamb Super Center, everyone always bragged about how friendly he was and how he always had a smile on his face. Even now when he chases down shoplifters in that golf cart he rides around the parkin' lot, he always sounds polite when he yells out, "Stop where you are, dirtbag scum." My momma on the other hand, well, she's a completely different story. I can't think of one Tupperware party she hosted that wasn't a disaster. She'd either run out of coffee or forget to thaw out the cake. She was horrible at it. Why, I even recall one Avon party she'd forgot she'd scheduled. God bless her, she served warm RC Cola and pickle slices. It was pathetic. It also goes to show that not everybody is a natural-born hostess. That's why in this chapter I'll show you how to be the kind of Christmas hostess you've always dreamed of bein'. And I'll also give you ideas for different types of Christmas parties.

As the hostess, you will be a social butterfly, goin' from person to person, makin' sure they're doin' fine. Of course even this easy task can be done wrong. You don't want to be like that waiter who keeps comin' by every two minutes to make sure you got enough tea nor do you want to be like that cafeteria tea lady whom you've got to hunt down just to get a refill. So just pace yourself, but make sure you meet and greet everyone when they arrive. If you can't, then have your husband do it, but make sure he puts his pants on first.

Party Idea

Cookie Exchange

Who doesn't love a good cookie? That's why a cookie exchange Christmas party is so much fun. If you ain't been to one of these, let me tell you how they work. Everybody is told to bring along three or four dozen cookies, which are then placed on a table. After some snacks or even a set-down meal, each person talks about their cookie. They say where they got the recipe or a little history about it. Then everybody grabs the empty container that they brought along as well, and y'all gather around the cookie table. Y'all walk around the table, grabbin' two or three cookies from each batch that's on the table until everyone has gone around the table a few times. You keep this up until all the cookies are gone. This way you get to eat lots of different cookies without havin' to bake all of 'em yourself. Naturally you can eat some of the cookies that you've collected durin' the party or you can just wait and enjoy 'em in the privacy of your own home. There are a few things that you really need to do when you throw a cookie exchange.

1. Make sure that none of your invited guests are bringing the same kind of cookies.

2. Ask the guest to either bring a lot of copies of the recipe to the party or if you got the time, have them give you the recipe in advance and you can put together a little cookie recipe book for all the guests to take home with them.

3. Since some of the cookies will most likely have chocolate in 'em, make sure that your pets are locked away in a separate room. The last thing you want is to have to make an emergency visit to the vet.

You will want to serve some kind of snacks as I mentioned or a whole dinner at this type of party as well. If you want to make it a potluck where everybody brings a side dish along with their cookies, that's fine too. Just have a good time and make sure that everyone eats before y'all do the cookie exchange.

Trailer Park Christmas Games

Everybody enjoys a fun party game, especially at Christmas. I know that at my Christmas parties, after we've eatin', game time is one of the highlights of the night. We all enjoy playin' "White Elephant / Dirty Santa," but the fun doesn't stop there. We also play "Hey, What's in My Sock," "Donna Sue's Boyfriend," "The Christmas Pea," "Pass the Aqua Net," "The Check Is in the Mail," "The Christmas Goose," "I've Never on Christmas," "Blow It Out for Santa," "Decorate the Christmas Tree Game," and "Kiss and Tell." Not only are these games fun, but they also help your guests get more acquainted. Just make sure you award a prize to each winner. The better the prize, the harder your guests will play. (FYI, food is not somethin' you win at Christmas parties, but rather it's somethin' you enjoy.) Make the prizes somethin' like a gift certificate for a movie rental or a coupon for a free popcorn at the local theater. And as usual one of my books, my sister's book, or any of the merchandise on my web page make great prizes as well. But most important, y'all have fun playin' these games.

Blow It Out for Santa

You light a candle and put it on a chair away from where everyone is seated. The story is that it's Christmas Eve, and Santa is up on the roof waitin' to come down the chimney. The only thing is, he won't budge until he sees that all the lights are out. So you have to blow out the candle for Santa. Then each player, in turn, is blindfolded and positioned two feet away with their backs to the candle and chair. The hostess then asks them to take three steps forward, turn around four times, and step three steps forward toward the candle. They then simply have to blow the candle out. Since most people will get disoriented, they'll end up in some other part of the room, blowin' on somethin' else. Just make sure you got somebody standin' behind or beside the chair just to make sure that nobody walks into the candle. The last thing you need while havin' a party is a trailer fire.

WHAT'S THAT SMELL?

Christmas is one of them holidays that the Anglicans like my friend Liz who lives in that great big house in London like to refer to as Bells and Smells 'cause their services are full of sound and odors that help 'em to celebrate Christmas. Of course this is true even in a good Baptist's home like mine. To be honest, regardless of your faith, Christmas is one of those very special holidays that call for usin' all your senses. We eat wonderfully delightful food. We listen to cheerful Christmas carols. We feel the felt and velvets. We see the colorful lights that brighten up our holiday. And we smell the delightful fragrances of pinecones or cinnamon that complete our experiences of Christmas. Of course from time to time when you're in a trailer, your Christmas smells can include the odors of pesticides, pets, your husband's shoes, and dirty laundry that you just ain't had a chance to get to, which is why I've written this section.

One quick note for y'all. Most of these potpourri recipes require that they set up in a container for several weeks, so you might want to make these well in advance. Then you can feature each of these potpourris on their mentioned day.

Traditional Potpourri

4

We all start makin' this around Halloween.

$1/4$ cup grapefruit peel	1 cup rosemary leaves
$1/4$ cup lemon peel	$1/2$ cup dried basil
$1/4$ cup orange peel	3 bay leaves, crumbled
$1/4$ cup lime peel	2 cups noniodized salt
1 quart of dried fir needles	

Put the first four ingredients in a blender and blend on medium for 10 seconds. Pour into a plastic bowl that has a lid. Add the remainin' ingredients. Put the lid on and shake well. Let it set for a few days, and then open the lid and enjoy the smells.

HOLLY JOLLY WOOHA!

❋ A Christmas wreath on your front door, mantel, or front window is a sign of welcome and long life to all who enter your trailer or home.

❋ In 1879, Edward H. Johnson, who worked for Thomas Edison's company, had the very first Christmas tree bulbs especially made for him.

❋ The very first state to declare Christmas a legal holiday was Alabama, and it did so in 1836.

HELPFUL HOLIDAY HINTS

Knowin' how much y'all just love the helpful hints from my neighbors, which I featured in all my other books, I've asked these folks to share their holiday shortcuts in this book as well. I'm sure they'll help your Christmas season go smoother as well as make y'all say, "Hey, that's a good idea."

By the way, we folks at the High Chaparral Trailer Park would love to hear some of your helpful hints, too. So please send 'em to rubylot18@aol.com. As my sister Donna Sue says, the more the merrier.

* Celebrate the season by usin' Christmas music on your answerin' machine.

* Want fresh bread for Christmas? Look at the twist tie color to find out when the bread was delivered to the store. Monday is blue, Tuesday is green, Thursday is red, Friday is white, and Saturday is yellow.

—Opal Lamb-Brown, Lot #1

* If you string up popcorn for your tree, after Christmas take it outside and hang it in front of your windows. The birds will come and eat it and you can watch 'em from the warmth of your trailer.

* Want your trailer to look even brighter for the holidays? Take all your glass light fixtures and run 'em through your dishwasher.

—Anita Biggon, Lot #2

Twelve Days of Yuletime Advice

If there's one thing that I sure like to do other than makeup or eatin', it'd have to be handin' out advice. Of course if you've read my *Dear*

Ruby book, you'd know that already. You'd also know that I'm real good at solvin' people's problems as well. I can't run my own life, but I sure can run everybody else's without even thinkin' twice. And just from the cards, letters, and emails I get from y'all durin' the Christmas season, it sure seems like Christmas is one of those times y'all would just as soon shoot as look at 'em with all the stress y'all seem to deal with on a day-to-day basis. That's why I've included this little section. I ain't got lots of space to handle all the questions I get about the season, but I've managed to throw some of the more common ones in here and there. I hope these examples and my answers help to make your next Christmas the best ever. If not, just drop me a card, letter, or email.

Dear Ruby Ann Boxcar,

We have a girl in our office who is just as ugly as a mud fence. She does not see it that way though; as a matter of fact she thinks she is next to perfection, which isn't a problem until Christmas. Well, at the last office Christmas party she had a couple of drinks, and before we knew it she was on the copier dancing. Now, for someone good looking that wouldn't have been a bad thing I guess, but oh my God, with her it was horrible. She almost ruined Christmas for the whole office. She thinks she was the life of the party and when she walks by and hears the other workers laughing she thinks they are talking about how great she was. This girl has been my friend for a long time and I don't want to hurt her feelings, so how can I keep her down off the copier at next year's Christmas party without hurting her feelings and losing her as my friend? Please help.

Denise

Dear Denise,

You can't, so don't even try. If this makes her feel good, then you as a friend should support her actions, and get on to them folks who are laughin' at her. Of course if you want her to fully see what the real experience was like for others, just press the print button when she gets up on the copier at next year's Christmas party. They say a picture's worth a thousand words.

Love, Kisses, and Trailer Park Wishes,
Ruby Ann Boxcar

Puttin' Your Best Face Forward

Seein' how this is the time of year that we spend makin' merry with our families and groups of our friends and even coworkers, the last thing we want to do is look like we've had a rough past twelve months. I know that for some of y'all, you just can't help lookin' that way, and that's okay, 'cause nobody expects you to ever look any better. But Christmas is a time for fantasy like in the *Nutcracker* where that little girl's nutcracker comes to life and she beats off the Mouse King with her shoe. Now that I think of it, I've known some folks who could kill a mouse just by takin' off their shoes so maybe that ain't as hard to believe as I'd first thought. In any case, y'all, and I'm includin' you ugly ones as well, can give your makeup that touch of fantasy and get away with it durin' the holiday season. With that in mind, here are five easy tips to look your best for Christmas.

Lipstick

Bright red lipstick is the deal for Christmas. I know that some of y'all are already tryin' to talk me down on this one by sayin' that bright red lipstick will make you look like a hooker. Well trust me, hon, nobody's ever gonna mistake you for a lady of the night. You see, people actually pay them. So get out that red lipstick and put it on. The brighter the better, I say. And not only will you be makin' yourself look beautiful, but you'll be doin' a public service as well, 'cause the older folks who have problems hearin' what you're sayin' will now be able to read your flappin' red lips a lot easier.

CHRISTMAS CHEER

I've always been the first to say that my sister put the "Ho" in "Ho-Ho-Ho." It's true! When it comes to holiday cheer my sister beats the drum, crushes the ice, and shakes the shaker. And bein' the drunk that she is, I can't think of anyone better to turn to when it comes to Christmas drinks. I'm not one to brag, especially when it comes to my sister, but Donna Sue is so skilled in the art of mixology that she can mix a cocktail with her eyes closed. Bein' the good Baptist that I am, I sometimes wish I had that skill, 'cause my curtains don't close all the way in the livin' room, and I ain't got a light in my hall closet. Anyways, Donna Sue is to the world of drinks what I am to the world of food, advice, and entertainment. That's right, she's an expert. Now I ain't just talkin' about adult beverages, which do happen to be her specialty, but I also mean old seasonal standbys with an added twist as well as a few nonalcoholic drinks that even the kids can enjoy. In each chapter y'all will find that I've listed two drinks that my sister has given me. One of the refreshments will be what she calls an adult beverage, which contains alcohol; the other will be one that the whole family can enjoy. And as y'all will soon see, she's also commented on each drink as well. So without any further ado, here are some drinks that will definitely put the "Merry" in your "Christmas."

Rudolph the Red-Nosed Reindeer

A couple of these and you'll know why his nose glows.

1¼ ounces light rum
1½ ounces lemon juice
½ ounce grenadine

Ice cubes
Hawaiian Punch
Lemon wedge for garnish

Mix the light rum, lemon juice, grenadine, and ice in a shaker. Pour over ice in a collins glass. Top off with Hawaiian Punch. Add lemon wedge and serve.

Orange Eggnog Float

I wouldn't be surprised if Bing didn't come back for a little glass of this on a White Christmas *night.*

Makes about 30 servin's

4 eggs
6 tablespoons sugar
5½ cups orange juice, chilled

½ cup lemon juice
1 quart vanilla ice cream
1 quart ginger ale, chilled

In a large bowl, beat your eggs and sugar until they're light. Add your juices and stir well. Gently pour this in a punch bowl. Scoop out small portions of ice cream and place 'em in the punch bowl as well. Slowly pour your ginger ale along the sides of the punch bowl so not to waste the carbonation. Stir gently. Serve in punch cups.

Trailer Park Christmas Grub

Boy, do we love to eat at the trailer park, which is a good thing for y'all, 'cause we've tried and tested near almost every recipe we've come across. That means all the recipes that are included in this section of each chapter are sure to be winners regardless if you're sharin' 'em with friends at a holiday gatherin', or eatin' 'em with your family.

In order to make your lives a little less stressful durin' the Twelve Days, I've decided to divide the food into four parts: cookies, fudge, pies, and supper.

The cookie part will give you some of our favorite recipes down here at the High Chaparral Trailer Park. These are tried and true, and they're sure to make Santa Claus come back to your trailer year after year.

And what would a Christmas be like without fudge? If you answered "Canadian Thanksgivin'," you're correct. And who doesn't like fudge? Nobody, especially at the High Chaparral, will turn down a good piece of melt-in-your-mouth homemade fudge. But I ain't just got regular fudge recipes. No, I've included a large assortment of different-flavored fudge that is sure to please everybody regardless of what their favorite might be. Just one little thing about fudge makin', the soft ball stage for y'all who won't be usin' a candy ther-mometer is reached when your boilin' mixture reaches around 234 degrees Fahrenheit. Oh, and if you've never made fudge or candy before, make sure you got a lot of room in the top of your pot 'cause your mixtures will boil up to almost double their size.

When it comes to pies, I'm tellin' y'all, the folks at my trailer park have gone all out to provide you with some of the best pies you'll ever put in your mouth. These delectable desserts would make the angels sing after just one bite. Typically in a trailer home durin' the Yuletide you'll find our tables filled with a variety of pies. Not only are these good tastin', but they're so basic and easy to make. Like I've said before, you find a good trailer park woman, and you'll find a good pie recipe.

And finally, I give you a supper menu that will have your family beggin' for more. They won't know what hit 'em with these blue-ribbon-winnin' recipes.

So there you have it, all the recipes you will need to bake your way into Christmas. Oh, one more quick thing. If you've read my past books, which you really should, y'all will know that at the High Chaparral Trailer Park, we prefer margarine over butter, which means all our recipes call for margarine. If your family happens to be wealthy and y'all can afford butter, then please feel free to substitute the exact same amount of butter for the called-for amount of margarine.

Now, before y'all fire up that stove and have a Merry Christmas, let me just add one thing. Since this, the first day of Christmas, is one of those holidays that starts when you wake up in the mornin' or afternoon, whichever the case may be, I've decided to include a breakfast item as well for this day. Actually this is also a great item to feed your family on any Sunday mornin' before y'all head out to church. Naturally my Jewish friends could change the dish's name to Sister Bertha's Breakfast Rolls, and enjoy the same breakfast dish before headin' off to temple on a Saturday, although I don't know how this will taste durin' Passover, if you substituted matzoh for the biscuits. Please let me know.

Away in the Manger Breakfast Rolls

Start your day off with the same breakfast that they ate in Bible times, or so says Sister Bertha.

Makes 24 rolls

1 bag frozen dinner rolls, 24 rolls
$3^3/_4$ ounces Jell-O cook-and-
   serve butterscotch pudding
$1/_2$ cup margarine

$3/_4$ cup brown sugar
$3/_4$ teaspoon cinnamon
$1/_2$ cup chopped pecans

Take two greased angel food cake pans and arrange your rolls in 'em. Open your Jell-O package and sprinkle the mix on the rolls. Set aside.

   Put the margarine in a saucepan over low heat. Once it starts to melt, add the rest of the ingredients and continue to cook until the sugar dissolves. Pour it over the rolls. Cover the cake pans with foil. Let them set in the fridge overnight. Fire up the oven the next mornin' to 350 degrees F. and bake for 30 minutes. Say a prayer over 'em and serve.

      —SISTER BERTHA, LOT #12

Christmas Cookie

Holly Jolly Eggnog Cookies

If you're feelin' real decadent, dip 'em in a glass of eggnog when you eat 'em.

Makes between 5 and 6 servin's

$1^1/_4$ cups sugar
$3/_4$ cup margarine, softened

$1/_2$ cup eggnog
1 teaspoon vanilla

2 egg yolks
1 teaspoon ground nutmeg
2$\frac{1}{4}$ cups all-purpose flour

1 teaspoon bakin' powder
$\frac{1}{2}$ teaspoon ground cinnamon

Get your oven goin' at about 300 degrees F.

Grab you a big bowl and combine flour, bakin' powder, and cinnamon. Set it aside. Get you another bowl and cream your sugar and margarine real good. Toss in the eggnog, vanilla, and egg yolks. Beat this until smooth. Add the dry ingredients and carefully mix these together until just combined. If you use a mixer, put it on low.

Drop about a teaspoon-sized portion of dough onto an ungreased cookie sheet. Once you've got your cookies on the cookie sheet, sprinkle them lightly with nutmeg. Bake 20 minutes or until the bottoms are a light brown color.

—LITTLE LINDA, LOT #20

Festive Fudge

Opal's Snow Fudge

Don't y'all in Florida worry none, this recipe don't call for real snow.

Makes a batch

2 cups sugar
1 cup evaporated milk
$\frac{1}{2}$ cup margarine
$\frac{3}{4}$ cup flaked coconut

1 teaspoon vanilla
8 ounce white almond bark
1 cup miniature marshmallows
$\frac{1}{2}$ cup chopped walnuts

Put sugar, cream, and margarine in a pot and bring it to a soft ball stage. Remove from heat. Add almond bark and marshmallows. Beat until melted. Stir in nuts, $\frac{1}{2}$ cup coconut, and vanilla. Put in 9- × 9-inch buttered pan. Sprinkle on remainin' coconut. Put in fridge to cool.

—OPAL LAMB-BROWN, LOT #1

Pies on Earth, Goodwill Toward Men

Anita's Bar and Grill up on the Housetop Chocolate Buttermilk Pie

Not only is this divine, but it also gives a good Baptist an excuse for goin' into a bar.

Makes 2 pies

$3/4$ cup margarine, melted
1 cup sugar
1 tablespoon self-rising flour
3 whole eggs, beaten

$1/2$ cup buttermilk
$1/2$ cup chocolate chips
1 teaspoon vanilla
2 unbaked 9-inch pie shells

Preheat oven to 350 degrees F.

Stir together margarine, sugar, flour, eggs, buttermilk, chocolate chips, and vanilla, mixing well. Pour buttermilk mixture into unbaked pie shells. Bake in preheated oven about 30 minutes.

—ANITA BIGGON, LOT #2

Seasonal Supper Sensation

Ollie's Old St. Nick Spam Stuffin'

It wouldn't be Christmas without a big helpin' of this.

Makes about 8 servin's

6 ounces dry bread stuffin' mix
8 slices bread, cut into tiny
  pieces

3 eggs, beaten
$1/2$ cup chicken broth
6 ounces Spam, diced

Preheat your oven to 350 degrees F.

Take a 2-quart bakin' dish and grease it up.

Make the dry bread stuffin' mix as per the directions on the box. Add the bread, eggs, broth, and Spam. Mix well and put in the bakin' dish. Bake in the oven for 1 hour.

—OLLIE WHITE, LOT #10

Vance Pool's 'Tis the Season Maple Ham

One bite and you'll know why he weighs almost 400 pounds.

Makes 10 to 12 servin's

5 pounds precooked smoked ham
1 cup maple syrup
$1/4$ cup all-purpose flour

1 cup water
$1/2$ teaspoon powdered mustard
2 teaspoons Worcestershire Sauce

Put your noncovered ham fat side up in a shallow roastin' pan and toss it in a 325 degrees F. preheated oven. *Don't add no water.* After 45 minutes of cookin', pull the ham out and pour the juices in a bowl. Pour your maple syrup over the ham. Put it back in the oven, bastin' it with the syrup from the pan from time to time. Let it back in another 45 minutes. Pull the ham out of the oven and drain the drippin's into a sauce pan. Put the sauce pan on a medium heat, and add the flour and blend it. Add the rest of the ingredients, mix well, and bring to a boil, stirrin' constantly. Remove from the heat. Serve on the side with the ham.

—VANCE POOL, LOT #19

Faye Faye's Fried Christmas Corn Dish Delight

This is so good it might be illegal in some states, which is why we only eat it around Christmastime.

Makes about 6 servin's

6 strips bacon
$1/3$ cup chopped onion
$1/3$ cup chopped bell pepper
16-ounce package frozen corn

1 large tomato, skinned & diced
$1/2$ teaspoon salt
Dash of pepper
1 teaspoon cumin

Fry, drain, and crumble bacon. Sauté your onion and bell pepper in $1/4$ cup of your bacon drippings. Add corn, tomato, salt, pepper, and cumin. Cook about 10 minutes, stirring frequently. Add the bacon.

—FAYE FAYE LaRUE, LOT #17

Momma Boxcar's I'll Be Home for Christmas Honey Buttermilk Bread

This is the reason I tried to continue livin' at home up till I was in my twenties.

Makes one loaf

$1/4$ cup honey
1 large egg, beaten
1 cup buttermilk
$1^1/4$ cups whole-wheat flour
$1/4$ cup ground flaxseed

$1^3/4$ cups all-purpose flour
$1^1/2$ teaspoons salt
$1/2$ teaspoon ground cinnamon
1 packet active dry yeast
1 teaspoon melted margarine

Add all your wet ingredients to your bread machine. Follow this with the dry ingredients except for the yeast. Make a well in the middle of the flour and finally add your yeast. Set your machine to the dough cycle and start it up.

When the bread machine is done, remove the dough from the pan and place it in a lightly greased loaf pan. Cover with plastic wrap that has been greased as well, and place it in a warm place until doubled in size.

Preheat oven to 350 degrees F. Gently brush the top of the loaf with melted margarine and bake bread for 30 to 35 minutes.

—Momma Boxcar, Lot #5

CHAPTER 2

The Second Day of Christmas

DECEMBER 14

It only takes four words to sum up Kenny and Donny's yearly Christmas display: be-you-tea-full!

Traditional Gift on This Day
  Two turtle doves

Trailer Park Gift on This Day
  Two dozen turtle candies (and don't think I'm sharin')

ABOUT THIS DAY

Traditionally we trailer folks have spent most the time leadin' up to this day gettin' the inside of our trailer in order. We've got it sparklin' and shinin' and our home is a doggone Christmas showplace that must be seen to be believed. So it's usually on this day of the year when we start on our outside. Naturally our lights are already strung up since we never take 'em down, but we might go ahead and add an additional string or two weather permittin' of course. And we might have already put out a few yard statues by now as well. In any case, it is today that we go on out and finish up the job. After all, the non-trailer park dwellers will soon be drivin' through pointin' and takin' pictures of all the lovely Christmas items that we've used to decorate the little space we have. We can only hope and pray that our yard display will help to enlighten them with their own outside trimmin's.

A CHRISTMASTIME TREASURE
FROM THE HIGH CHAPARRAL TRAILER PARK

Kenny and Donny have always brought a special spirit of Christmas to our little part of the world. And I got to tell y'all that they are some of the most creative men I've ever known. It's just amazin' what they can do with an old wreath, a can of spray-on snow, and some glitter. Them boys just baffle our minds with their talent. They always have one of the most beautifully decorated trailers both inside and out. I tell y'all, it's like a doggone winter wonderland that you'd expect to see only in your dreams, which is why we were so disappointed in 1992 when Kenny stood up at our annual yearly High Chaparral Trailer Park residents meetin' and announced that he wouldn't be goin' all out for Christmas that year. "Y'all can beg at my feet and shed tears till y'all are blue in the face," Kenny said as he held back tears, "but I simply refuse to dedicate one more second of my life to a chore of this magnitude when it's not appreciated." Naturally we all told Kenny that we loved what he did to Lot #15, and how not havin' it would be like not havin' Christmas. Well, if you knew Kenny, you'd know that by now he *was* in tears, cryin' like a baby. He's a very emotional man, which is most likely why he always has a tissue tucked into the cuffs of his shirts. "I know y'all appreciate my work," he said through his tears, "but unfortunately there's someone in this meetin' who doesn't, so I'm sorry, but there will be no Christmas this year at Lot #15." As we gasped, Kenny spun around and ran out the door into the cold with his mullet blowin' in the wind. Well, it would later turn out that Kenny felt like he'd worked his behind off to make their trailer beautiful for the season and Donny didn't give him his propers, as they young'ens like to say. I got to tell y'all that even though I understood where he was comin' from, I still don't understand why he can get so upset with Donny like he does. God bless him, he's just so sensitive. I can't imagine what it's gonna be like when he gets a wife.

Anyways, long story short, later that night Donny and Kenny had either a heart-to-heart or a knock-down drag-out fight. Me and my husband, Dew, heard some yellin' goin' on over at their trailer, but it didn't sound like it'd turned to violence. Still when I talked to Donny about the whole thing he said that Kenny was fine after he'd "pounded the Christmas spirit into him," and that Kenny would be decoratin' after all. Maybe he meant "hammered the Christmas spirit into him," as in gettin' drunk on eggnog toddies, which I know they both highly enjoy durin' the holiday season. Regardless, this news just made everybody's Christmas. When Kenny came out and started to work on his display, I called up some of the gals and told 'em to come on over. Now I don't want y'all to think that while we set there in the heat of my livin' room and watched a single man doin' manual labor in December that we was havin' lustful thoughts in our hearts like them gals do in that old Diet Coke commercial. No, we just enjoyed watchin' Kenny take a pretty yard and make it magical. The passion he puts into settin' out and stringin' up them 20,000 lights, 24 rope lights with 216 bulbs in each, 7 sets of icicle lights with a chasin' option, 12 lighted 4-foot-high hollow plastic candles, a hollow plastic Rudolph with a flashin' red nose, 26 lighted hollow plastic toy soldiers, 8 Santa-hat-wearin' pink flamingos with their own personal spotlights, 6 lighted hollow plastic Frosty the Snowman, 2 lighted hollow plastic Nutcrackers that stand guard at their front door, a 6-foot lighted star for the top of the trailer, 2 lighted hollow plastic angels that stand on each side of the big star, 1 fake chimney with animated Santa legs sproutin' from the top that sets behind and to the left of the big star, 1 rainbow-colored fake tree with mirror balls that sets on a turnin' musical pedestal—which softly plays "We Are Family"—a white PVC pipe manger with track lightin', 3 lighted hollow plastic Wise Men, 2 identical lighted hollow plastic shepherds, an assortment of hollow plastic barn animals, 1 hollow plastic camel, a lighted hollow plastic Virgin Mary with an added yellow neon halo, a lighted hollow Saint Joseph with an added yellow neon halo, and last but never least a lighted hollow plastic baby Jesus with an added yellow neon halo wrapped in a blue sequined baby blanket layin' in a crib. Oh, and I can't forget the searchlights.

Folks drive from all over the area to see Kenny and Donny's light display. And as you can guess, none of the local businesses mind either. But if you think their yard is somethin', you should see what them boys do together on the inside of the trailer. The decorations are just breathtakin'. It sure is a blessin' havin' those two around, even if they did frighten us that year with the horrific thought of them not doin' up their yard. All I can tell y'all is that it sure made us realize how important them boys and their Christmas display really are to makin' our holidays special. That's why December of 1992 will always be known around the High Chaparral Trailer Park as the "Christmas that almost wasn't." It's also known over at the electric company as the "Christmas that we almost didn't get bonus checks."

CHRISTMAS CRAFTS FROM THE HEART

Donna Sue's Beer Bottle Reindeer

SUPPLIES

1 beer bottle (shaped like the rounded Michelob bottle), washed and dried
Large-size Styrofoam egg
8- × 10-inch tan felt
8- × 10-inch dark brown felt
2 12-mm crystal animal craft eyes
14-inch strip Christmas ribbon
3/4-inch plastic craft eyelashes
1 small red pom-pom
2-inch tan pom-poms
Gold self stickin' craft braid
Brown Styrofoam paint
Medium-sized paint brush
Craft glue
2 pipe cleaners

1. Paint egg completely with brown Styrofoam paint. Set aside to dry.

2. Usin' the patterns on the next page, cut out ears, antlers, chest, body, and toes from the felt.

3. Match and glue 2 antler pieces together with a pipe cleaner in between to make the antler bendable. Do this with the other 2 antler pieces and the additional pipe cleaner.

4. Once the egg is dry, position it sideways on the top of the bottle so that the thick part of the egg is on the bottle and the thinner top of the egg hangs over the bottle. The thick part will be the head and the thinner portion will be the reindeer's muzzle. Once positioned, press down on the thick part of the egg so that it enters the bottle slightly. Take the egg off and put glue along the rim of the bottle. Place the egg back on the rim and let the egg and bottle dry.

5. Usin' the finished photo, glue the felt body piece to the front of the bottle and let dry.

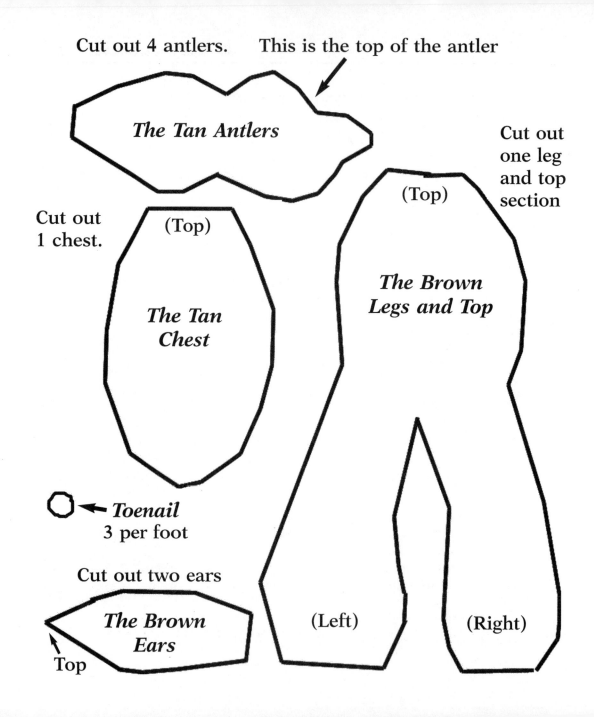

6. Glue the chest piece on to the dried body piece so that the front of the reindeer matches the completed photo.

7. Glue on the toes.

8. Take the self stick decorative braid and make a circle around the brown egg muzzle. Attach another piece from each side of the circle around the back so that it creates a "bridle." Again, refer to the completed photo.

9. Glue the small red pom-pom on the tip of the muzzle to make the nose.

10. Press the eyes into the position on the egg head.

11. Press antler pieces into the position toward the back of the head.

12. Glue ear pieces in front of the antlers.

13. Glue eyelashes behind eyes.

14. Tie the ribbon around the bottle neck.

15. Glue the tan pom-pom directly on the back of the bottle to make a tail.

16. If you like, feel free to decorate the front tan felt section with sequins or glitter.

17. Display.

TIPS FOR THE HOLIDAY HOSTESS

As hostess, it's your job to do the invitin'. Usually I try to include all my relatives unless it's a private party where it'll just be me and my husband, Dew, and, say, members of my bowlin' team. I also invite the neighbors on either side of me. This way they can't complain about the parkin' or the noise. I also let my guests know when I invite 'em that this is a party for adults only. I love children just as long as they ain't in my trailer or out in my yard. Your guests shouldn't have a problem with leavin' their little ones at home. If they do, well, that's just too bad. Paper invites are always nice, but in the trailer park they're not needed. A simple phone call a week prior to the event is fine. Just make sure you follow up that call on the day of the party. It ain't that your guests are all that busy, but you certainly don't want to find out after the party has started that the gal who was supposed to bring the Dr Pepper is in jail for bad checks. That could be a fiasco. So be sure you make that follow-up call.

Party Idea

Lingerie Christmas Party

For the past two years Little Linda has invited me, Donna Sue, Connie Kay, Nellie Tinkle, Dottie Lamb and her daughter Opal, Anita Biggon, and Flora Delight over to her little RV in Lot #20 for what she calls her "Naughty Girl Lingerie" Christmas party. Mind you, I was a little worried about attendin' one of her parties. I figured that it'd be nothin' but a big booze hounds blowout, but I couldn't have been any more wrong. Sure there was booze, after all, my sister Donna Sue was there, but there was no pressure to drink or nothin' like that. And even though it was a bit crowded, I still had a blast. I'd never been to a lingerie party let alone bought the stuff, but I was ready to give it a try. Now, if you've never been to a lingerie party, let me just give you an idea of what it's like. Imagine a Tupperware or Mary Kay party but instead of lookin' at products that will lock in freshness, you're lookin' at clothes that will lock in some lovin' from your husband. The first one sure was somethin'. Since Little Linda's

RV ain't all that big, she had to have the models dress in a van that she had runnin' just outside her door in the driveway. When one of the gals was ready, she'd knock on the door, Little Linda would introduce the product, and the girl would come in. She'd model the item and we'd mark it down on our order sheet if we wanted it, and then when we was done with her, she'd go out and the next gal would come in. It was really simple how they had it all done. Of course that all changed once the menfolk found out that there were lingerie models in the park. They congregated together out in the cold street and hooted and hollered as them gals would go from the van to the RV and back. It really started to upset the models and led our party in a whole new direction. After all, do you really think Mickey Ray is gonna find them hunter orange lace panties excitin' on Connie Kay after he's seen 'em on some well-built twenty-two-year-old girl? Heck, Connie would have a better chance of gettin' her man's attention with a rack of ribs danglin' from her neck after he'd seen all that madness. So all the married ladies got up and went outside to chase their other halves back to the trailers. Of course, I didn't have to get up and chase my man back home 'cause me and my husband, Dew, have a good, long-lastin', committed marriage that is different from the ones the rest of the gals in my trailer park have. I just stayed seated and yelled out, "I hope I ain't got to leave this heat to see if my husband is out there bein' all perverted like."

"You ain't," he muttered back and then turned around to go back over to Lot #18 where he belonged.

A good time was had by all, and we saw some things that I just couldn't believe anyone would even think about runnin' around in. But then we ladies saw some items that I personally liked. The only problem was that it was hard to tell just what them pieces was gonna look like on me with these tiny models runnin' around in the outfits. For example, I wanted that red velvet full back stretch thong with the stretch rhinestone embellishments, but exactly how much stretch will them rhinestones put out was my question. You just couldn't tell on them gals. So I just ordered a dozen assorted leg garters and a pair of Christmas boxers that play "Jingle Bells" for Dew. Let me tell you, when them leg garters arrived and wouldn't go past my ankle, I sure was glad that and them boxers were all I ordered, and I told that to Little Linda as well. I quickly found out I was preachin' to the choir when she opened her RV door and stood there in a lace panties and a matchin' mis-sized bustier that can best be described as lookin' like somebody tied a batch of bread dough in a bag, which once it rose wound up burstin' on both ends. It was then that both Little Linda and I were probably glad that she went with the matchin' panties option rather than the thong.

"I thought you was the fire department," she said as she tried to catch her breath. "The panties fit just fine so I tried to get this bustier on as well. All I got to say is somebody at that lingerie company must be on drugs." Luckily for her, our volunteer fire department showed up just a few seconds later and used the Jaws of Life to free her from that contraption. The firefighters quickly headed back on their way without sayin' a word to her or even a word about what had happened. I guess they've been called over to Little Linda's on business enough times over the past year to become desensitized to any kind of trouble she manages to get herself into.

This past year Little Linda assured each of us gals that she was bringin' in 300-pounds-and-up-size models this time around so we big gals could see what we was actually buyin'. It did make a difference, and I felt like I was buyin' with confidence this go around. Unfortunately I had to leave and head back home right in the middle of the party on account of feelin' ill. All that rockin' Little Linda's RV was doin' from them large gals walkin' back and forth as they modeled had made me seasick. A few weeks later when she stopped by with my order, she assured me that before her next Christmas lingerie party she'd have new shocks put on the RV and use cinderblocks as counter weights. Of course, I told her to count me in!

Trailer Park Christmas Games

Decorate the Christmas Tree Game

This is a great way to get your tree decorated just as long as you don't care what it looks like. You divide up into two teams. Each team is given an equal amount of garland and Christmas ornaments. When the hostess gives the go sign, each team has to decorate the pre-lit tree. The winnin' team is the first one to put all its garland and ornaments on the tree. Naturally, they can't just throw the items on the tree. They have to be hung tastefully and with care.

WHAT'S THAT SMELL?

Nothin' is as welcomin' to company durin' the holiday as a lovely smellin' trailer home, and this mixture will surely bring 'em inside.

Mrs. Claus's Favorite

A whiff of this and you'll know why she stays at home enjoyin' the smells of Christmas.

3 cinnamon sticks
3 bay leaves
$^1/_4$ cup whole cloves

$^1/_2$ lemon, halved
$^1/_2$ orange, halved
1 quart water

Put everything in a Crock-Pot and bring it to a boil. Reduce the heat to the lowest temperature settin', and let it simmer in your trailer all day long. Keep an eye on the water level, and add more when needed. You can reuse this potpourri just as long as you cover it and store it between times in the fridge.

HOLLY JOLLY WOOHA!

* There are thirty-four "Reindeer" place names in the United States; twenty-seven are located in Alaska alone.

* In 1851, Mark Carr hauled two sleds loaded with trees from the Catskills to the streets of New York and opened the first retail tree lot in the United States.

* It takes ten years for a Christmas tree to grow to full maturity.

HELPFUL HOLIDAY HINTS

* Take a plastic grocery bag, fill it with a few whole cloves, pinecones, and cinnamon sticks, and tie it closed. Punch a few small holes in the bag and put it in with your holiday dec-

orations. If you do this in each box, your decorations will fill the air with the smells of Christmas every year when you take 'em out of storage.

❋ You can clean them metal filters in your range fast and easy by washin' em in the dishwasher.

—Lois Bunch, Lot #3

❋ Sprinkle potpourri over the soil of houseplants. Since the petals and leaves in the potpourri eventually decompose, it won't hurt your plants, and it will add color and Christmasy smells, too.

❋ Those little packages of cheese and crackers make wonderful stockin' stuffers unless you got mice or roaches.

—Nellie Tinkle, Lot #4
—Wendy Bottom, Lot #4

Twelve Days of Yuletime Advice

Dear Ruby Ann,

At our last office Christmas Party I got a bit tipsy and got up on the copy machine. I was dancin' and havin' a good time. Everybody loved it. I have a good friend in the office who has treated me differently ever since. It's like she is embarrassed to be seen even talking to me. I can't for the life of me figure it out. Everyone loved it and thought I was the hit of the party. Could it be that she is jealous? I mean, she isn't as pretty as me, but she is real smart! Help me get my friend back.

Love,
Tipsy

Dear Tipsy,

Don't let this friend get you down. And if you want to get to her real feelin's, be your wild and crazy self at next year's party as well. You'll know that she's with you if she presses the print button while you're on the copier just so you can have more light on you while you dance.

Love, Kisses, and Trailer Park Wishes,
Ruby Ann Boxcar

PUTTIN' YOUR BEST FACE FORWARD

Eye Shadow

Your eyes are the windows of your soul, so just like the windows in your trailer, they should be frosted as well. Naturally if you'd read my *Down Home Trailer Park Guide to Livin' Real Good*, you'd know that I always suggest wearin' blue eye shadow, so you most likely guess that I'd suggest frosted blue eye shadow for the holidays. That's right, so follow the King's advice and make this Christmas a blue Christmas, frosted of course.

CHRISTMAS CHEER

Donna Sue suggests . . .

White Russian Winter

It took twelve of these and a little bit of flirtation, but I can now say I danced at the Bolshoi!

3 ounces Kahlua
2 ounces vodka
$^1/_2$ cup coffee ice cream

$^1/_4$ cup milk
1 cup ice

Put everything into a blender. Cover and blend until smooth. Serve in a brandy snifter.

Reindeer Power Punch

This is what Santa's reindeer drink to fly. If you feel like flyin', add some rum.

Makes about 15 to 20 servin's

32 ounces Hawaiian Punch
1 small can frozen orange juice
1 small can frozen cranberry
   juice

$^1/_2$ the combined water the cans
   on the frozen juices say to use
Pineapple chunks for garnish
1-liter bottle Sprite

Add everything but the Sprite into a punch bowl and stir. Cover and chill in the fridge overnight. Add the Sprite by pourin' it down the sides of the bowl. If you want more carbonation, add more Sprite. Serve chilled.

TRAILER PARK CHRISTMAS GRUB

Christmas Cookie

Quickie Kris Kringle Cookies

The only thing easier than these is my sister Donna Sue.

Makes about a dozen

1 cup sugar
1 cup white corn syrup
1¹/₂ cups peanut butter

4 cups corn flakes or sugar-
   coated corn flakes

Put a pot on the stove and add the first two ingredients. Bring it to a boil, and stir. Take it off the heat once the sugar has dissolved and add the peanut butter. Stir until it's mixed well. Add the corn flakes. Drop the mixture by the spoonful onto a wax paper–lined bakin' sheet. Let 'em cool down and set, which should take just a few minutes.

—JUANITA HIX, LOT #9

Festive Fudge

Velveeta Cheese Fudge

I know it's hard to believe, but this stuff is better than a Mickey Rooney movie and is a tasty holiday treat.

Makes a batch

¹/₂ pound Velveeta cheese, cubed
¹/₂ pound margarine
2 pounds powdered sugar

¹/₂ cup cocoa powder
1 tablespoon vanilla extract
1 cup nuts, optional

Put the cubed Velveeta and margarine in a microwavable bowl. Microwave for 2 minutes. Take out the mixture and stir. If the cheese has not melted all the way, put it back in the microwave for another minute or so.

In a separate bowl, sift the powdered sugar and the cocoa together. Add it to the Velveeta cheese mixture. Stir well. Add the vanilla extract. Mix well. Add the nuts if you decide to use them, and mix well. Spread the mixture out into a lightly greased pan or cookie sheet. If you use the cookie sheet, I'd also line it with wax paper. Let it cool in the fridge for an hour or so. Once it has set, slice it into pieces. You can actually put these pieces in plastic bags and store in the freezer for months.

—ANITA BIGGON, LOT #2

Pies on Earth, Goodwill Toward Men

Taco Tackle Shack's North Pole Lemon Cheesecake Pie

Lois offers this at Christmas time at her Tex-Mex restaurant. You order up a Mexican Wienie platter and a free slice of this pie comes with it.

Makes one pie

8 ounces cream cheese
2 tablespoons margarine
$1/2$ cup sugar
1 egg
2 tablespoons flour

$2/3$ cup milk
$1/4$ cup lemon juice
2 tablespoons grated lemon peel
1 graham cracker crust, unbaked

Thoroughly blend the cream cheese and margarine together. Add sugar and egg. Mix well. Add flour, milk, lemon juice, and peel. Pour into graham cracker crust, and bake 35 minutes in a 350 degree F. oven. Put it in the fridge to chill for at least an hour.

—LOIS BUNCH, LOT #3

Seasonal Supper Sensation

Connie Kay's No Time to Cook 'Cause I'm Christmas Shoppin' Hawaiian Sandwiches

My husband, Dew, says these go good with an ice-cold Dr Pepper.

Makes 4 sandwiches

8 slices cooked ham (use some of the ham you got from last night's dinner)

8 tablespoons chopped pineapple

4 tablespoons Miracle Whip

8 slices bread (If you got any left, you can use the Honey Buttermilk Bread, page 47.)

Some margarine to spread on bread

Chop your ham up into real fine slivers. Add this and the pineapple and Miracle Whip into a bowl and combine. Put in fridge.

Spread margarine on one side of the bread slices and grill in a skillet until they're nicely toasted. Spread the ham mixture on the bread and make into sandwiches. Serve with pickles.

—CONNIE KAY, LOT #13

Ruby Ann's Homemade Joy to the World Potato Chips

These are so good, you can actually put 'em in decorative sacks and hand 'em out as Christmas gifts.

Makes 4 servin's

8 russet potatoes, cleaned and
  peeled
2 quarts water
3 tablespoons salt
Oil for fryin'

3 tablespoons garlic salt
1 tablespoon pepper
1 tablespoon onion salt
1 tablespoon oregano

Combine the water and salt in a bowl. Slice your potatoes up real thin and put 'em in the water. Push the potatoes down until all have been submerged at least once. Cover and put in the fridge overnight. If you ain't got that kind of time for them to set, an hour would be just fine, but overnight is much better.

Drain your potatoes and pat dry. Get your oil up to 350 degrees F. Add the potato chips. Turn the chips from time to time until they've almost reached their desired brownness and then place the chips on paper towels to drain. They'll keep cookin' for a little while more after they've been placed on the paper towels.

Mix the remainin' ingredients together and put in a salt shaker. Sprinkle this mixture over the chips. Store the remainder of the seasonin' that's in the shaker with your other spices.

—RUBY ANN BOXCAR, LOT #18

CHAPTER 3

The Third Day of Christmas

DECEMBER 15

Both the dry, bland turkey that Faye Faye brought to
the Christmas party and the steps outside her trailer
could have used a lot more salt that year.

Traditional Gift on This Day
Three French Hens

Trailer Park Gift on This Day
Three French perfumes (from one of them 99-cent stores)

ABOUT THIS DAY

By the third day of Christmas we got our ovens fired up and goin' 24/7. We're bakin' more Christmas goodies than we can possibly eat, although somehow we manage to eat 'em anyway. Of course, as I've said earlier, this is the season that we do bake like the Dickens and for good reason. Our food is our way of sharin' the Christmas spirit, which we do daily at the High Chaparral Trailer Park with both our neighbors as well as guests who stop by. December 15th happens to be the traditional day for the residents' trailer park Christmas party. With all the good food that's consumed on that evenin', I really do think that we have more fun with our neighbors on that day than a good Baptist is allowed. Oh, well, it is the holidays.

A CHRISTMASTIME TREASURE
FROM THE HIGH CHAPARRAL TRAILER PARK

There are three things I remember about Christmas of 1964:

1. Some of us young uns at the trailer park were rockin' to the Beatles song "I Feel Fine," which was climbin' up the charts

(Pa-Pa swore that Paul, George, John, and Ringo was the Four Horsemen of the Apocalypse).

2. It was wet and cold.

3. Faye Faye LaRue had an astonishin' prediction about our trailer park Christmas party.

Now, y'all who've read my earlier books will recall that when Faye Faye and my sister Donna Sue had their big fallin' out (where Donna Sue ended up goin' to jail and Faye Faye moved out of state in the middle of the night), Faye Faye was livin' in Lot #3. Well, back in 1964 she was livin' with her older sister Divina Lee, in Lot #17. It wasn't until Divina moved to Louisiana to run that string of adult theaters that Faye Faye bought a used trailer and moved over to Lot #3. Anyway, now that we're on the same page, let me continue with my story.

Every year we'd all gathered at the trailer park community center, which used to be located where the dumpster and mail boxes are today (there's a map in my first book and one on my web page). Of course that was before the community center was struck by lightnin' and burnt to the ground. But back then everybody would volunteer to bring somethin'. Seein' how I was just fourteen at the time, I just helped Momma with her side dish and dessert that she'd selected for the Christmas gatherin'. Well, that year Divina and Faye Faye agreed to bake the turkeys, which everyone in the park had chipped in on, since the two birds would be the main meat items at the event. They put the first twenty-five-pound turkey in the oven around 6 in the mornin' so it could cook, but seein' how they'd never roasted turkeys this big before, they kind of messed 'em up by over-stuffin' 'em. That first bird blew up, blowin' the doggone door right off the oven. When Momma got the call to come over quick, she brung me along. I tell you, we couldn't believe our eyes. There was stuffin' everywhere. It was hangin' from the ceilin', off the fridge, on top of the couch in the livin' room. Why, I wouldn't be surprised if Faye Faye still ain't pullin' the occasional piece of turkey or bread-crumb from her hair. Luckily, Momma was able to unstuff part of the other turkey so it didn't suffer the same fate. Of course Faye Faye and Divina had to take turns holdin' the oven door on till the bird was done cookin'. As me and Momma left, Faye Faye looked both of us right in the eye and said, "Y'all be careful out there, 'cause somebody could slip and fall with all that ice." I'll never forget them words as long as I live, 'cause it'd turn out that even back then Faye Faye was already showin' signs of havin' the gift of predictin' the future. Well, me and my momma made it back just fine, and, feelin' bad for Divina and Faye Faye, she popped a ham in the stove just to make sure that there would be plenty of meat for everyone. Around six that night Momma and Daddy and me headed over to the com-munity center with our food items, but after sayin' hello to every-body, Momma noticed that my sister Donna Sue hadn't arrived. She sent me over to Donna Sue's trailer to see if she needed help carryin' her side dish to the gatherin'. Even though my sister was just eight-een at the time, she was already drinkin' for four and the whole trailer park knew it. Obligingly I went back out into the cold and carefully made my way down the street toward my sister's place. Sure enough, I found Donna Sue passed out on her couch, and there was no wakin' her drunken behind up. So I did what any good sister would do, I dumped a bag of Fritos into a bowl of leftover chili I found in her fridge, topped that off with some sour cream, mixed it up real good, and slapped a lid on it. Then I stuck her hand in a bowl of warm water and exited out her trailer with the bowl of Donna Sue's South of the Border Mix. I figured I'd just tell everyone that she wasn't feelin' good so she decided to stay at home and just send her side dish with me. Even though everyone knew she was most likely laid up with either a bottle or a man, it would at least make my folks feel like they'd saved face in front of their neighbors. Knowin' I'd done a good deed, I begin to make my way back to the community center, which was when I came up on Faye Faye and her sister Divina comin' out of their trailer. Since Divina used a cane on account of her bad leg, she let Faye Faye carry the turkey. Well, Divina came down the front steps, clingin' on to that handrail for dear life. Once Divina was safely down, Faye Faye handed her a bowl of stuffin', which they'd taken from the turkey. Then, as I got closer, Faye Faye went back into the trailer, shut the lights off, closed and locked the door, and began makin' her way down the icy stairs. She did real good balancin' the turkey in her hands while tryin' to be careful on those treacherous steps. That is, until her foot hit a patch of slick ice on the next to the last step and then both Faye Faye and that turkey she was carryin' took to flight. I got a feelin' that big bird most likely hadn't flown as high when it was alive as it did on that freezin' December night. You can only imagine that it took all I had not to bust a gut right there. Not only had Faye Faye fallen flat on her behind, but she'd also managed to throw that Christmas turkey up into the nearby tree. Once Faye Faye managed to get up from the ground she and Divina, who had not seen me standin' across the street, tried to figure out a way get that turkey down. At first they did everything they could to shake the tree, but it didn't budge. Faye Faye even tried to climb the tree, but the freezin' rain from earlier that day made that tree slipperier than a greased pole. Finally Faye Faye took Divina's cane and began swingin' at that poor roasted bird. After several tries she finally made contact, and that bird flew out of that tree like Mickey Mantle had hit it. It landed in the street and slid under the front of my Pa-Pa and Me-Ma's trailer over in Lot #16. Luckily for the girls, my grandparents were already at the community center, so Faye Faye climbed under the trailer, wiped off the bird, and stuck it back in the bakin' pan. They then swore not to tell a soul about what had happened and went into the community center. Naturally no one had the slightest idea as to what had taken place. And Faye Faye's prediction had come true. I also learnt two things that night before Christmas:

1. Turkeys can fly.

2. If you ever look at a dish at a potluck, and think to yourself, "I wonder if that stuff on top is dirt," it most likely is.

Needless to say, when given the choice as an adult, I'll almost always select the ham over turkey.

CHRISTMAS CRAFTS FROM THE HEART

Christmas Card Placemats

Now, not only do these look fabulous on your kitchen table, but they make great gifts as well. And they're so fun to make. Plus they're both clever and cheap, and we like that, now don't we?

SUPPLIES
16 Christmas cards
Scissors

1. Cut off the fronts of each card, and then cut 'em all down so they're all the same size.

2. Take the matching-size front artwork to a copy place that laminates. Show the clerk how you want them to be laminated. Lay out four cards and then lay out four more below those, all with the artwork face down. Next lay the remainin' eight cards on top of the first ones, but this time with the artwork face up. When the clerk finishes laminatin' the cards, you should have a holiday placemat with artwork on both sides.

Tips for the Holiday Hostess

If you've invited a new guest to join y'all, check with them to make sure that they ain't allergic to any of the food you're servin'. Why, I'll never forget the time I was havin' a Mexican theme party and had gotten Lois Bunch from the Taco Tackle Shack to cater it. I'd invited this new gal from church to come and join us, you know tryin' to be all nice and all. Luckily I asked her if there was anythin' she was allergic to, and she said she couldn't eat nothin' spicy. Needless to say that knocked out all the food Lois was servin', and had I not asked that simple question, I'd have felt terrible havin' her show up and not bein' able to indulge. Instead I acted like a good hostess and I simply informed her that we'd be servin' Mexican food so she might want to bring a sandwich or a salad or somethin' else so she could eat with the rest of us. The last thing you want is a guest just settin' in the livin' room while the rest of y'all are feedin' your faces.

Party Idea

A Trailer Park Christmas Party

Now I got to tell y'all that I really don't see what's so special about this gatherin', but I've been told that several folks across the United States held parties like this last year, which is why I'm sharin' it. It seems that the host invites people to his home but tells 'em that they have to come dressed up like someone from a trailer park (of course I have no idea what that's supposed to mean) and while the invited guest is on the phone, the host makes him pick a number between 1 and 20. The host then rattles off a list of recipe names from my books for that lot number. For example, if the guest had said "8," then the host would name a whole bunch of recipes that have been credited in my books to Lot #8. The guest has to pick one of the dishes, and the host marks that one off the list. The host later emails or hand-delivers the recipe for that dish to the guest. He does this until all the guests have selected a lot number and a dish to bring to the party. The host or hostess, who dresses up like me, decorates the house with crafts from my *Guide to Livin' Real Good* book as well as items picked up at the local thrift store. They play either country music or Elvis tunes for background music at the party. If liquor is served, they have my sister's *Bartending Guide* on hand so the guest can pick out a drink from the many recipes it features. After dinner, they play games like "The Check Is in the Mail" or "Donna Sue's Boyfriend," and the winners of each game get a copy of one of my books. And either on the wall or up on the fireplace if they have one, they hang a knee high with my name written on it, a man's white sock with my husband Dew's name on it, and a fishnet stockin' with a piece of paper bearin' my sister Donna Sue's name attached to it. Guests are encouraged to put a small cash or check donation in one or all of the stockin's, and the next day the host or hostess takes that money and donates it to the charity of her choice in the name of Ruby Ann, Dew, and Donna Sue Boxcar. I don't understand the whole trailer park thing, but I sure do like the idea of givin' to others who are less fortunate.

Trailer Park Christmas Games

Pass the Aqua Net

Line up in two teams. The first person in each team is given a can of Aqua Net to place under his or her chin. The team member must pass the can to the next in line, but neither may use his or her hands. The first team to get the can of hairspray all the way to the last person in line is the winner. If the can drops between two players, they have to pick it up, give each other's hair a quick spray, and continue from there.

WHAT'S THAT SMELL?

This will bring the smells of a citrus Christmas to your trailer.

Christmas in Florida

Not only does this one smell good, but accordin' to my senile Me-Ma, it tastes good, too.

Makes a batch

6 oranges
3 tablespoons of cloves
2 ounces orange oil

10 drops cinnamon essential oil
12 cinnamon sticks

Take your potato peeler and cut long strips from the orange. You only want the orange-colored skin and none of the white from the orange. Place the strips in a big jar. Add the cloves, orange oil, cinnamon oil, and cinnamon sticks. Let it set for three weeks before usin', shakin' it every few days.

HOLLY JOLLY WOOHA!

❋ Regardless of how you pronounce them, poinsettias are the number-one flowerin' potted plant in the United States.

❋ The Pennsylvania Germans first introduced the Christmas tree to the United States back in 1820. Most likely if you went to their house you could still find some of the original tree needles in their carpets.

❊ More than three billion Christmas cards are sent annually in the United States.

Helpful Holiday Hints

❊ The beautiful pictures on old Christmas cards can be clipped off and used as lovely gift tags.

❊ Wrap oversized gifts in a holiday-patterned tablecloth.

—Momma Boxcar, Lot #5

❊ You can get rid of any bad kitchen smells by cuttin' up a lemon or an orange, puttin' it in a pie pan, and bakin' it in the oven at 200 degrees F. for 20 to 25 minutes.

—Donna Sue Boxcar, Lot #6

Twelve Days of Yuletime Advice

Dear Ruby Ann,

Last year I was robbed at gunpoint on Christmas Day. It was a very traumatic experience for me, and I'm afraid that this is going to ruin my Christmases from now on. Have you or anyone you know gone through an event like this, and then managed to get over it? I love Christmas and don't want to have to give up the joy and fun because of one person's actions. I'm sure somebody at the trailer park has had to have had a horrible Christmas like me.

Troubled About Tinsel Time,
Tony

Dear Tony,

I personally haven't had any kind of holiday trouble like you talk about, but I know some folks over in Lot #13 that sure have. You might want to grab a tissue for this one.

Gaylord Ray Kay, his wife, Wanda, and their three kids—Benton Ray, Mickey Ray, and Lovetta Raye—moved into Lot #13 back in December 1968. But Gaylord Ray didn't stick around at the High Chaparral for too long. Just three short years later he'd up and leave Wanda in the middle of the night, which I personally think explains why she had so much trouble with them kids of hers. Of course, when I say "kids," I mean Benton Ray and Lovetta Raye. I'd bet them two seen a lot more coal in their stockin's than any normal child. That Mickey Ray was always a good son to Wanda as well as a good citizen and Baptist. But for those other two kids, well you could've had 'em as far as I care. That Benton was nothin' but trouble lookin' for a place to happen. And the company he kept was simple low-life gutter trash. Why, he even dated my sister for a time. But that boy treated his momma like she was nothin' more than swamp water—until he needed money, or wanted a good gift for Christmas, and then he'd come runnin' right back to her as if he'd never done her wrong. And I can't begin to tell you how many times he'd seen the inside of a jail cell. That he got from his daddy, who would later surface himself in Mississippi, where he'd been livin'. After locatin' her then husband, Wanda filed for divorce. Well, it turned out that Gaylord Ray was well known in the Mississippi court system, and up until his death, he'd had the distinction of appearin' on Mississippi's John TV more times than any other man arrested for payin' a prostitute. And God bless him, the idiot was arrested eight times in five years by the same undercover police officer. Soon Wanda was a free woman, but that Benton son of hers just got worse. And to make matters even worse yet, Wanda's only daughter, Lovetta Raye, handed her waitressin' apron to the night manager at the truck stop and left her job to run off with a trucker. If that wasn't enough for Wanda to bear, Benton finally ended up in the state prison facin' a two-year term for bad checks and mail fraud. But twenty-two months later, on an unusually warm Christmas night, Wanda got up from the supper table to answer a phone call that she'll always remember. It was Sheriff Gentry on the other end with news about Benton. It seemed that he'd managed to escape from prison, but was hit and killed a few minutes later by a semitruck just two blocks away. The worst part was that it was the rig that killed Benton was bein' driven by Lovetta Raye while her boyfriend was takin' a nap in the back. Talk about your bizarre *Twilight Zone* kind of coincidence. As you can imagine, Wanda was devastated. Mickey Ray and his wife Connie, whom he'd married in May of that year, said they had to help lead Wanda to the bathroom just so she could splash some cold water on her face before she could come back and finish her piece of butter chess pie and cup of coffee. As for Lovetta Raye, she understandably ended up in the nuthouse there for a while, but now if I recall correctly, lives in Tennessee, where she works on the line at a thumb tack factory. Of course with Mickey Ray and Connie, who as you might recall is our rep for Avon, Amway, Shaklee, Tupperware, Mary Kay (no relation mind you) and Merle Norman, takin' care of her, Wanda is doin' just fine, and has managed to not let that tragedy ruin her Christmases. That gal's a trooper all right, and I know if she can turn a bad Christmas around so can you. You just have to let things go and keep on truckin'.

Love, Kisses, and Trailer Park Wishes,
Ruby Ann Boxcar

PUTTIN' YOUR BEST FACE FORWARD

Eyebrows

I understand the pain that comes when you groom your eyebrows. Why, I've even been the victim of hot wax burns. But there is no reason for bushy eyebrows at Christmastime. I don't care if you're ten or a hundred and ten, your eyebrows should look good. That don't mean you have to go out and have 'em plucked, waxed, or even shaved. Instead you can just follow my simple brow secret, Aqua Net. Just give each brow a blast of hairspray, and then use your fingers to slick each of 'em back toward the side of your head. You'll be amazed at how tame that unruly brow can become with just a little Aqua Net.

CHRISTMAS CHEER

Donna Sue suggests . . .

Jingle Bell Punch

A couple glasses of these and you'll be laughin' all the way.

Makes about 10 to 12 servin's

6 cups apple cider
12-ounce can frozen lemonade
  concentrate
1 cup sugar

1 cup peach schnapps
1 cup rum (light, dark, or spiced
  is fine)

Combine the apple cider, lemonade concentrate, and sugar in a big pot, and bring to a boil. Pull off the heat and mix in the schnapps and rum. Stir well. Pour into a punch bowl and serve hot. You can also simply stir together the cider mix in a bowl and pour it in a big coffeemaker to brew. When it finishes brewin', add your booze and swish it around a bit.

Sugar-Free Holiday Nog

Now everybody can enjoy a bit of the old nog.

Makes 8 servin's

9-ounce package sugar-free
  instant vanilla puddin'
7 cups skim milk, divided
1 teaspoon vanilla extract

$^1/_4$ cup Splenda
1 cup evaporated skim milk
$^1/_2$ teaspoon nutmeg

In a large bowl combine the puddin' mix, 2 cups of milk, vanilla, Splenda, and nutmeg. Follow the directions on the puddin' box for how long you should mix it and at what speed. Pour the mixture into a large container that has a lid, and add 3 more cups of milk. Put the lid on and shake well. Take the lid off and add the evaporated milk. Snap that lid back on and shake well again. Pop the lid off and add the remainin' milk. Put the lid back on, shake well, and put in the fridge to chill. If you like the taste of rum in your eggnog, but can't have it for whatever reason, add about $1^{1}/_{2}$ to 2 drops of rum flavorin' to the mixture and shake.

TRAILER PARK CHRISTMAS GRUB

Christmas Cookie

Lulu Bell's God Bless Everyone Bisquick Puddin' Cookies

These are as simple as my niece or her new husband for that matter.

Makes 3 dozen

$^{3}/_{4}$ cup Bisquick
1 regular package instant
   chocolate fudge puddin' mix,
   you can use sugar-free as well

$^{1}/_{4}$ cup oil
1 egg

Mix all of the above together in a bowl. Form into small balls and flatten with your hand onto an ungreased bakin' sheet. Take a fork and run it across like you do them peanut butter cookies. Bake 8 minutes at 350 degrees F.

—LULU BELL BUTTON, LOT #8

Festive Fudge

Wanda's Traditional Trailer Park Bumblebee Christmas Fudge

What would Christmas be like without a few pieces of this stuff?

Makes a batch

4 cups sugar
1 cup water
2 egg whites
1 cup honey

$1/2$ cup peanut butter
1 cup chopped nuts
1 teaspoon vanilla

Boil 1 cup of the sugar and $1/2$ cup of the water to soft ball stage. Pour slowly over stiffly beaten egg whites, stirrin' constantly until stiff. Set aside.

Boil together remainin' 3 cups sugar, honey, peanut butter, and remainin' $1/2$ cup water to soft ball stage. Add to first mixture. Beat constantly until the mixture will hold its shape when dropped from a teaspoon. Add nuts and vanilla. Drop by teaspoonfuls onto waxed paper. Let it cool and then eat.

—WANDA KAY, LOT #13

Pies on Earth, Goodwill Toward Men

Santa's Soda Cracker Pie

I don't know if this is really Santa's own recipe or not, but if it is, thanks, Santa.

Makes one pie

3 egg whites
Pinch salt
1 cup sugar
1 teaspoon vanilla
³/₄ cup chopped pecans

³/₄ cup soda cracker crumbs,
  finely ground
1 teaspoon bakin' powder
1 cup whipped cream
2 tablespoons chopped nuts

Beat 3 egg whites until stiff. Add the salt and sugar a little at a time. Add vanilla. Beat until stiff. Fold in pecans, soda cracker crumbs, and bakin' powder. Spread into buttered pie pan. Bake 25 minutes at 325 degrees F. Top with whipped cream. Put in refrigerator over night. Sprinkle chopped nuts on top.

—VANCE POOL, LOT #19

Chess Pie

All I Want for Christmas Is My Chocolate Chess Pie

This pie takes two good things and makes 'em even better.

Makes one pie

2 whole eggs
1 small can sweetened
  condensed milk
1 teaspoon vanilla

¹/₄ cup margarine
1¹/₂ cup sugar
2 tablespoons cocoa
9-inch unbaked pie shell

Beat your eggs real good, add everythin' but the pie shell. Beat the mixture until its beat real good. Pour it into the pie shell, and bake at 350 degrees F. 40 minutes or until set. Cool and serve.

—LOIS BUNCH, LOT #3

Seasonal Supper Sensation

Trailer Park Bubble and Squeak

Even my friend Liz with the crown and her friend Tony would put down their figgy puddin' for a helpin' of this Americanized version of a classic English dish, which by the way is eaten at our trailer by itself with nothin' else.

Makes 3 to 4 servin's

3 to 4 servin's of prepared instant
  mashed potatoes
1 small onion, chopped
6 ounces Spam, cut into small
  cubes

1 small can sweet peas
1 pound Velveeta cheese,
  cubed
4 strips crisp bacon, crumbled
8 tablespoons vegetable oil

Mix everything but the oil together in a large bowl. Put 4 tablespoons of the oil in a large Teflon skillet and let it get hot. Add the mixture to the skillet, and smash down with a spatula until it's about an inch thick. Cook 5 to 10 minutes or until it takes on a very dark color. All the oil should be soaked into the mixture. Take your spatula and carefully lift the mixture all around to make sure it's not stuck to the skillet. Put a plate on top the mixture, hold the plate tight, and flip the skillet so that the mixture comes out on the plate. Then add the remainin' oil to the skillet, and slide the mixture into the pan so it can cook. When both sides are dark brown or blackened, slide out of the skillet and serve.

—RUBY ANN BOXCAR, LOT #18

CHAPTER 4

The Fourth Day of Christmas

DECEMBER 16

Even though Arkansas is landlocked, with Ollie White around it's always easy to have the same type of nautical Christmas feel as the folks who actually live where sailboats are commonplace.

Traditional Gift on This Day
Four callin' birds

Trailer Park Gift on This Day
Four cars on blocks (and not one tire among 'em)

ABOUT THIS DAY

Even though I decided way back when me and my husband, Dew, got married to have my tubes tied since I knew no child could ever live up to the shadow I cast in life, I still try to help out with the little ones when I can. I always take an active role in the Toys for Tots campaign as well as buyin' more Girl Scout Cookies than a person can possess at one time by law. I volunteer locally to help out at the school's Christmas party, which is held on this day every year, regardless of the day of the week it falls on. Typically what happens is that all the kids, no matter their grade, gather around 3 P.M. in the high school gymnasium and eat. They sing Christmas songs afterward and then open up the little boxes of store-bought candies provided by the school. As you can imagine, the candy doesn't make it out of the buildin'. I usually help pass out the candy or serve the meals. And with all the excitement that these kids are experiencin', they can sometimes become little monsters—but I don't mind. You just have to know how to handle 'em. Personally I've found that a jab with a teasin' comb usually does the trick—turnin' any child's bad behavior around almost instantly.

A CHRISTMASTIME TREASURE
FROM THE HIGH CHAPARRAL TRAILER PARK

When I think back to Christmas when I was a child, Ollie White of Lot #10 can't help but come to mind. Ollie worked in the school cafeteria, and all durin' the holiday season she would always give me a little more than the rest of the kids when she was servin' up the meat item. She later told me this was 'cause all us trailer folk have to stick together. Needless to say, more food at lunch meant a lot to me. Heck, she might as well have been puttin' gold on my plate durin' the Christmas season. Her kindness might also be why I always try to include her in my Christmas plans when I'm in residence at the High Chaparral Trailer Park over the holidays. I know that even though her husband has been gone for many years now, the months of November and December can most likely still be a little lonely, especially since she never had any kids. But even when I'm not spendin' the holidays at my trailer, I always make sure that my momma, daddy, or sister Donna Sue stops by to visit her frequently. Of course, since my sister drinks like a fish, this means that sometimes Ollie finds Donna Sue's Christmas cheer bangin' at her door at all hours of the night. This led me to simply instruct Ollie to hang a sign on her door when she goes to bed at night that reads, "Bar Is Closed!" That seems to work.

The one Christmas I'll never forget that involved Ollie in a special non-food-item-related way took place back in 1979. Actually the story started durin' the summer of '79. Ollie liked to take her clothes that she'd just given a good washin' to and hang 'em up on the line outside to dry. Since they didn't have them dryer sheets back then to add a fresh smell to the clothes, this method of doin' just that was real big and often practiced. As a matter of fact, my mother swore by this way of dryin' clothes even though her temporary clothes line always ran inside from the picture of Elvis in the livin' room to the hangin' lamp over the kitchen table. Momma did this inside on account of how she'd had a bird relieve itself as it flew over her when she was a teenager, and she's never trusted "winged devils" since. In any case, Ollie kept complainin' when she'd get all her clothes back in, some of her panties would be missin'. To this, Orville her husband, who was still alive at the time, would simply tell her she was crazy, and must have just mislaid 'em somewhere. "After all," Orville would add, "you know I love you like a hard roll, but who'd want to steal your panties?" Orville did have a point, which Ollie couldn't argue with. Bein' a size 34 did make the whole idea of someone wantin' your panties a bit absurd, but still it didn't stop Ollie from peekin' out her windows when she noticed someone was washin' his car just to make sure he wasn't usin' her good cotton drawers as a chamois. Needless to say, as the summer went on, Ollie never did see her panties reappear in the form of some kind of wipe, cover, or replacement curtain. She did, however, swear up and down that at least one pair of her underpants would come up missin' every time she put her clothes out to dry. Orville would always add that if her underwear was truly bein' stolen, there'd have to be more than one person involved (or a very strong individual). Ollie never found that funny. When it got just too cold to hang her laundry outside, she went back to usin' her dryer, but it broke down from wear and tear durin' the first week. In the meantime, the Janssens, who lived in Lot #11 in those days, said that Ollie could come over and use their dryer until the new one she'd ordered from the Lamb Department Store arrived. Again, Ollie claimed in the privacy of her home that she was still comin' up short on her panties. These freakish disappearances wouldn't come to a stop until the new dryer had arrived and Ollie would be able to keep an eye on her laundry at all times. Of course October and November passed by and by then everyone, includin' Ollie, had forgotten about her missin' undergarments. That was until one December afternoon when Ollie stepped outside the school cafeteria to catch a breath of fresh air and get away momentarily from all the cigarette smoke. She couldn't believe her eyes. Several of the kids out on the playground had built up snow forts around the freezin' monkey bars and swing set, and were now engaged in snowball fights. That was natural childhood behavior of course, but what had taken her breath away was that these kids had her panties. These little sons of guns had knotted up the leg hole openin's and were usin' her panties to carry their snowballs in. She wasn't crazy after all. Her panties had been lifted. We'd later find out that it was those evil-spirited Janssen twins, Jack and Josh, that had been stealin' Ollie's undies all this time, and had sold 'em for 25 cents each to the fifth- and sixth-graders as snowball carriers. They also swapped them out for food with the younger kids, tellin' 'em that they was miniature pup tents. As you can probably imagine, Jeannie Janssen made those little hoodlums go and buy all of Ollie's undergarments back, usin' their own allowance money, and then she made 'em unknot each pair and wash 'em before returnin' 'em to Ollie. She even made 'em apologize to her as well, and shovel her driveway after every snow for the rest of that winter. I felt sorry for poor Jeannie Janssen. She was so embarrassed that as soon as Lot #19 on the other side of the trailer park opened up, her and her husband, Jimmy, hitched up their trailer and moved into it. I don't think she ever talked to Ollie again until Orville died. Of course what Jeannie never knew was that Ollie had no hard feelin's toward her. How could she? After all, she took all those pairs of old panties, which she'd already replaced, down to the flea market in Heber Springs and sold 'em as snowball carriers for 75 cents each. When you figure out how many you can carry at a time, I think that comes out to about a penny a snowball. You can't beat that with a stick.

CHRISTMAS CRAFTS FROM THE HEART

Clay Pot Christmas Tree

Even though you could easily get a hernia from cartin' around this lovely craft, it sure does scream "Merry Christmas." Not only is it fun, but it's pretty too. And I bet once your guests see it in your livin' room, they'll be amazed.

SUPPLIES

1 large clay pot
1 medium clay pot
1 small clay pot
Hot glue gun and glue sticks
Green paint made for clay
    surface
Large paint brush

1 small bow like you'd put on
    a Christmas gift
Spray adhesive
Glitter
Assorted buttons of all colors,
    at least 20

1. Turn the pots upside down so the openin's are all facin' the ground. We're gonna stack 'em on top of each other facin' this way. So go ahead and glue the pots together, startin' with the medium-sized pot on top the large pot. Then glue the small on to that. Let 'em dry.

2. Paint the pots green. Set aside to dry.

3. Take your bow and lightly spray it with the adhesive. Sprinkle some glitter on the bow.

4. Glue the buttons all over the pots just like they were tree ornaments.

5. Glue the bow to the bottom of the small pot. This is your clay pot tree topper.

6. Spray the pot tree with adhesive and then sprinkle glitter all over it. Set it aside and let it dry before findin' the perfect place in your livin' room to display it.

Tips for the Holiday Hostess

Usually all my parties are potluck, but from time to time as I mentioned previously, I'll either have a party catered or cook the whole meal myself. On these latter occasions, I find that some of my guests will volunteer to bring a dish along anyway. To say no to these folks is just out and out impolite. You should always accept their offer by simply sayin', "That's very kind and somethin' that you ain't got to do since I'll have food there, but if you want to bring your Spam noodle bake with you, please feel free to." Ain't that nice? Don't that sound real fancy and all? Just remember to never turn down food, even if you know it's gonna stink up your trailer. All you have to do is make sure that the person who brought it is first in line. Once they've gone through the food line and have taken their seat, snatch that dish from hell along with a trash bag, and take it back to your bedroom. Dump the contents in the trash bag, toss the bag out the back door, wash the dish, and give your trailer a few shots of air freshener. If your guest gets up for seconds, and notices that her food item is missin', just thank her for bringin' it, 'cause it went like wild fire. You can then show her the clean container dryin' in the rack. Also make sure that you insist on a copy of that recipe. This will come in handy if somebody's dog tears into that trash bag and has to be taken to the vet.

Party Idea

Tree Decoratin' Party

I know that some of y'all out there hate decoratin' your tree, and that's understandable. Why do you think I got mine on wheels? If you happen to be one of them people who would rather have your teeth pulled than fix up the tree, I got a full-fired plan to help you. All you got to do is get your tree and all your decorations. Put the tree up where you want it and string up the lights. Then invite your friends over for a Christmas tree decoratin' party. Or you could have some friends over for a night of games, and include everyone's favorite "Decorate the Christmas Tree Game." All you got to do is provide the food and drinks and your tree will be finished in no time without you even breakin' a sweat. Bah humbug, my big behind, with a tree decoratin' party, you ain't got no reason not to give out a big, "God bless us everyone."

Trailer Park Christmas Games

The Check Is in the Mail

I love this game. First every player puts in a dollar bill. Then the hostess takes all the money that has been collected and puts it in an open envelope that has the word BILLS written on it. Then all the players get in a big circle. When the hostess starts up a song on the CD player, everyone starts passin' the envelope. When the music stops, the person holdin' the envelope is either out or has to put two more dollar bills in the envelope in order to continue playin'. If that same player gets stuck with the envelope a second time, he don't put any more money in the envelope 'cause he's out for good this time. The last person to not get stuck with the envelope is the winner and gets to keep the cash. Or if you're in need of cash yourself (and who isn't), you keep the cash and award a nice gift like some Tupperware or one of my books.

WHAT'S THAT SMELL?

Even if your Christmas tree is made out of coat hangers and toilet paper, with this potpourri scent fillin' your trailer, folks will swear it's real.

It's Beginnin' to Smell a Lot Like Christmas

Makes a batch

2 quarts pine needles   1 tablespoon pine oil
1 cup orrisroot

Put your pine needles in a food processor and grind 'em up. Pour 'em into a big jar or container and add the remainin' ingredients. Shake gently till well blended. Every three days stir the contents to refresh the piny fragrance.

HOLLY JOLLY WOOHA!

❋ In 1856, President Franklin Pierce decorated the first White House Christmas tree.

❋ In 1907, Oklahoma became the last U.S. state to declare Christmas a legal holiday.

❋ Theodore Roosevelt banned Christmas trees from his home as well as the White House when he was in office.

HELPFUL HOLIDAY HINTS

❋ Always look your best at the holiday parties and functions regardless of the advance time you might have. Put a denture cleanin' tablet in a glass of water, throw in your jewelry, and walk away. While you're busy doin' other chores your jewelry will be cleanin'. Come back in an hour for sparkly jewelry that looks great.

✻ If you serve one of those canned hams for Christmas, save the can. They make great cake forms for Easter cakes.

✻ Save those 2-liter soda pop bottles durin' the holiday season. Not only can you just throw in a funnel, add your Kool-Aid, sugar, water, and shake, but they also make great travel holders for leftover gravy and sauces when you want to send some home with folks.

—PASTOR IDA MAY BEE, LOT #7

TWELVE DAYS OF YULETIME ADVICE

Dear Ruby Ann Boxcar,

Recently I attended a potluck that my family has every Christmas. We always gather at my Aunt Viola's trailer since she has a double-wide that has room for everyone. My deviled eggs are always the hit of the party. This year, while I was carefully arranging my tasty morsels, a man walked up to me. I can only describe him as perfection. He was a cross between Elvis and Tom Jones. Anyway I found out he is my Aunt Viola's long lost son Luther who was recently released from prison. The spark between us nearly melted the paneling right off the walls. Everyone gave us their blessing. Heck, I think they were just glad to see me meet someone. I was wanting your advice though. Do you think it is wrong that I am in love with my own cousin?

Sincerely,
Juanita J.

Dear Juanita J.,

The reason everybody is givin' you their "blessin'" could also be 'cause they know you'll be marryin' into a good family. Did you know that it's legal for cousins to marry in nineteen states? Did you have any idea that cousins marry all the time in both Europe and Canada? Why, President Franklin Roosevelt and Eleanor Roosevelt were cousins. Both Darwin and Einstein married their cousins. So you and Luther can hold your heads up high and feel good about rockin' each other's worlds.

Now I want to know about this deviled egg recipe of yours. Please send me more information and the recipe.

Love, Kisses, and Trailer Park Wishes,
Ruby Ann Boxcar

PUTTIN' YOUR BEST FACE FORWARD

Mascara

There is only two times that colored mascara is okay to wear, and Christmas ain't one of 'em. Stay with black. It's nice, classy, and will set your eyes on fire with passion. So again, if it's St. Patrick's Day or you're showin' your team spirit for your favorite sports team, colored mascara is fine to apply. Any other day, includin' Christmas, make it jet black.

CHRISTMAS CHEER

Donna Sue suggests . . .

Christmas Shot

If this don't put you in the holiday spirit, nothin' will.

1^1/$_2$ ounce Chambord raspberry liqueur
1^1/$_2$ ounce Midori melon liqueur

Pour the Chambord into a tall thin liqueur glass. Slowly pour the Midori over the back of a spoon into the glass. You are wantin' to layer this drink so it is red on bottom and green on top. If you pour it too fast, it'll turn out an ugly brown and the drink name then changes to "Dirty Snow."

Happy Elves Punch

If you want your elves even happier, add a couple cups of vodka.

Makes about 25 servin's

2 cups sugar
^{1}/$_2$ cup water
12 whole cloves
2 cinnamon sticks
46-ounce can unsweetened
  grapefruit juice

6-ounce can frozen orange
  juice, prepared and mixed
  accordin' to the instructions
  on can
1 quart apple juice

Combine the sugar, water, cloves, and cinnamon sticks in a large pot over medium heat. When it gets to a boil, reduce the heat and let it simmer for 25 minutes. Strain the mixture and put it back in the large pot. Add the remainin' ingredients and bring it almost to a boil again. Take off the heat and serve it hot or put it back in the fridge after the reheatin' and let it chill for two hours, and serve it cold.

TRAILER PARK CHRISTMAS GRUB

Christmas Cookie

The Sweat Scarves of Elvis Fan Club Blue Christmas Cookies

Since it's a must that you have to have Elvis Christmas music playin' while you make these cookies, I always end up cryin' in my hot oil.

Makes a couple dozen

2 eggs
1 tablespoon sugar
3 tablespoons heavy cream
1 teaspoon brandy (it's okay to use the brandy, 'cause you're mournin' Elvis)

$^1/_2$ teaspoon salt
$1^3/_4$ cups flour
Oil for fryin'
1 cup powdered sugar
Bottle of blue decorating sugar

Beat eggs lightly. Add sugar and cream, beat well. Blend in brandy and salt. Add flour and mix well to make a smooth dough. Roll out the dough so that it is very, very thin. Cut into 2- by 2-inch squares. Deep fry in 350 degree F. oil until delicately browned. Drain on paper towels. Cool and shake in a plastic bag with powdered sugar. Sprinkle on blue sugar. Serve.

—RUBY ANN BOXCAR, LOT #18

Festive Fudge

Pastor's First Noel Pumpkin Fudge

By popular demand, Pastor Ida May Bee makes this every week from October to December. It only takes one batch of this to find out why.

1 cup milk	$^1/_2$ teaspoon cinnamon
3 cups sugar	$^1/_2$ teaspoon allspice
3 tablespoons light corn syrup	4 tablespoons margarine
$^1/_2$ cup canned pumpkin	1 teaspoon vanilla
Dash of salt	

Combine milk, sugar, corn syrup, pumpkin and salt in a pan, and cook over medium heat. When the mixture starts to bubble, reduce heat to simmer and cook to soft ball stage. Remove from heat and beat in spices, margarine, and vanilla. Allow to cool. Then beat until thick and the mixture loses its gloss. Spoon into greased dish. Let it set till it gets firm. Cut into squares.

—PASTOR IDA MAY BEE, LOT #7

Pies on Earth, Goodwill Toward Men

Eggnog Pie

Momma Ballzak likes to dunk her piece of eggnog pie in brandy.

Makes one pie

9-inch baked pie shell	$^1/_2$ teaspoon salt
$^1/_2$ cup granulated sugar	3 eggs, separated
1 envelope unflavored gelatin	$1^1/_4$ cups milk

1¹/₂ teaspoons light rum
¹/₄ teaspoon cream of tartar
¹/₂ cup granulated sugar

1 cup whipped cream
1 tablespoon nutmeg

Stir together ¹/₂ cup sugar, gelatin, and salt in pan. Blend together egg yolks and milk in separate bowl, then stir into sugar mixture. Cook over medium heat, stirrin' constantly, just until mixture boils. Place pan in bowl of ice and water, stirrin' occasionally until mixture mounds slightly when dropped from spoon. Stir in rum. Beat egg whites and cream of tartar until foamy. Beat in ¹/₂ cup sugar, 1 tablespoon at a time; continue beatin' until stiff and glossy. Do not underbeat. Fold gelatin mixture into meringue mixture. Fold meringue mixture into whipped cream. Pile into baked shell. Sprinkle generously with nutmeg. Chill 3 hours. Enjoy.

—TINA FAYE STOPENBLOTTER, LOT #17

Seasonal Supper Sensation

Here We Come A-Wassailin' Chicken Casserole

A scoop of this on a paper plate, a can of cheap beer, and a candy cane are the traditional items you hand out to Christmas carolers in the trailer park.

Makes about 6 servin's

8¹/₂-ounce box corn muffin mix
1 tablespoon chili powder
4 boneless, skinless chicken
    breast halves, cut into ¹/₂-inch
    pieces
2 tablespoons oil
16-ounce can baked beans

14¹/₂-ounce can Mexican-style
    stewed tomatoes, undrained
1 tablespoon BBQ sauce
14¹/₂-ounce can green beans,
    drained
1 tablespoon maple syrup

Mix up the corn muffin mix followin' the directions on the package. Set aside.

Sprinkle chili powder on chicken chunks; toss with fork to coat well. Put your oil in a large skillet and get it up to a medium heat. Add the chicken pieces and cook until they're done. Drain the fat. Reduce heat. Stir in baked beans, stewed tomatoes, BBQ sauce, and green beans. Simmer mixture 5 to 10 minutes, stirrin' occasionally. Spoon mixture into greased 9- by 13-inch baking pan. Spoon the corn muffin batter on top of bean mixture. Bake in a 400 degree F. oven for 20 to 25 minutes or until topping is golden. Remove from oven and brush the top lightly with maple syrup.

—RUBY ANN BOXCAR, LOT #18

CHAPTER 5

The Fifth Day of Christmas

DECEMBER 17

I always keep a camera handy durin' the holidays 'cause you never know when a Christmas memory might happen that you want to cherish for the rest of your life.

109

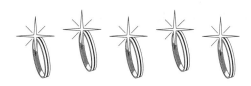

Traditional Gift on This Day
　　Five golden rings

Trailer Park Gift on This Day
　　Five onion rings (and six packets of ketchup)

ABOUT THIS DAY

Since we put Me-Ma in the Last Stop Nursin' Home, which is located at the last stop before you get to the lake, me and my husband, Dew, usually round up Momma, Daddy, my sister Donna Sue, and Lulu Bell and all go out and see her on this day. Usually we'll bring along a few ornaments and decorations to hang up in her room as well as a can of pepper spray, since some of them residents just don't understand the words, "Get back, these ain't for you." After probably a good thirty minutes of mindless conversation we tell her good-bye and promise to pick her up for the church Christmas party as well as Christmas itself. Then on our way out we pick up her Christmas cards that she needs mailed. On the way back home we drop the ones that she remembered to stamp off at the post office and throw the others without postage in the trash. Naturally we check the unstamped ones for money before droppin' 'em off in the dumpster, and we split the take. As you can guess, Me-Ma is always happy to see us when we arrive, which is one reason we go on the same day each year.

A CHRISTMASTIME TREASURE
FROM THE HIGH CHAPARRAL TRAILER PARK

Kyle Chitwood's family moved into Lot #11 shortly after the Janssens vacated the lot. When his momma and daddy up and moved to Missouri, Kyle kept the family trailer, which he now shares with his wife of twelve years, Kitty Chitwood. I just love Kitty to death and Kyle has always been a breath of fresh air, although I do my best to keep him and Dew apart, 'cause you never know what that boy is likely to talk my husband into tryin'. For example, Kyle just loves sled ridin' so much that when snow is forecast, he sets by his window in the front livin' room dressed up in his winter coat just waitin' for it to fall. Once he talked Dew into tryin' to jump the stream that's back behind the office with his sled. He told Dew that he should be goin' fast enough down that hill that when he hit the angled embankment, he'd soar over the four-foot-wide stream of ice cold water and land on the thick snow that laid on the other side. Well, God bless him, after a successful test run usin' just the unmanned sled, my husband agreed, and sure enough he came flyin' down that hill, hit that embankment, and soared . . . for about a tenth of a second. What Kyle and my husband had forgot to add in their calculations was Dew's 165 pounds of body weight. I tell y'all, he dropped like a dang stone straight down into the ice-cold waters below. Luckily the stream was only about a foot deep, 'cause when Dew came crashin' down, the force of the impact knocked the air right out of him and all he could do was roll over on his back so as not to drown. Kyle had to pull him up out of the water until he was able to get back on his feet. My poor Dew was almost frozen solid when he got back up to the trailer. Needless to say, he didn't get back on a sled for a good long time. When I asked him why he trusted Kyle, he said he didn't have any reason not to. It was then that I remembered my husband had not grown up in the High Chaparral Trailer Park, and he'd most likely never heard about the Christmas that Kyle would love to forget.

It was 1973, and it'd been snowin' for two days straight. With the high winds and all it looked like Christmas might just blow past us that year. Well, it didn't, naturally, and come Christmas Day, the snow had stopped and the sun had come out. It was as beautiful as it can get in Arkansas durin' December. Naturally, after openin' their presents, all the kids wanted to go out and play. Who could blame 'em? They'd been out of school and cooped up inside for two whole days. The mothers all told their little ones to be good and be careful, gave 'em a kiss, and sent 'em outside so they could get some peace and quiet as well. So off Kyle and the rest of the kids went to go sleddin' down the hill where him and Dew would later attempt their Evil Knievel–style jump. When they got there, no one could believe all the snow that had almost filled the space between the two hills. Bein' children, they still decided to try and slide down what was left of the hills. But before six-year-old Kyle Chitwood could even climb aboard his trusty sled, his Christmas adventure would take a turn for the worse. It seemed that the snow under little Kyle's feet had given way and he slid down the hill, under the snow embankment. He was trapped, and even at six he knew that if he tried to climb out, he could easily cause the snow to cave in on top of him. So instead he just laid there and prayed somebody had seen him go under. As it turned out, somebody had. Connie Kay, who back then was better known as Cootie Connie Cone, yelled at the other kids to hurry up and come over. She frantically screamed that Kyle had fallen down in a hole. But since she was only seven years old herself, and nobody really liked her, they didn't pay much attention. Besides everybody knew that Connie Cone was a bald-face liar. So there was only one thing left to do—she would have to go tell her momma, Mrs. Cone. As Connie took off, Kyle laid there deep in his little snow shaft. And as the time passed, Kyle began to grow thirsty and hungry. Finally out of sheer desperation, he gently started to nibble away at some of the snow around him, bein' careful not to eat too much from one spot. The last thing he wanted was for the snow to fall in around him. Then the unthinkable hit Kyle. He had to pee. He tried to hold it for as long as he could, but finally, he gave in to nature. Well, at least he'd be warm for a little bit, from the waist down anyway. Within what had seemed a lifetime to Kyle, but in all actuality had been no more than twenty minutes, Cootie Connie showed back up with half the trailer park. Kyle would be all right. He would pull through, or so he thought until some of the menfolk lowered down a rope and told him to grab hold. Try as he might, Kyle just couldn't. His fingers were too numb from the cold to hold tight on to anything. He couldn't even bend them enough to tie the rope around his arms. The parents would just have to come up with a plan B, which they quickly did. They raced over to Frank Goodshaw's place and told him what had happened. Without thinkin' about it, Frank left the warmth of his Christmas dinner and jumped into his tow truck. Carefully Frank drove across the field until his truck was at the top of the hill. With the help of the menfolk guidin' the line into the hole, Frank lowered the towin' hook slowly down to Kyle. Kyle hooked it to the back of his shirt and then very softly told the concerned parents up above that he was ready. Once he had the high sign, Frank turned the crane on and began to lift the hook and Kyle up from the hole to safety. The only problem was that not every-thing was ready to come out from the hole. The urine had frozen Kyle's pants to the packed snow, and just like that stubborn ice cube that won't loosen from the tray, they were goin' nowhere. This of course meant that when the crane had finally come to a complete stop, little Kyle Chitwood was danglin' over the back of the tow truck naked as a jay bird. God bless him, by the time everyone had stopped laughin' and had returned from runnin' to their trailers to grab their cameras, the cheeks on his face weren't the only ones rosy from the cold. As you can imagine, Kyle was fine and they got his pants back after the thaw. Of course his wife Kitty Chitwood now says that Kyle is still very peculiar about the coolness. She claims that even today as a grown man he won't set down on a toilet seat if the bathroom is even the slightest bit cold.

CHRISTMAS CRAFTS FROM THE HEART

Mrs. Claus Tissue Box Cover

When I was just a little girl, I use to lock myself in the bathroom and fix the hair on Momma's little girlie head tissue box cover. Even then I knew what my callin' was to be.

SUPPLIES

$20^1/_2$- × $9^1/_2$-inch fake white long fur

Flat-backed doll face

Glue

Needle

Tan thread

Hairbrush

Aqua Net

Old lady doll eyeglasses

Seasonal brooch

1. Take your fur and cut out two pieces. One should be $4^1/_2 \times 4^1/_2$ inches while the other comes out to 16×5 inches.

2. Turn the 16- $\times$ 5-inch piece inside out and whipstitch the two short ends by hand.

3. Whipstitch the one end of the piece that you just sewed to the $4^1/_2$- $\times$ $4^1/_2$-inch piece, inside out of course. This should form an open-ended box.

4. Cut a slit in the top of the box to allow tissues to be pulled through.

5. Flip the box back so that the fur is now showin' on the outside. Brush the hair straight down on all sides.

6. Glue the doll face on the very bottom of one of the sides.

7. Glue the eyeglasses to the doll face.

8. After it has dried, put the "fur box" on a tissue box. Next, style the hair so that it has a flip all the way around. Spray with Aqua Net and brush it out from time to time. You can also spray it with lacquer, but it will never move if you do.

9. Add a seasonal brooch to the hair and display it in your favorite room.

Tips for the Holiday Hostess

What would a good party be without music? Normally I'd tell you to put on a country station and just turn it down so folks could talk over it, but durin' this blessed time of the year, it's Christmas music all the way. Of course as host it's your job to pick the music and to make sure that when the music stops, you're right there to start it back up again. This task can be handled in two ways: Either load up your multi-disk CD player with music or stick in an 8-track tape. One positive thing about goin' with the 8-track tape is that since they ain't made new ones in at least twenty years, the musical choices that you'll have are sure to bring back fond memories of Christmases gone by. Just remember every hour or so to go and pop in a new 8-track so your guest ain't got to hear the same songs over and over.

Party Idea

Fondue Party

If you read the first part of this book, you know what my feelin's are on fondue, but still, it can make for a fun party. When the hostess calls up the guests and invites 'em, she tells 'em to bring along their favorite fondue sauce in a Crock-Pot. The hostess provides the dippin' items (bite-size hot dog pieces, French bread cubes, ham cubes, bite-size pieces of beef, cubed Spam, vegetables, cubed pound cake, apple slices, pineapple squares, strawberries, pear slices, seedless grapes, strips of chicken, banana pieces, brownie chunks, or whatever sounds good to dip into the many sauces), the napkins and small paper plates, and the wooden skewers or long toothpicks to be used for spearin'. The hostess also needs to have a Fry Daddy or some such thing set out so folks can cook their bites-size meats in it. Personally I suggest that you set up several small tables with power strips on each one or one long table with several power strips. This allows you to put several Crock-Pots on a table. I suggest that you push your tables or table up against a wall so that nobody accidentally trips on the electrical cords. And set your Crock-Pots on medium so that the sauces stay melted but not hot enough to burn somebody. If you want to make it even more fun, you can play lounge-style Christmas music that dates back to the 1960s and 1970s—when fondue parties were all the rage. For that matter, if you're up to it, you could invite your guests to dress in clothin' from that time as well. Regardless, here are a few recipes to get your party started right.

Donna Sue's Beer Batter Dip

Pastor Ida May Bee has ruled that this is allowed at the church's Christmas party just as long as she don't catch nobody drinkin' the batter.

Makes about 2$\frac{1}{2}$ cups

1$\frac{1}{2}$ cups Bisquick
$\frac{1}{2}$ teaspoon salt
$\frac{1}{2}$ teaspoon black pepper

1 egg, beaten
1 cup beer
Vegetable oil for fryin'

Combine the Bisquick, salt, pepper, and the egg in a bowl. Slowly add the beer, and stir the mixture until it's well blended. Cover and store in the fridge till it's time to Fondue. Heat oil in a deep metal pot to 375 degrees F. Dip your bite-size hot dogs, beef, Spam, or veggies in the batter first, then put in hot grease to cook.

—DONNA SUE BOXCAR, LOT #6

Pastor Ida May Bee's
White Chocolate Fondue Dip

It's nice to know our pastor makes enough money to afford white choco-late. Me and the board will have to look into that.

Makes about 2 cups

3/4 cup heavy cream
12 ounces white chocolate or
   white chocolate chips

1 teaspoon vanilla

Put your cream in a pot and heat it over a medium heat for 3 minutes. Add your white chocolate. If you're usin' solid white chocolate, make sure to chop it up first before addin'. Stir until all the white chocolate has melted. Add the vanilla and stir. Pour this mixture into your Crock-Pot and set the temperature to medium. Dip in strawberries, bananas, apples, pears, or anythin' else that sounds good.

—PASTOR IDA MAY BEE, LOT #7

WHAT'S THAT SMELL?

Every guest is sure to leave your trailer with a feelin' of Christmas hangin' in their nostrils thanks to the following potpourri.

Santa's Smell

This is what he smells like now after the Fab Five got a hold of him.

Makes a batch

2 tablespoons ground cloves
3 tablespoons ground cinnamon
26 drops nutmeg essential oil
1 cup dried rose petals

1 cup sandalwood chips
1 cup dried mint leaves
2 cups cedar chips

Mix the cloves and cinnamon together. Add the oil, followed by everything else. Screw on the lid and shake it up. Let it set for two weeks, gently shakin' it every three days.

HOLLY JOLLY WOOHA!

❊ Nova Scotia leads the world in exportin' Christmas trees.

❊ "One Horse Open Sleigh" was "Jingle Bells" original title.

❊ Mr. Joel Poinsett first brought the poinsettia to America from Mexico, where it originated, in 1829.

HELPFUL HOLIDAY HINTS

❊ When makin' cookies on greased bakin' sheets, you can stop the dough spreadin' out too much by first dustin' a little flour (or cocoa, for chocolate cookies), on the bakin' sheet.

❊ If you're makin' cookies on nongreased bakin' sheets, you can stop 'em from spreadin' if you cook 'em on cold bakin' sheets.

—LULU BELL BUTTON, LOT #8

❋ Don't get your presents under the Christmas tree wet when you water it. Instead of pourin' in water, just drop in ice cubes into the tree stand.

❋ If you use a real tree for Christmas, cut about an inch from the trunk, and put it in a bucket of cold water mixed with a cup of sugar. Let it set in the bucket for 3 to 4 days before bringin' it in the house. You will have a greener tree by doin' this.

—JUANITA HIX, LOT #9

TWELVE DAYS OF YULETIME ADVICE

Dear Ruby Ann,

I know I should know this, but it slips my mind every year. Who should we give a holiday tip to, and how much should we spend?

Yours truly,
Mellody

Dear Mellody,

Not to worry, hon, 'cause I think everybody forgets who and what amount to tip each holiday season. Go ahead and grab your pen and I'll give you the list of who and how much.

Personal Care Professional

Persons included in this category are your beautician, barber, nail tech, or anybody else who does any kind of personal groomin' for you. You should give them a Christmas tip that equals the cost of one visit. For example, after you get your hair done, you should give your beautician the $3 you normally pay for her to do it plus an additional $3 for her Christmas tip.

Child Care Providers

A box of chocolates will make your momma and mother-in-law happy enough.

Landlord / Trailer Park Manager

Considerin' all the times that your late rent check bounced from here to Mars, you need to give some kind of gift to this person. An unopened bottle of Avon's Black Suede cologne is appropriate regardless if the landlord or trailer park manager is a man or a woman.

House Cleaner

It must be a blessin' to have someone come and clean up after you once or twice a week. In any case, you will make their Christmas with coupons from Taco Bell.

Family Doctor / Vet / Dog Groomer

These three people or in some cases, one person, provide you with services you can't get no place else. Your doctor (or vet in my case, when the doctor is out of town) not only does what he can to keep you in good health, but he's also seen you naked. And the dog groomer always treats your pet with love and kindness. So make sure you relay your thanks this Christmas with a $15 gift certificate from Fingerhut.

Mail Carrier / Garbage Man / Newspaper Delivery Boy

Postal workers ain't allowed to accept money or gifts that are valued at over $20, but garbage men and delivery boys ain't got no such rules. Still, since they all do the same type of service for me, I make sure that their gifts are of equal value. By this I mean that I set in the same chair wearin' the same bra leavin' the curtains open exactly the same amount for all of 'em.

Auto Mechanics

Just leave $2 or $3 in change in your car console.

Pastor

If you want to do somethin' special for your pastor, I always suggest a check. Wait until the church Christmas party and let others give your pastor their presents first. Naturally the bearer of the gift will announce how much it cost either openly or by leavin' the price tags on. If you have your check almost completely written out, when the last gift is given, you can quickly write in a dollar amount that tops everyone else's. It might not get you to heaven, but it'll sure get you invited over to the pastor's family place a lot more often.

Well, Mellody, that ought to about do it. Of course if you want to do somethin' for your favorite author, simply buyin' more books and givin' 'em out as presents will do just fine.

Love, Kisses, and Trailer Park Wishes,
Ruby Ann Boxcar

PUTTIN' YOUR BEST FACE FORWARD

Glitter

And last, but not least, my number-five tip for Christmas makeup is glitter. That's right, put a little glitter on your face to make your holiday look festive. Now I don't mean for you to just throw it on. The last thing I want is for you to look like a Christmas ornament exploded in your face. A little glitter goes a long way. You can find the spray-on kind in stores all over this country. Just make sure that it's the stuff intended for your face. I don't want nobody to accidentally give her face a good coatin' of that spray-on glitter for clothes and crafts, 'cause that stuff don't come off real easy. You might be wearin' your Christmas makeup all the way up to Easter if that should happen. So just read the labels and sparkle pretty for Momma.

CHRISTMAS CHEER

Donna Sue suggests . . .

Christmas Tree

No extension cords required.

$^1/_3$ ounce Bailey's Irish Cream $^1/_3$ ounce crème de menthe
$^1/_3$ ounce grenadine

Pour the Bailey's in a shot glass. Next, layer the grenadine by slowly pourin' it over the back of a spoon. Layer the crème de menthe in the same manner. Serve.

Hot Buttered Apple

They love to drink these at the Holier Than Most Baptist Church Christmas party on account of how the rum tastes, even though it's nonalcoholic, makes 'em feel like they're Episcopalians.

$^3/_4$ cup packed brown sugar $^1/_4$ teaspoon ground allspice
$^1/_2$ cup margarine   1 cup cider
$^1/_4$ teaspoon lemon juice   1 teaspoon rum extract
$^1/_4$ teaspoon ground cinnamon

Combine the brown sugar, margarine, lemon juice, cinnamon, and allspice in a bowl. This mixture, which makes around 10 servin's, will keep in the fridge for a long while, just as long as you've got it covered. Place 1 tablespoon of this mixture in a coffee mug. Add the cider and 1 teaspoon of rum extract. Stir and serve.

Another idea is to go ahead and put the margarine mixture in 10 cups, wrap the cups in foil, and put 'em in the freezer. This way when guests come over you can just pull out a mug, add your cold cider and rum extract, and pop it in the microwave for 2 minutes or so.

TRAILER PARK CHRISTMAS GRUB

Christmas Cookie

Wendy's Old-Time Let It Snow Sour Cream Cookies

Dear old sweet Wendy Bottom always brings over a batch of these durin' the Christmas season, and once we've checked 'em for hair, me and my husband, Dew, gobble these up in no time with a big glass of milk.

Makes 3 to 4 dozen

2 cups flour
1 cup brown sugar
1/2 teaspoon ground cinnamon
1/4 teaspoon ground nutmeg
1 cup chopped pecans
1 teaspoon bakin' powder

1/2 teaspoon bakin' soda
1/4 teaspoon salt
1/2 cup margarine, softened
1 egg
1/2 teaspoon vanilla
1/2 cup sour cream

Put all dry ingredients into large bowl and mix. Add the margarine, egg, and vanilla. Mix for a minute and then add the sour cream. Continue to beat the mixture.

Put teaspoon-size balls of dough onto greased cookie sheet and bake at 375 degrees F. for 8 to 10 minutes. Cookies should be lightly browned. Take cookies out of oven and immediately place them on a wire rack so they don't get soggy. Eat like they are or frost 'em with your favorite frostin'.

—WENDY BOTTOM, LOT #4

Festive Fudge

Flora Delight's Winter Wonderland Rum and Butter Fudge

Even though the newest dancer at the Blue Whale Strip Club, Flora Delight, only actually lived in a trailer durin' her short stay in Lot #19 while she was waitin' to collect the insurance on her home that burnt to the ground, one taste of this fudge and you'll agree that this is all just a technicality.

Makes 1 batch

2 cups dark chocolate chips
3 cups brown sugar
3 cups sugar
$1/3$ cup corn syrup
$1^3/4$ cups cream

$1/4$ pound margarine
$1/2$ cup mini-marshmallows
$1/2$ cup of either dark rum, spiced rum, or coconut rum, overproof

Get you a great big pan and add both your sugars, corn syrup, and cream. Heat it on medium heat until it gets to the soft ball stage. Take off the heat and add margarine, stirrin' until the glossy look is gone. Add your chips and marshmallows and stir until everythin' is smooth and melted. Pour in your rum. Stir well. Pour immediately into well greased and floured cookie sheet. Carefully bang pan on counter until completely level. Let cool well. Cut, and enjoy.

—FLORA DELIGHT, FORMERLY OF LOT #19

Pies on Earth, Goodwill Toward Men

Half and Half Cream Pie

This one will have your family and friends guessin' how you made it.

Makes one pie

1^1/$_2$ cups graham cracker crumbs
^{1}/$_2$ cup packed brown sugar
^{1}/$_2$ cup melted margarine
1 regular package chocolate
  puddin'

1 regular package vanilla
  puddin'
1 cup heavy cream, whipped

We start off by makin' the crust. You do this mixin' the first three items together in a bowl. Pour the mixture into a greased pie plate and press the mixture down evenly with the bottom of a spoon. Set aside.

Followin' the directions on the boxes, make the chocolate and vanilla puddin's, but use heavy cream instead of milk, and only half the amount it calls for. Cover the surface of the puddin's with waxed paper and refrigerate for an hour. Fold half of the whipped heavy cream into each puddin', then usin' a 17-inch piece of foil, make a collar 4^1/$_2$ inches in diameter and 3 inches high. Place the collar in the center of the crust and spoon the chocolate mixture into the center and the vanilla around the outside of the collar. Carefully lift out the collar and refrigerate the pie for 2 hours. You can also use any two flavors of puddin'.

—KITTY CHITWOOD, LOT #11

Seasonal Supper Sensation

O Come, All Ye Faithful Pot Roast Supper

Not only is this good, but it's also magical. Regardless of how cold it gets outside, the aroma from the Crock-Pot manages to make its way through the trailer, around the trailer park, and magically into the nose of the exact same neighbors who'd planned on headin' over for a visit. It's just like that star that shined on the first Christmas.

Makes around 4 to 6 servin's

1 boneless roast
1 can RC Cola
1 bottle Heinz chile sauce
1 package Lipton's Onion
   Soup mix

1 regular package stew
   vegetables

Put everything in a Crock-Pot, cover, set on medium, and let it cook for 4 to 6 hours. Serve with corn.

—BEN BEAVER, LOT #14

CHAPTER 6

The Sixth Day of Christmas

DECEMBER 18

Drivin' at Christmastime can be such a pain.

Traditional Gift on This Day
  Six geese a-laying

Trailer Park Gift on This Day
  Six coon dogs bayin' (or is that my neighbor Little Linda
    singin' Christmas carols?)

ABOUT THIS DAY

It was back in 1979 on this very day that my first thoughts of bein' a professional entertainer came about. You see, each year on December 18, we hold the Christmas talent contest at the high school theater/gymnasium. Everybody in the surroundin' area turns out to enjoy a night of fun and raw entertainment as well as Christmas cheer. You can count on my sister to spike the free punch as well. Anyway, that year the gal that was playin' the accordion up on stage got stage fright and ended up gettin' sick all over the place. Well, the only problem was that the next act, which was little sweet Tommy Turner who did a knife-throwin' routine, wasn't ready to go on 'cause his grandma's tranquilizer pill hadn't kicked in yet, and she could still move. So the school principal saw that I was settin' up front and he asked me over the PA system to come on up on the stage and sing a number. I'd always sang at school when I was young as well as at church, but I didn't know about singin' for such a large gatherin'. Well, long story short, after several of my friends managed to push me up on stage, I belted out "Stand By Your Man,"

133

and the rest is history. All these years later, I still attend the Christmas talent show on this day every year, although I ain't sung on that stage since 1979 on account of how now I charge 'em out the wazoo just to hold the microphone, let alone sing in it. After all, I ain't cheap. That's my sister.

A CHRISTMASTIME TREASURE
FROM THE HIGH CHAPARRAL TRAILER PARK

If there is one thing that trailer park folks just out and out enjoy, it'd have to be a good old-fashioned demolition derby, which is why back in 1999 when Harland Hix of Lot #9 proposed his idea at our annual High Chaparral Trailer Park residents meetin', which takes place on the first Monday of December, we all fell for it hook, line, and sinker. It seemed that Harland, who'd always dreamed of drivin' a derby, had found a car on one of them online auction places that'd be just perfect for this year's traditional "Do You Hear What I Hear Holiday Demolition Derby" up by Hickory Flat. He thought he could get it for a real good price, but he didn't have the cash on hand to buy it. It was there that Hubert Bunch of Lot #3, who been approached first with this idea, jumped in and explained how this was a once-in-a-lifetime chance, for all of us could be sponsors, which meant that we'd all give a little donation and get our names written somewhere on the car (or we could do this as a community and just have the High Chaparral Trailer Park spray painted on the hood of the car). Hubert went on to assure us that the Taco Tackle Shack, with the Bunches' half Tex-Mex food restaurant / half fishin' supplies store, would sponsor the remainin' price of the car and any other cost that might arise. To this news, Sister Bertha of Lot #12 jumped up and said that she thought it was an outrage supportin' a demolition derby durin' this season of joy and peace. Of course, after Harland said that he could get a public address system for free, and that he'd be happy to play a recorded tape from the car of whatever Sister Bertha wanted while the derby was goin' on, the devoted Baptist changed her tune. This led Connie Kay, who at the time was our local Amway rep, to ask if small businesses like hers could pay a little bit more to get their names painted a little bigger on the car. Since neither Harland nor Hubert had a problem with that idea, the trailer park took a vote, and unanimously agreed that each of the twenty lots would put in $1.37. Both Sister Bertha and Connie Kay agreed to pay an additional $5 each for their extras for a grand total of $37.40. Harland couldn't have been any happier. With that and the promise from Hubert to cover any additional cost up to $200, Harland thanked us all and headed back over to his trailer to place a bid on that vehicle. About a week later this tow truck showed up with our demolition car, a 1979 Ford LTD. Harland wasted no time gettin' it ready for the race. As he stenciled HIGH CHAPARRAL TRAILER PARK across the hood as promised and then in much larger letters added the Taco Tackle Shack on the sides, Hubert and my husband, Dew, carefully took out all the windows and other glass items along with the backseat. With just a few days left until the race, the boys added the public address system and then chained the doors shut. On the back of the car Harland hand painted the slogan and information that Connie Kay had personally written down for him, IF YOU WANT THE GOOD LIFE, IT'S TIME TO BUY AMWAY FROM CONNIE KAY, followed by her home phone number. With the last stroke of the spray can, the car was finished, and nobody in the park could think of anything other than Friday night's main event. Even as we watched

Harland practicin' his drivin'-in-reverse skills from the warmth of our trailers, it seemed that the derby day would never arrive. But as it always does, the anticipated evenin' did finally arrive, and we found ourselves heavily dressed in long johns, sweaters, coats, and even blankets shiverin' in our seats up in the stands at the racin' arena waitin' for the official start of the derby. There, down on the racetrack was our car, number 137, which was selected by Hubert in tribute to the amount each of our lots had sponsored. For most of us at the High Chaparral, this was a dream come true. And even though Harland Hix would be doin' the actual drivin', he wouldn't be alone, 'cause each one of us would be right up there with him, behind that Ford steerin' wheel on this very evenin' even if it was in spirit only. Then our dreams were interrupted by the words, "Drivers, start your engines." Before we could worry about would she start, the engine in #137 turned over. She started right up. It was actually here! The moment we'd all waited for! We was all so excited that for a brief moment we forgot just how cold we were up there in those open stands. We didn't care, 'cause boy golly we were here to see a demolition derby. And then out of nowhere the startin' shot from the starter pistol blasted through the crisp air. The rampage was on! Every one of the forty-five cars headed backward toward the middle of the blocked-off arena area, every one, that is, but our #137. It just stood there motionless. What could be wrong? we all wondered. There was smoke comin' out of the tail pipe, so it was still runnin'— but it wasn't movin'. Then came a voice that pierced the cold night air like the steel of a razor blade.

"Are you on the highway to hell?" blared the prerecorded voice of Sister Bertha through the loud speaker on the top of #137. We suddenly realized that Harland, upon hearin' the gunshot, had been tryin' to start the tape with Sister Bertha's message. That was why his car hadn't taken off. But now it was movin' thank goodness, 'cause the last thing you want to do is get trapped along a wall in demolition derby. That's sure death in this ball game. But luckily no one had noticed that Harland hadn't moved when the race started or they'd had been on him like a fat man on a Ding Dong. But Harland's anonymity didn't last long. With Sister Bertha's loud voice tellin' folks to "turn away from the fires of hell," and to "turn your keys over to Jesus, and let him do the drivin'," it wasn't long until every car in the arena was aimin' for him—as if they all of a sudden had it out for our LTD. They was chasin' him down like a toupee in a wind storm, and Harland was doin' all he could do not to get hit. Then for some reason unexplainable even to this day, just as the cars were closin' in, the public address speaker blew up into a million pieces. The explosion made the drivers slam on their brakes and gave Harland the chance to pull out from the middle of the group. He had emerged unscathed. And you should have seen the crowd as they rose to their feet in cheer! Of course I don't know if they was cheerin' for Harland's escape or if it was 'cause the loudspeaker had blown up and you couldn't hear Sister Bertha's tape preachin' no more. In any case, Harland had made it into the clear and was now takin' aim to strike his first blow. We all could see it comin'. Car #55 had stalled out and was settin' there like a lame duck. Its frantic driver continued to try to restart the old Malibu, as Harland lined up the back of #137 and then floored it. Dirt and mud went flyin' from his wheels as he headed right for the front of #55. The excitement ran through the crowd like bad potato salad at a family reunion.

"Knock his lights out, Harland," Connie Kay screamed from the bleachers.

"Show him what for!" my momma added at the top of her lungs. We was in the demolition derby spirit, there was no doubtin' that, and we was ready to root our car all the way to the checkered flag. And then the strangest thing that any of us had ever seen happened just as Harland rammed into the front of that 1975 Buick LaSabre. A 1973 Impala hit the back of that Buick with such force that it acted like a brick wall to Harland's hit, causin' the car body of #137 with Harland still in it to come flyin' clean off its frame. Even the axles had separated from the rest of it. We'd later find out that this "perfect car" Harland and Hubert had told us about was completely rusted out underneath, and the slightest bump from any of those derby cars or even just the motion of my sister climbin' up on the hood would have been enough to cause the damage that we saw happen right before our very eyes on that December night. Our Ford LTD had come from upstate Wisconsin, which, with all the salt that they used to put on the roads back in the 1970s and 1980s owing to the snowy winters, ain't the place to get a derby car. It was a miracle that Harland wasn't hurt. But even though he was out of the competition, the rules said he had to stay strapped into that piece of junk until the race was over, which was just fine with us 'cause we'd now switched our allegiance to anyone else who was gunnin' for car #137. Why, even Hubert and Lois Bunch were cheerin' with each gut-wrenching crash that Ford LTD took. Finally after the other cars got tired of playin' smash-up with the piece of junk, they went on to continue the derby. I guess now that we look back on it, all that we folks at the trailer park lost on that cold December night was our pride and $1.37. We had fun, and we even believed in somethin' that wasn't church related, kind of havin' our dreams and fantasies played out on the derby arena. All in all, it really wasn't that bad for us. Well, except for Connie Kay. That poor gal. After all that crashin' and bangin' from the other cars into #137, the rear end of that car was so bent up that from the stands all you could make out were the words GOOD, TIME, CONNIE, and her phone number. God bless her, it's years later and she still gets telephone calls at all hours of the night.

CHRISTMAS CRAFTS FROM THE HEART

Clothespin Santa

This is one of my favorite crafts. You can put it about anywhere, includin' in your hair or pinched to your front pocket. It even makes a great bookmark.

SUPPLIES

1 new clothespin	1¹/₂- × ¹/₂-inch black felt
Red spray paint	1¹/₂- × 1-inch red felt
1¹/₂- × 2-inch white felt	Scissors
1¹/₂- × ¹/₂-inch pink felt	Glue

1. Spray-paint the entire clothespin red and let dry.
2. Cut out the felt to match the patterns on the next page.
3. Usin' the completed picture as a guide, glue on the pink felt first.
4. Then glue on the red felt hat next.
5. Follow this by gluin' on the white felt mustache, beard, and hat trim.
6. Lastly glue on the black eyes and boot pieces. Let it dry and have fun.

Eyes 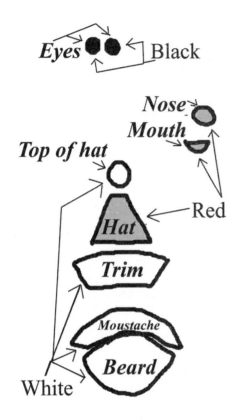 ← Black

Nose
Mouth

Top of hat

← Red

Hat

Trim

Moustache

Beard

White

TIPS FOR THE HOLIDAY SEASON

Make sure to let everyone know what kinds of drinks you'll be servin' and whether booze is allowed. Normally I offer sweet tea and coffee. When I mention this to my guests when I invite 'em, at least one of 'em will offer to bring somethin' so I ask 'em to pick up some diet soda and Dr Pepper since you'll always have at least one guest who don't drink sweet tea or coffee. Both regular and caffeine-free diet pop are always good choices since sure as shinola somebody won't be able to drink sweet tea on account of the sugar. And as far as the Dr Pepper goes, well, who don't like Dr Pepper? And if a guest requests decaf coffee, tell 'em you'll be happy to make it for them if they just bring the decaf, the filter, and a coffeemaker since you only got the one. Of course if you want to be a really good hostess like me, just keep a jar of Sanka instant around for them decaf drinkers.

Party Idea

Bring a Can Party

This party idea not only allows you to have a great evenin' with your friends and family durin' this joyous time of year, but it also allows you to help others. What I do is have everybody bring a covered dish so we can eat first. Of course they also have to bring a can of somethin' like beans or corn or whatever. Then after dinner you gather all the cans together, divide 'em into two or three or four stacks, dependin' on how many families you plan on takin' 'em to. Place 'em in brown paper bags, and throw a ribbon on each bag. Then y'all divide up into groups, one group per needy family, and y'all deliver the canned goods. If you don't know no needy family, take 'em to your closest homeless shelter and donate it to them. And if you ain't got one of those, then ask your pastor who might need it. If anyone knows who's in need of a Christmas miracle, your pastor will. Once y'all are finished, have your guests meet back at your trailer for hot chocolate and a second helpin' at the potluck. By the way, just for the record: Since this is your party, there ain't nothin' wrong for you to exchange some of the canned goods you have in your cupboards for a few good ones that your guests have brought. Just remember that a can of beets is not an equal tradin' value for a can of Spam. You'll need to put in two cans of beets for that item.

WHAT'S THAT SMELL?

If this don't remind you of Christmastime, you're dead.

Peppermint Stick

For some reason this one always makes me hungry.

Makes a batch

2 cups dried peppermint leaves
1 tablespoon peppermint
   essential oil
2 cups dried orange mint
2 cups dried spearmint leaves

2 cups dried lavender blossoms
1 cup dried thyme
1 cup dried rosemary leaves
$1/2$ cup orrisroot

Combine all ingredients in a jar and let it set for 5 or 6 weeks. Stir every other day.

Holly Jolly Wooha!

* Back when Christians were persecuted, a simple candle in the window meant that Christian services would be celebrated there that night, which is how Christmas lights came about.

* The Puritans forbade the singing of Christmas carols.

* The largest wreath was constructed on September 4, 1982, by the Gothenburg Florists at Liseberg Amusement Park, Sweden. It measured 68 feet 4 inches in diameter and weighed 4,368 pounds.

Helpful Holiday Hints

* When washin' dishes by hand, add a little vinegar to the rinse water, and you won't get a soap film.
>   —Ollie White, Lot #10

* Use Sunday's colored newspaper comic pages instead of expensive paper for wrappin' gifts.
>   —Kitty Chitwood, Lot #11

Twelve Days of Yuletime Advice

Dear Ruby Ann Boxcar,

Last year at the annual neighborhood Christmas party, I brought one of those Whitman samplers with all the chocolates. Toward the end of it, someone cleared all of the wrappers out of the box leaving just the candies, so we had no way of knowing what the flavors were. I stuffed a strawberry parfait in my mouth, thinking it was a chocolate caramel. Seein' how I'm allergic to strawberries, that thing went right back in the box in no time. Ruby Ann, how can I convince my neighbors to leave those little wrappers in their place so we can use the candy map?

Sweet Tooth Katie

Dear Sweet Tooth Katie,

This one is easy. Open the candy box and simply super glue the wrappers to the bottom of the box and the thick paper that lays between the two or three layers of candy before you take it to the party. That should solve your problem. But now I want to talk to you about puttin' a piece of candy that you've had in your mouth back in the box. Not only is that nasty, but it's rude. Next time you bite into one of those small candies, and realize you can't have it 'cause it's strawberry or that you simply don't like the taste, spit it out and either throw it in the trash or do what I do, and give it to your husband to finish. My husband just loves chocolate.

Love, Kisses, and Trailer Park Wishes,
Ruby Ann Boxcar

PUTTIN' YOUR BEST FACE FORWARD

Eyeliner

Regardless if your eyeliner is liquid or pencil, stay away from the holiday colors. Green liner should be saved for St. Patrick's Day while red eyeliner will make you look sickly. And we all know the last person we want to be around durin' the holiday season is somebody sick. So keep those lines black or brown.

CHRISTMAS CHEER

Donna Sue suggests . . .

Christmas Tree Water

Now you know why your cat likes it under the tree.

1 ounce gin
3 ounces 7-UP

Place the gin and 7-UP in a cocktail glass. Gently stir and serve. For a fun effect, you can add a little dry ice.

Christmas Mimosas

These are perfect at any Christmas party for the nondrinker.

$1/3$ orange juice
$2/3$ club soda or ginger ale

Serve in a champagne glass or fruit jar.

TRAILER PARK CHRISTMAS GRUB

Christmas Cookie

Hark! The Herald Angels Eat No-Sugar Raisin Cookies

It's hard to believe these cookies have less than one gram of carbohydrates each.

Makes a couple dozen

3/4 cup raisins
3/4 cup peeled and cored apples, chopped into really, really small bits
1 cup water
1/2 cup margarine
1 cup all-purpose flour
1 teaspoon bakin' soda

Pinch of cinnamon
1 teaspoon vanilla extract
1 1/4 cups quick-cookin' oats
2 eggs, beaten
3/4 cup chopped walnuts (You can use other nuts, but check the label for carbs.)

Take a pan and add the raisins, apples, and water. Mix and bring to a boil and let it cook for 3 minutes. Take the pot off the heat and add margarine. Stir and set aside.

In a bowl, add the flour, bakin' soda, and cinnamon. Mix well. Add the vanilla, eggs, and the apple mixture. Blend well. Fold in the oats and nuts. Cover and put in the fridge overnight or 8 hours. Drop by spoonfuls onto greased cookie sheet and spread the raisins out in the cookies. Bake for 8 to 10 minutes in a preheated oven at 350 degrees F. Let the cookies cool on the bakin' sheet for 5 minutes, then cool on a rack. If these ain't sweet enough for you, sprinkle on a little Splenda.

—DONNA SUE BOXCAR, LOT #6

Festive Fudge

Christmas Grasshopper Fudge

Now, don't go thinkin' Nellie has lost her mind, 'cause she ain't. This fudge gets its name 'cause it tastes like the chocolate mint drink or ice cream.

Makes a batch

13¹/₂ ounces sugar
5¹/₂ ounces light cream
6 ounces mint-flavored
   chocolate bits

Few drops oil of
   peppermint

Combine the sugar and cream in a pan, then cook over medium heat until the sugar dissolves and the mixture comes to a boil. Boil and stir constantly for 5 minutes. Remove from heat and blend in 6 ounces mint-flavored chocolate bits and a few drops of peppermint oil. Stir until thick. Pour into buttered pan. Cool until firm. Remove from pan and cut into small squares.

—NELLIE TINKLE, LOT #4

Pies on Earth, Goodwill Toward Men

I Heard the Bells on Christmas Day Brown Sugar Pie

This recipe is older than my Me-Ma's remainin' tooth.

Makes 2 pies

2 unbaked 9-inch pie shells
1 box brown sugar
¹/₂ pound margarine

3 eggs
2 cups milk

Mix ingredients well, divide the mixture between the two shells, and bake at 350 degrees F. for 35 to 40 minutes until crust is lightly browned. Serve as is or topped with whipped cream.

—ELROY DaSAFE, LOT #19

Seasonal Supper Sensation

Preacher's Peace on Earth Pork Chops

Here is yet another reason we thank the Good Lord for our pastor, Ida May Bee.

Makes 2 to 4 servin's

4 pork chops

3 tablespoons soy sauce

3 tablespoons ketchup

2 teaspoons honey

Trim the fat off your chops and set aside.

Mix up your remainin' three items. Set aside.

Put your chops in a bakin' dish, spoon the sauce over the chops, cover and bake at 350 degrees F. for 45 minutes. Uncover and bake an additional 5 minutes.

—PASTOR IDA MAY BEE, LOT #7

CHAPTER 7

The Seventh Day of Christmas

DECEMBER 19

Bob Beaver's Human Christmas Light Display truly lit up
our holidays.

Traditional Gift on This Day
Seven swans a-swimming

Trailer Park Gift on This Day
Seven Swanson dinners (them great big ones, of course)

About This Day

With Christmas Day just a spit away, this is what we at the High Chaparral Trailer Park call our "Ain't here day." We rest on this day, soak our feet on this day, and just lay back on this day. If you come a knockin' on the door or callin' on the phone, you're gonna get a "Ain't here!" So if you know what's good for you, turn around, walk away, or hang up the doggone phone.

A Christmastime Treasure
from the High Chaparral Trailer Park

It was durin' the mid-1990s that Ben Beaver, who manages the High Chaparral Trailer Park, decided to do somethin' that has brought cheer to both children and adults alike durin' the holiday season. Of course this was back before his late wife, Dora Beaver, passed away as well as before his recent marriage to Dottie Lamb of Lamb Super Center. One January down at the racetrack they had this fella who was gonna attempt to jump a whole mess of lighted Christmas decorations on a Yamaha motorcycle. Well, as fate would have it, the fella didn't make it and ended up all tangled in them Christmas lights. Upon seein' this two things flashed in Ben's mind,

1. Regardless of what you're doin', if it ain't on a Harley-Davidson you might as well forget it.
2. I want to be the Human Christmas Light Display.

When Ben told his wife later that evenin' about his idea of bein' wrapped up in thousands of Christmas lights and participatin' as an entry in one of them nighttime parades, she was dead set against it. She, just like all us wives when our husbands come to us with some harebrained idea, told him that she thought it was too dangerous, he was an idiot, and she'd have nothin' to do with it. Of course this just made Ben even more determined. He'd prove to Dora that there was nothin' dangerous about it, but he'd have to bide his time for just the right moment, which luckily came later that very week. You can imagine the surprise on Dora's face that night when she awoke after fallin' asleep watchin' TV to find several strings of Christmas lights wrapped around her and the recliner. At first she was fit to be tied, which she of course already was, but then after she calmed down and Ben agreed to unplug her, she gave in and told him that if he wanted to break his neck then he could go for it. Ben spent the rest of the year workin' on his idea. He experimented with outside lights and indoor lights, and he tried both the older models and the newer ones. Once he'd settled on the type of lights, he tested out colors to see if the multicolored strands had a better effect than just the plain old white ones. And as the year progressed and Christmas season grew near, Ben had to decide on if he should go with the lights that blink, chase, or just stay solid. After hours of tests, Mr. Beaver was finally ready to go, or so he thought. The one thing that had skipped his mind was how to keep the lights lit. With his first parade of lights just a day away, Ben turned to Mickey Ray Kay of Lot #13. Mickey Ray was known around the trailer park as bein' what we call a tinkerer, which basically means somebody who plays with gadgets. If any of us was ever havin' a problem with somethin' from a clock to a car, we'd always get Mickey Ray to take a look at it. Usually he could get it back to workin', but like any tinkerer, he also had his failures. In this case, though, he was the perfect person to ask. After thinkin' about it for a minute or so, he told Ben that he could rig up a place that could hold a battery and then do a little wire workin' and hook 'em up to that. Ben was thrilled until Mickey Ray said that with the double he was workin' at the Dr Pepper plant, he couldn't get to it till the day after tomorrow. After Ben told him he had a parade to do the next evenin' Mickey Ray came up with a temporary solution. He'd hook up one of those chargers you see on them bicycles that power up the headlights. They work off the wheels, where the faster the wheels turn the brighter the lights run. Ben couldn't have been happier with Mickey Ray's idea. He'd use this now, and then have him rig up the battery holder later that week.

As you can probably guess, the followin' day Ben was, well, happy as a beaver. He was gonna finally get to live out the dream he'd been workin' on all year long. That afternoon him and Dora loaded up the truck and headed on over to the parade location, which was just outside of neighborin' Newport, Arkansas. Ben had managed to talk Dora into wearin' an elf costume while she pushed him and his wheelchair along the parade route. Well, they was just as cute as could be, and those of us who'd showed up to see the Human Christmas Light Display make his virgin run were tickled pink. We was all plannin' to yell and scream out his name as he passed our way and tell everybody that he was our trailer park manager. Well, that was what we'd originally planned, but we soon changed our minds. You see, when the parade started off, Ben was shinin' like a brand-new dime. I tell you, even some of the United Church of Christ folks that was around us admitted that Ben all lit up in that wheelchair was somethin' to behold. But then when the first entry slowed down in order to turn a corner, everybody else had to slow down as well, eventually comin' to a momentary halt. Needless to say, Ben's lights also came to a slow halt and then complete darkness while he and Dora waited for the parade to continue. Some of those folks along the route started to shout out mean things about Ben's light display. Other's picked up candy and trinkets that some of the other floats had tossed to the crowd or made snowballs and sent 'em flyin' toward Ben and Dora. It was terrible. Before you knew it, the whole crowd had turned against the couple. Luckily it was dark and most of the snow and flyin' candy missed its mark completely, but then Dora panicked and started pushin' Ben forward in order to move away, which in turn juiced up the lightbulbs just enough to see what you was aimin' for. I mean what they was aimin' for. Anyway, it was a disaster. Ben and Dora were all bruised up (there ought to be a law against kids puttin' rocks in snowballs), and half the lightbulbs were busted. The Human Light thing was an utter flop, and we were sure that Ben would put his dream aside. But no, he was more determined than ever. Ben wouldn't ever let some snowballs, a bunch of candy, and a few beer bottles upside the head get him down. This next weekend when he did the light parade over by Beebe, Arkansas, he'd be ready. By then Mickey Ray would have the battery holder rigged up and there would be no dimmin' lights.

Mickey Ray had no problem installing a holder in the back of Ben's wheelchair, but what kind of battery would Ben want to use? After the last parade he wanted to make sure that his thousands of lights were real bright, so after replacin' all the broken bulbs, he wrapped himself up with the strings of lights and had Mickey wire him up to one of those never-die-type batteries that are guaranteed to start under any condition. Well, Ben lit up all right. God bless him, people called up the sheriff's department and reported seein' a burst of unusual lights that evenin'. Why, even to this day if you get down wind of his wheelchair you can catch a slight smell of burnt flesh. After a thick coatin' of aloe vera cream, Ben decided that a lawn mower battery would probably be just fine. With that solved, there was only one detail left to deal with. Dora had refused to push Ben through the second parade even though it was bein' held in a different city, 'cause she wasn't gonna be turned on and pelted by a crowd like she been just a few nights before. And even though everybody in the park loved Ben to death, after seein' how ugly folks at a Christmas parade can get, none of us were gonna volunteer to push his old behind either. So after a bit of thinkin', Ben came up with the idea of hookin' up a rope between the truck bumper and his wheelchair and havin' Dora pull him along that route. With the protection of steel, glass, and locked doors between her and those in attendance at the parade, Dora caved in and agreed.

To the glory of everyone around, Ben shined like the top of a Christmas tree while bein' pulled slowly down the parade route. The multitude of colors that he put out sparkled even brighter off the reflection of his aluminum wheelchair. Ben had done it. He had truly become the Human Christmas Light Display, and despite the rumors and naysayers that had preceded that night's light procession, everyone in attendance was utterly in awe of the beauty one man had brought to each of them. As Ben rolled down each block, it was as if a miracle was happenin'. The real meanin' of Christmas was comin' alive in everyone's hearts. Through the brilliant flashin' glow the story of the Christ child could be seen. The story of how one single child long ago had come to show the world the light of love and compassion for your fellow man. Of course this abruptly ended when the float in front came to a sudden stop, causin' Dora to slam on the brakes. The insurance said it'd easily cost around $2,000 to get the dents out of the back bumper and fix the tailgate so it would open again, but with the emergency room bill, Ben and Dora decided to wait until the followin' year to get it fixed. Plus Ben was gonna need some of that money if he was gonna get his wheelchair bent back into shape and replace those broken bulbs in time to participate in the next week's light parade by Greer's Ferry.

Luckily Ben was able to get his act together in time to roll down the parade route, although this time he'd made a few changes. Ben had decided to wear a motorcycle helmet and one of them big umpire chest protectors, and to cover himself in foil to create an even more brilliant light, and to let Kitty Chitwood come, who'd also dreamed of bein' in this particular light parade since her grandparents had brought her to see it when she was just a little girl. And instead of havin' Kitty pull him, Ben decided to have her nudge him along with the truck. He'd installed thick squares of rubber to the back of his wheelchair that would work as bumpers and absorb the gentle impact from the truck. He'd also had temporary mirrors added to the grill of the truck so Kitty could see him at all times, as well as a portable headset in the helmet so they could keep in contact as well. And unlike the last parade when Dora was drivin', Kitty and Ben practiced this pushin' procedure several times around the High Chaparral Trailer Park just to make sure they had worked out all the kinks. Needless to say, Kitty and Ben were wowin' those in attendance. It was even better than the last go around. People were yellin' and screamin' out as Ben made his way down the street with Kitty ever so gently pushin' him. The feelin' of accomplishment filled both their hearts as the end of the parade route came into sight, which also might explain why Kitty didn't see that pothole that knocked her cigarette out of her mouth. In a frantic attempt not to get burnt, Kitty brushed the cigarette off into the floorboard with her free hand while pushin' herself up from the seat with her shoulders and feet. Of course since she happened to have her foot on the gas pedal at the time, she also sent Ben and his chair flyin' down the road like a rocket ship. Luckily he managed to avoid the float in front of him, but he wasn't so lucky when it came to the boat dock, which he hit at top speed. The sight of all those thousands of Christmas lights tied around Ben and his chair, streakin' across the night's sky before landin' in Greer's Ferry Lake, was compared by most in attendance to the comet that passed by this way several years past. As you can imagine, he got a standin' ovation for that one. All these years later, with Dora now dead and gone, and residin' over in Lot #14 with his new wife Dottie Lamb, Ben still on occasion dresses up as the Human Christmas Display Light and does a parade or two, but now he has one of those fancy powerchairs from Lamb Super Center. Of course the thrill of not knowin' whether Ben will finish the parade is finally gone, which to be honest, also kind of leads to a real big letdown once you've seen his act.

CHRISTMAS CRAFTS FROM THE HEART

Shotgun Shell Santa

If you ain't got no empty shotgun shells around your house, just call the National Rifle Association and ask 'em if they can help. Oh, and regardless of what they say, you ain't got to join the NRA to get free empty shells from 'em.

SUPPLIES

1 used shotgun shell
1 8-inch-long gold spring
1 $2^1/_2$- × $3^1/_2$-inch piece of red felt
Skin-tone craft paint
Black craft paint
White puff paint
Small paint brush
Box knife
Hot glue gun and glue sticks
$3^1/_2$-inch-long piece white yarn

1. Take the used shotgun shell and turn it so the metal part is face down. Use your box knife to punch two small holes directly across from each other $^1/_4$ of an inch from the top of the shell.

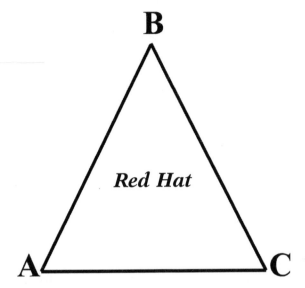

To make hat, simply glue end A to end C, which forms a circle. Fold end B backwards, and glue a white pom pom to the end.

2. Take the gold spring and shape both ends into hooks. Place each hook in the small holes. Apply a small amount of hot glue to each of the little holes, makin' sure that the gold spring is facin' up in an arch shape. This will be the handle that you use to hang your shell on the tree when it's finished. Set shell aside.

3. Usin' the pattern on page 159, cut out Santa's hat from the red felt. Take the felt and hot-glue it along the top of the shell. Make sure that the material meets in the back of the shell. Cut off any of the extra and discard.

4. Take the white yarn and hot-glue it around the top of the shell. This is Santa's fur trim. Cut off any extra, but save it.

5. Now take the extra and cut off a little corner of the white yarn to make the fluffy ball on the top of Santa's hat. Put a little hot glue on the tip of his hat and carefully press the little piece of yarn onto it. Fold Santa's hat backwards and hot glue it down so the tip of his hat touches the back of the shell.

6. Take your skin-tone paint and paint on the face. Wipe your brush clean and make eyes and a mouth with the black paint.

7. Now, use the photo of the completed Santa shell as a guide, and apply the white puff paint beard. Once it dries, hang him up, and enjoy.

TIPS FOR THE HOLIDAY HOSTESS

While we're at it, let's talk about drunks and you. As a hostess, it's your job to make sure that none of your drunken guests ever drive themselves home. Drunk drivin' ain't funny or a laughin' matter. You can laugh at 'em and make fun of 'em when they're at your party, but the laughin' stops when they pull out their car keys or truck keys. Regardless if you know 'em well or not, as host it is your job to step in. Call the police and tell 'em you got a drunk driver in your neighborhood. Then try to stall the drunk for a few minutes before walkin' 'em to his or her car. Let 'em get in the vehicle and continue to chat until the police car is in sight. Say goodnight, go back inside, and know that you did your duty as a good hostess.

Party Idea

Singin' Party

Each year at the High Chaparral Trailer Park we have a singin' party where we all bring a covered dish or just appetizers, eat, and then go out carolin'. We really have fun and it costs the hostess next to nothin' to put this one on. The only problem you have to deal with is folks who don't sing. Just put 'em in charge of carryin' the jug of hot chocolate and they'll fit right in. You'll want to make sure you have plenty of Christmas carols printed out so all your guests have the words to the songs. Make sure to remind your guests to dress warm, which includes socks and slacks for the ladies and gloves for everyone.

TRAILER PARK CHRISTMAS GAMES

Hey, What's in My Sock

The hostess takes a thermal sock and fills it with twenty-five different objects that pertain to Christmas (mistletoe, a bow, a figure from a nativity scene, pinecone, tinsel, unbreakable ornament, etc.). The hostess then takes a second thermal sock and puts the exact same things in it. When it's time for the party, the hostess passes out a blank sheet of paper and pen to each guest, and then she explains that the socks contain twenty-five Christmas objects. Each guest must take a sock, stick their hand inside, and, without lookin', try to figure out what all the items are in one minute's time. Each guest must write down as many items as he can. When his time is up, he passes the sock on to the next person. The reason you pack up two identical sockfuls is simply to speed up the game. This way you can have two people rather than just one trying to guess the items in the sock in that same one-minute time period. Make sure to tell your guests not to call out an object. The winner is the person or persons who has the most correct items on their paper after everyone has had a chance with a sock. This can be a hoot as well.

WHAT'S THAT SMELL?

Your guests won't want to leave your trailer on account of this wonderful smell.

Christmas Apple Pie

I put on five pounds from the smell of this alone.

Makes a batch

1 cup dried apples, cubed
4 cinnamon sticks
1 tablespoon nutmeg essential oil

2 tablespoons whole allspice
1 cup whole dried cranberries
2 tablespoons whole cloves

Combine everything in a jar and put the lid on it. Let it set for a week, stirrin' it every other day.

Holly Jolly Wooha!

❋ The Puritans in America tried to make Thanksgiving Day the most important annual festival rather than Christmas.

❋ Saint Francis of Assisi introduced Christmas carols to formal church services.

❋ *White Christmas* (1954), starring Bing Crosby and Danny Kaye, was the first movie to be made in Vista Vision.

Helpful Holiday Hints

❋ When you've got holiday recipes that require you to use a frozen juice concentrate, just mash it with a potato masher, and you won't have to wait to thaw it out.
—Sister Bertha Fay Bluemoker, Lot #12

❋ Real unbuttered popcorn works great for packin' around Christmas foods to be sent in the mail.

❋ If you use a real tree and it's time to throw it away, lay it down into an old bed sheet, wrap it up, and carry it outside that way to avoid gettin' needles all over your trailer. Of course, hang on to the sheet when you throw the tree out your door and it rolls down the hill into the gully.
—Connie Kay, Lot #13
—Wanda Kay, Lot #13

Twelve Days of Yuletime Advice

Dear Ruby Ann Boxcar,

During the holidays, I want to invite my entire family over, but someone is always mad at someone else and those folks don't get along. What should I do if I want to make everyone happy?

I Love My Family

Dear Love,

The answer is easy. Find out who it is that's fightin' this year, and then put your feelers out. Once you've gathered all the information, simply schedule two family gatherin's on Christmas, one in the mornin' and one in the evenin'. Invite one of the feudin' family members and all their supporters to the mornin' gatherin' and then invite the other fightin' members and their supporters over for the evenin' event. Make it a potluck so you don't do nothin' but offer your place for the meetin' point. That way nobody can say you did somethin' for one and not for the other. Of course I don't care what you do to not show favoritism, somebody is gonna say somethin'. But since you have to be a martyr and just have to have the family gather for the holidays, then it's on your head. If it was me, I'd just tell the families, "No party this year," and go on vacation. But again, that's just me.

Love, Kisses, and Trailer Park Wishes,
Ruby Ann Boxcar

Puttin' Your Best Face Forward

Beauty Mark

Your beauty mark is to your face what an artist's signature is to his paintin'. With that said, I always suggest that you keep your beauty mark black. I've personally found that if you change its color to red or even green, regardless of where you place your mark, folks will think you've got somethin' on your face. I also suggest that you stay away from tryin' to make your simple mark resemble a snowflake. My sister tried that one year and ended up with a concussion from all the people who hit her upside the head 'cause they thought she had a spider on her face. So just keep it simple.

Christmas Cheer

Donna Sue suggests . . .

Christmas Cake

Leave some of this for Santa Claus, and I'll guarantee you get a good gift.

1 ounce brandy
1 ounce Amaretto di Saronno

2 ounces Bailey's Irish Cream
$1/2$ cup ice cubes

Mix all the liquors in a cocktail glass, add the ice, and dust with powdered sugar if you like.

Little Drummer Boy Beverage

This drink will just look like you're bangin' your drum.

$^1/_3$ white grape juice
$^2/_3$ club soda

Serve chilled. You can use regular purple grape juice, too, if you like.

TRAILER PARK CHRISTMAS GRUB

Christmas Cookie

M&M Bisquick Cookies

Durin' the holiday season at the Blue Whale Strip Club, my fifty-eight-year-old sister tapes these to her legs and arms when she dances, and lets the patrons take one when they tip. They must be good, 'cause a batch of these only lasts one night, and anybody that's seen her up on stage can tell you they ain't tippin' her for her beauty.

Makes a couple dozen

$^3/_4$ cup Bisquick
1 package instant cheesecake- or
   vanilla-flavored puddin'
$^1/_4$ cup vegetable oil

1 egg
$^1/_4$ cup M&M's

Mix all ingredients together. Roll into balls and place on greased cookie sheet. Bake at 350 degrees F. for 15 minutes.

—DONNA SUE BOXCAR, LOT #6

Festive Fudge

Kenny and Donny's White Chocolate Carol of the Bells Fudge

Leave it to two single men sharin' a trailer together for the past sixteen years to come up with somethin' this good. It still amazes me that with the kind of cookin' skills them boys got, that they ain't found wives yet.

Makes a batch

2 cups sugar
³/₄ cup sour cream
¹/₂ cup margarine

12 ounces white chocolate
7-ounce jar marshmallow cream
³/₄ cup walnuts

Mix the first three ingredients together and bring to a boil. When it gets to a soft ball stage, take it off the heat. Add chocolate and stir until melted, add marshmallow cream and nuts, and put in greased 9-inch pan. Cool at room temperature, cut in squares.

—KENNY LYNN AND DONNY OWENS, LOT #18

Pies on Earth, Goodwill Toward Men

Nellie's Jolly Old Saint Nicholas Apple Chess Pie

With his dentures bein' the way they are, Nellie says this is the only way her husband, C.M., can eat apples.

Makes one pie

1 unbaked pie shell
1 cup sugar
1 stick of margarine
1 tablespoon flour

2 eggs
1¹/₂ cups chopped apples
¹/₄ teaspoon cinnamon

Cream sugar, margarine, flour, and eggs in a bowl. Fold in chopped apples and cinnamon. Pour into an 8-inch unbaked pie shell and bake at 400 degrees F. for 10 minutes. Then lower the oven down to 325 degrees F. and bake for an additional 40 minutes.

—NELLIE TINKLE, LOT #4

Seasonal Supper Sensation

Wendy's Mistletoe and Holly Rooster Taters

Despite the name, there is no chicken in this dish, but rather it came from the rooster on the Corn Flakes box. Of course there ain't no mistletoe or holly in it either, but it sounds a whole lot better than just plain "Wendy's Taters."

Makes 4 to 6 servin's

4 medium bakin' potatoes, sliced
 $1/4$-inch thick
2 tablespoons melted margarine
1 teaspoon salt

$1^1/_2$ cups grated Cheddar
 cheese
2 cups Kellog's Corn Flakes,
 crushed

Put your potato slices in a bowl and drizzle the margarine over them. Now toss 'em to make sure that all are covered. Lay these out on a greased bakin' sheet. Sprinkle on the salt and bake at 375 degrees F. for 15 minutes. Sprinkle on the cheese and crushed corn flakes, and put back in the oven to cook for another 25 to 30 minutes.

Mickey Ray's Here Comes Santa Claus Sandwich

These are great to make when you can fit 'em in durin' the day, and then you can forget about 'em until later on when you got time for a little holiday dinner.

Makes 8 sandwiches

$^1/_4$ pound Velveeta cheese, cubed
   into small pieces
3 hard-boiled eggs, chopped
1 7-ounce can tuna
2 tablespoons chopped onion

2 tablespoons diced celery
2 tablespoons pickle relish
1 to 1$^1/_2$ cups Miracle Whip
8 hamburger buns

Mix everything but the buns together. You might want to add more Miracle Whip dependin' on how creamy you like it to be. Put on the buns and wrap 'em up in foil. Put in a Crock-Pot, put the cover on, and set it to low. If you want to eat 'em in less than an hour, turn the settin' to high and let 'em go for 30 minutes.

—MICKEY RAY KAY, LOT #13

CHAPTER 8

The Eighth Day of Christmas

DECEMBER 20

The Spirit of Christmas and the Drive of Passion unite to form the face of Christmas.

171

Traditional Gift on This Day
Eight maids a-milking

Trailer Park Gift on This Day
Eight midgets wrestlin' (on Pay-Per-View)

ABOUT THIS DAY

When I'm in town, I have a standin' appointment each year to get my hair done over at the Beauty Barge, a beauty shop out on the lake. As all who've read my sister's book might recall, neighbor Little Linda won that old houseboat durin' a card game. Well, with the holidays upon us, as well as the Holier Than Most Baptist Church Christmas party just around the corner, I like to get my hair and nails done. Usually I just do my own hair; after all, I am a former licensed beautician, but since it is Christmas and all, I like to treat myself to goin' to the Beauty Barge. And the staff is just wonderful. I told y'all in my other books about the Asian Siamese twins that Little Linda has doin' nails. They both work on you at the same time so it only takes half as long to get your nails done. Of course you got to double-tip 'em. Well, she also got a gal there who does hair who is a hoot. She's in her sixties if she's a day over twenty and she can't stand up for very long, so she cuts your hair while settin' in one of them motorized scooters. She's really good as well as a joy to talk with. Of course she did mess up my hair one time. She didn't realize her scooter's front tire had partially gone flat so my hair was

173

cut crooked. But other than that and the fact that sometimes she runs into you with that doggone thing, Vonda Lee Cooder is just a pleasure.

A Christmastime Treasure
from the High Chaparral Trailer Park

Durin' the 1970s everybody in the United States had a CB in their cars, trucks, or homes, and all of us at the High Chaparral Trailer Park were no different. Why, I even had a CB set up in my kitchen area and I'd talk on it from time to time. After all, I was a single woman back in those days, and it was fun talkin' to the truckers, pretendin' that I was ridin' along with 'em as they went from state to state. Even though I did manage to waste away many an hour gabbin' back and forth, the actual queen of the CB radio at the trailer park was none other than my sister, Donna Sue Boxcar. She had turned her trailer in Lot #6 into one mean CBin' machine. She had a home base that would have put our local sheriff's department's communication system to shame. Sure, when folks would pass by our area they'd always give a shout out to the "Hairspray Honey"— which was me—but turn your CB on day or night and them menfolk would be yellin' for my sister, "Lot Lizard." Even later on when Donna Sue changed her name to "Boozy Beaver" 'cause she found out that lot lizard is also slang for the cheap nasty hookers that hang out in the back row of truck stops, them truckers would still try to reach her on the CB at all hours of the day and night. I don't know what it was about Donna Sue that set them men off, but hear tell, some of them truckers would sign up for next-to-no money just to haul a load through our part of Arkansas, in hopes that they might meet up with my sister. Maybe it was the way she presented herself on the CB, or her tone of voice. Of course it could have also been that she always had a place for weary truckers to lay their heads for the night when they was up her way.

It was on one of those nights that my favorite Christmas memory was formed. Even though the weather forecastin' had gotten much better by 1975, no one had the slightest idea that we'd get as much snow as we did on that chilly Christmas Eve. The weather was so bad that Roy Peters, owner of the Grin and Bear It, called up Donna Sue at three in the afternoon and told her not to come in to work that evenin'. With all the snow that was comin' down and the wind blowin' as hard as it was, Roy had decided to just close down the nightclub, where my sister was the guest dancer that week, and head on home. That was good news for Momma's and Daddy's ears I can tell you. They didn't like the fact that Donna Sue was drivin' almost an hour to as well as an hour back that late at night durin' those two weeks she worked there. Of course they also didn't understand why a taxidermist would be open those kinds of hours either. It'd be several years later till they'd find out that their oldest daughter was a cheap drunken exotic dancer. No, now that I think back on it, they already knew she was a cheap drunk. They just didn't know that she danced around on stage takin' her clothes off for dollar bills or in most cases, loose change. Still, they were happy that Donna Sue would be off those snow-packed roads that evenin' 'cause they were bad, and my Daddy knew that first-hand. Since 4:30 that afternoon he'd been usin' the then trailer park owner Ben Beaver's John Deere tractor to help pull many of our neighbor's cars and even trucks out of the snow. Yes, the roads were bad, but as the snow continued to fall, they got even worse.

Accordin' to the TV, motels and even them top-dollar hotels were plum near full with stranded motorists. Even if you didn't leave the comfort of your trailer, you could still tell that nobody was drivin', just from the silence on the CB radio that night.

"Breaker breaker one nine. Is there anybody out there in radio land?" the husky voice asked as it cracked the silence of the late night in my sister's trailer. "Breaker breaker one nine, does anybody copy?" My sister, who'd been drinkin', just like any other day, since she got up at 2 P.M., came to just in time to hear the male tones comin' from her CB radio. "Breaker breaker one nine, this is 'Dan the Man.' Is there anybody out there that copies me?" With that Donna Sue sprang up from the couch and to her feet only to fall face-first into her recliner. But without missin' a beat she pulled herself back up and made her way to the CB table by feelin' the wall. To this day my sister feels her way through her trailer by runnin' her hands along the wall with each step. This is why if you're ever in her trailer, you'll notice she ain't got no pictures or photos hung any higher than three feet from the floor.

"Roger, Dan the Man," my sister answered back, once she'd set herself down at her desk and located her base mic, "this is the Boozy Beaver, and you're bendin' the needle at my base station." (Basically translated for all you non-CBers, *"Hi, I hear you."*)

"Boozy Beaver, it sure is good to hear somebody's got their ears on out there. I got a convoy here that could sure use some help if you don't mind." *("I'm glad you're listenin', 'cause several of us need help.")*

"Well, Dan the Man, if you and your convoy are lookin' for a good time, I could certainly help." *("I'm a tramp.")*

"That's a big ten-four. What are your numbers, Boozy Beaver?" (*"Oh, really?"*)

"I'm single and blond with no rug rats." (*"I'm a peroxide tramp with no kids."*)

"I copy. Go ahead." (*"Good."*)

"I'm five foot nine and have a fridge full of brown bottles . . ." (*"I ain't a midget, and I got beer."*)

"I copy. Go ahead." (*"Good."*)

"I'm twenty-nine years old and a double D . . ." (*"Even though I'm not an old barfly, my chest could still be used as a flotation device."*)

"That's a big ten-four! Go ahead." (*"That's real good."*)

"I weigh around 348 lbs . . ." (*"On occasions I've been mistaken for a futon."*)

"Negatory, negatory on the good time!" (*"Oh, hell no!"*)

"But, Dan the Man, I got lots of brown bottles!" (*"I got beer!"*)

"Ten-four, Boozy Beaver, but I'd need a gas pipe." (*"I know, but I'd still have to be dead first."*)

"Well, Dan the Man, if you don't need a little Christmas noogy from the Boozy Beaver, what can I do for you?" (*"Since you don't want to get violently ill on Christmas, what else can I do to help?"*)

Dan the Man went on to explain to Donna Sue that him and twelve other truckers had been stuck along the highway for the past six hours and needed help. When she explained to them that all the roads had been closed due to the blizzard that had hit the area, he went on to ask if she'd call the sheriff and see if someone could at least pick 'em up and take 'em to a motel. Most of the guys hadn't eaten since lunch, and they didn't have enough gas to keep runnin' their rigs durin' the storm, which had now been predicted to last for another twelve to twenty-four hours. Donna Sue agreed to try and get in touch with the sheriff, but he told her what she already knew. They had no way to do anything for these men until mornin', and in the meantime they'd just have to do what they could. Not bein' one to take no for an answer, and also believin' that out of thirteen men, one of 'em might possibly get drunk enough to enjoy her company, Donna Sue took action. She called and woke up Ben Beaver. She told him the story and asked him if she could use his tractor and a couple of the inner tubes he had locked up by the pool. Ben, who'd been in a wheelchair since the Korean War, told her she could use whatever she needed, but that she'd have to get it herself, which she did. After hookin' up ropes between the inner tubes and the tractor, Donna Sue got back on her CB and told the fellas to keep an eye out for her. She then put on her long johns, a pair of overalls that one of her one-night stands had accidentally left at her trailer after fleein' when he'd come to, and her fake wool coat that she'd gotten on her birthday from one of her admirers. After slippin' on a pair of our daddy's boots, and puttin' on a pair of gloves, Donna Sue stood in her bathtub and poured three bottles of vodka all over herself. It was bitter cold outside with winds gustin' up to 15 miles an hour, but my sister didn't care. She knew it would be hard work rescuin' them men, but with the possibility of holiday loving in the back of her mind and the knowledge that liquor doesn't freeze, she made her way to the tractor and headed out to do her Christian duty.

The doctor would later say that if Donna Sue hadn't been as drunk as she was that night, the cold might have killed her. She made it to those thirteen stranded truckers and loaded up the trac-tor with a few of 'em while the rest rode on the inner tubes back to the trailer park. Then, with their help, she ran a few industrial-size extension cords from her trailer down to the pool, which had months earlier already been drained and covered with a canvas for the winter, and she hooked up some space heaters. The fellas used some old pillows and blankets that me and most of the other folks in the trailer park had temporarily donated. We'd also given up some of our leftovers and pitchers of sweet tea for the boys to enjoy while they camped out in the pool. As long as they kept the electric heaters goin', the canvas, which completely covered the pool, trapped the heat in, creatin' what was most likely an even warmer environment than the drafty trailers all of us were in. And of course Donna Sue's vast quantity of beer and liquor along with her personal charms, if you know what I mean, did a lot to keep those boys warm as well. As for Donna Sue, well let's just say she was right. All her hard work on that Christmas Eve did pay off in the end after all, although she said she'd have done a lot better job showin' those truckers a real good-time Christmas if only her drunken behind hadn't kept rollin' down into the deep end of the pool. And you wonder why the CB craze died out?

CHRISTMAS CRAFTS FROM THE HEART

The Trailer Park Christmas Mouse

With the exception of Mickey or Minnie Mouse, most of us trailer park folks can't stand mice. It ain't that they're ugly or nothin', but simply that we don't like sharin' our food with nothin' that ain't at least payin' rent. However, this crafty little Christmas Mouse is one that we all look forward to seein' in our homes in December.

SUPPLIES

25 paper Christmas napkins
25 small paper plates
25 Oreo cookies
6 ounces semisweet chocolate chips

1 jar maraschino cherries with stems (about 25)
25 Hershey's Kisses, unwrapped
2½-ounce bag sliced almonds
50 M&M's Minis

1. Set the small plates out on a table.

2. Place a paper napkin on each plate.

3. Take your Oreo cookies and gently open each one.

4. Set the cookie half with the most crème frostin' left on it down on a napkin, cookie side down. Discard (eat) the other half of the Oreo cookie 'cause you won't be needin' it to complete the project.

5. Next take the chocolate chips and melt 'em in the microwave.

6. Take a spoon and dip the very tip of it in the melted chocolate. Take the chocolate that's on the spoon and carefully place it on one of the M&M's Minis. Press the M&M's on the side of a Hershey Kiss. Do this again to another M&M's Minis of the same color and press the second one right next to the first. These are the eyes, and the Kiss is our mouse head. Repeat this process on each Kiss.

7. Dip the end of an almond slice in the melted chocolate and then press it on the bottom of the Kiss, just to the right of the M&M's Minis eyes. Do the same thing with another almond slice, but this time press it to the left of the eyes. These are your mouse's ears. Set the heads aside.

8. Take a chocolate cherry by its stem and dip it in the chocolate.

9. Set the dipped cherry on the Oreo half, makin' sure that its stem sticks up slightly on the side. This will be the body of our little Christmas mouse and the stem is its tail. Repeat this with the remainin' 24 cherries.

10. Press the end of the Kiss onto the chocolate-covered cherry so that the ears and eyes are facin' up. You may have to use your spoon and add a little more melted chocolate to the cherry area where the head goes. Hold the head in place for just a minute or until the chocolate hardens. Now, make some more, and pretty soon you got yourself a trailerful of chocolate mice.

TIPS FOR THE HOLIDAY HOSTESS

Every good hostess should always have a special somethin' to give each guest as they arrive. It don't have to be fancy or expensive, but it should be creative like the Trailer Park Christmas mouse that we just made. Not only is this little critter cute as a button, he's also edible. Who don't like an edible chocolate mouse? And as you just seen, he's pretty easy to make as well.

Party Idea

A Color Party

This one is real easy. Pick a holiday color, like white for example, and tell all your guests to come dressed in nothin' but white, with shoes bein' the exception to the rule. Put up white decorations in the livin' room, white towels in the guest bathroom, and serve white food in white dishes. This is also the perfect time to play White Elephant. Other fun colors are red and green. You might want to stay away from gold, since not everybody has gold clothin' unless you happen to live close to that 8 Mile place.

Trailer Park Christmas Games

White Elephant / Dirty Santa

This game is always a winner. You tell everyone to wrap up an item that they have lyin' around the house and don't really use anymore. It could be anything from an ugly coffee mug to an unopened box of corn pads. Anyway, you go around and have everybody pick a number from 1 to however many people you got playin'. The person with #1 picks a gift and opens it. When they've finished then next number, #2, gets the choice of either takin' #1's gift or openin' a new gift from the pile. If they take #1's gift, then #1 has to open a new gift. Then it is #3's turn, and they can either open a new gift or take #1's or #2's gift. This continues until all the gifts have been opened, and everyone has a gift. A gift can be stolen over and over again, but it can't ever be reclaimed by someone who's had it already. This one is a lot of fun and can get evil.

WHAT'S THAT SMELL?

This is one of those aromas that's even better when it's heated up.

The Three Wise Men's Stovetop Potpourri

This will make your trailer smell like heaven.

Makes one batch

3 whole cloves

3 whole allspice

3 cinnamon sticks

3 cups water

Put everything in a pot, bring it to a boil, reduce heat to simmer, and enjoy. Keep an eye on the water level and add more as needed.

HOLLY JOLLY WOOHA!

❋ A traditional Christmas dinner in early England was the head of a pig prepared with mustard *(and folks wonder why I don't feel bad servin' Spam for the holidays)*.

❋ The Friday and Saturday before Christmas are the two busiest shopping days of the year.

❋ The United States' official national Christmas tree, "General Grant Tree," which was made official in 1925, is located in King's Canyon National Park in California.

HELPFUL HOLIDAY HINTS

❋ If you spill eggnog on you, lift off the excess with a spoon. Blot up as much of it as you can with a napkin, and then rub the spot with a damp cloth. Wash it when you get home.

❋ Keep some lip balm in your car's glove compartment. Not only is it great for chapped lips, but you can apply it to a nose that's sore from a cold.

❋ Put those alcohol towelettes in your purse just in case you have to use a phone while at a Christmas party. Wipin' the phone receiver before you use it is a great way to kill those cold germs that another guest might have left on it.

—DOTTIE LAMB-BEAVER, LOT #14

Twelve Days of Yuletime Advice

Dear Ruby Ann,

As you know I love a man in uniform. Especially one bearin' gifts. But, things is different ever since my run-in with the Arkansas State Police at the big Outlet Mall over in Fort Smith, back in June of 2002. (I am sure you remember the big to-do about me borrowin' a few pairs of shoes for the big Fourth of July Festival pageant that the Blue Whale Strip Club was havin'. I was gonna take 'em back!) Well, I am no longer allowed in the mall, and I really want to see Santa. What am I to do? I tried waitin' till after the mall closed to see if I could catch him leavin', but he never came out. Help me!

Your friend,
Little Linda

Dear Little Linda,

I would've thought that you'd have known by now that Santa ain't your very own personal love doll; he belongs to everyone everywhere who celebrates Christmas. I'm afraid that when it comes to men in uniform durin' the holidays, you're just gonna have to be happy with the school custodial crew that you've dated in the past, any poor stray drunken soldier that passes out at the Blue Whale Strip Club, or the slow-runnin' Salvation Army bell ringers. Merry Christmas, hon!

Love, Kisses, and Trailer Park Wishes,
Ruby Ann Boxcar

Puttin' Your Best Face Forward

Lip Gloss

With mistletoe hangin' up all over the place, I think people tend to kiss more durin' Christmas than they do on Valentine's Day. Even if you don't kiss nobody, with all the food around, you're sure to at least eat it off. With that in mind, if you decide to wear lip gloss durin' the holidays, make sure you keep the tube close to the top of your purse, 'cause you'll need to reapply often. And yes, glitter lip gloss is allowed durin' the holiday season.

Christmas Cheer

Donna Sue suggests . . .

Santa Shot

This is the real reason his cheeks are red!

1 part peppermint schnapps
1 part green crème de menthe

1 part grenadine

Add the peppermint schnapps to a shot glass. Pour the crème de menthe over the back of a spoon so you layer it on top of the grenadine. Add the grenadine in the same fashion. Your drink should be from the top to the bottom, red, green, and clear.

Dirty Snowman

If only there was some vodka in this, I'd even drink it.

2 scoops vanilla ice cream   1 ounce grenadine
8 ounces orange juice

Blend all in a blender and pour in a glass over crushed ice.

TRAILER PARK CHRISTMAS GRUB

Christmas Cookie

Connie Kay's Attention-Christmas-Shoppers Cheesecake Cookie Bars

When the trailer park fills with the smell of these wonderful cookies, you know Connie Kay is gettin' ready to cut prices on her door to door beauty-and-health items for the holidays.

Makes one pan

$^1/_3$ cup margarine   8 ounces cream cheese
$^1/_3$ cup brown sugar   1 egg
1 cup flour   2 tablespoons milk
$^1/_2$ cup chopped nuts $^1/_2$ teaspoon vanilla
$^1/_4$ cup sugar   1 tablespoon lemon juice

Preheat oven to 350 degrees F. Cream margarine and brown sugar until light and fluffy. Add flour and nuts; blend until mixture resembles crumbs. Set aside 1 cup mixture. Press remainder into 8- × 8-inch pan.

Bake for 12 to 15 minutes. Let cool. Beat sugar and cream cheese until smooth. Add remainin' ingredients and beat well. Spread over crust. Sprinkle reserved crumbs on top, pressin' down lightly with fingers. Bake for 25 minutes, cool, and cut into bars. Keep in the fridge.

—CONNIE KAY, LOT #13

Festive Fudge

Sister Bertha's O Holy Night Sanctified Sour Cream Fudge

This stuff is as good as Sister Bertha's Sanctified Sour Cream Frostin' from my first book.

Makes a batch

2 cups sugar
2 tablespoons white corn syrup
2 tablespoons margarine
1 cup sour cream

1 teaspoon vanilla
$\frac{1}{2}$ cup pecans
$\frac{1}{2}$ cup candied cherries

Mix your sugar, corn syrup, margarine, and sour cream together in a bowl and place on medium heat till it gets to the soft ball stage. Pull it off the heat and add the vanilla. Let it cool to room temperature. Add the nuts and candied cherries and beat until thick. Pour it into a buttered bakin' dish. Put it into the fridge and let it harden a bit.

—SISTER BERTHA, LOT #12

Pies on Earth, Goodwill Toward Men

Chocolate Pecan Pie

*If Joseph and Mary would've had one of these with 'em, I got a feelin'
that there would've been room for 'em in the inn.*

Makes one pie

1 cup light corn syrup
$^1/_2$ cup sugar
$^1/_4$ cup margarine, melted
1 teaspoon vanilla
3 eggs
1 6-ounce package semisweet
   chocolate chips

$1^1/_2$ cups pecan halves
2 tablespoons reserved
   semisweet chocolate chips
10 pecan halves
Whipped cream
1 9-inch pie crust

Preheat the oven to 325 degrees F.

Combine the first five ingredients, beatin' well. Add your chocolate chips and the pecan halves. Stir well. Pour into pie crust. Spread it evenly. Pop it in the oven and bake for 15 minutes. Cover the crust edges with foil, and continue to bake for another 50 minutes or until the fillin' is set. Take it out of the oven and let it cool for 1 hour.

Melt 2 tablespoons of chocolate chips in the microwave. Dip the 10 pecan halves in the chocolate and then set 'em on a wax paper–lined plate. Put the pecans in the fridge and let 'em set. Put the whipped cream on top of the pie and add the chocolate covered pecans. Keep the pie in fridge until time to serve.

—TINA FAYE STOPENBLOTTER, LOT #17

Chess Pie

Lamb's I Saw Momma Kissin' Santa Claus's Assistant at the Mall Lemon Chess Pie

Now you can enjoy the same taste that you'd get at Lamb Super Center, but without havin' to pay $3.75 per slice. Sorry, Dottie.

Makes one pie

1¹/₂ cups sugar	4 eggs
2 teaspoons cornmeal	2 tablespoons margarine, melted
Juice of three lemons	1 9-inch unbaked pie crust

In a bowl, mix the flour and sugar. Add the lemon juice and margarine. Add your eggs one at a time, beatin' each one in before addin' the next one. Pour your mixture into the pie crust and bake for an hour at 300 degrees F. The pie should be set and golden brown.

—DOTTIE LAMB-BEAVER, LOT #14

Seasonal Supper Sensation

Christmas Is Comin' Trailer Park Beef Bourguignon

When you serve this dish you're gonna want to pull out and use the good paper plates that you drew Christmas-themed patterns on with them colored felt pens.

Makes 4 to 6 servin's

1$\frac{1}{2}$ pounds beef chuck, cubed
5 carrots, chopped
1 onion, diced
1 clove garlic, smashed
2 shallots, minced
$\frac{1}{4}$ pound bacon, chopped

1 can cream of mushroom soup
1 cup water
1 cup white grape juice
2 tablespoons flour
Margarine to sauté with
$\frac{1}{2}$ cup water

Get you a skillet and heat up your margarine. Add the carrots, onions, and garlic, and sauté 'em for about 3 to 5 minutes. Put in a large casserole dish.

Take your empty skillet and add the beef. Brown all sides of the beef cubes. After that add your 1 cup water and white grape juice. Stir. Then gradually add your flour. Stir well, makin' sure to get out all the lumps. Pour this mixture in with your sautéed vegetables and pop in an oven to cook for 1 hour at 375 degrees F.

Clean your skillet and then fry up your bacon till it's next to crisp. Add your shallots and cook for an extra few minutes. Add your cream of mushroom soup and $\frac{1}{2}$ cup water. Stir well. Let it cook for another 5 minutes. Cover and reduce the heat to low until your beef is done cookin'. Pour the bacon mixture on top of the beef mixture and enjoy. If you don't mind cooking with wine, substitute all the water and grape juice with burgundy wine.

—Donny Owens, Lot #15

CHAPTER 9

The Ninth Day of Christmas

DECEMBER 21

Don't worry. Luckily she landed on that great big behind of hers, so she was just fine.

Traditional Gift on This Day
Nine ladies dancing

Trailer Park Gift on This Day
Nine go-go dancers (workin' for loose change and food items
at the Blue Whale Strip Club)

ABOUT THIS DAY

You can bet my sister won't be answerin' her phone till after 2 P.M.
on December 21. Nor will Little Linda for that matter. No, they're
tryin' to rest up for their annual Blue Whale Strip Club Christmas
party. Typically if it falls on a Sunday, which seein' how most of the
dancers as well as both the owners are Baptist, is the only day of the
week the Blue Whale is closed, they hold their party around 7 that
night. But if it falls on any other day of the week, they have to wait
until the bar closes at 2 A.M. to have their party. Although since they
close the kitchen and stop servin' food around 11 P.M. rather than
1 A.M. on the twenty-first, the bar clears out a lot earlier and the
party gets a head start. And yes, the food is that good. All you have
to do is go to my sister's Web page at www.donnasueboxcar.com,
click on her link to the Blue Whale Girls, and take a good hard look
at the girls, who are all clothed, to see just how good the food really
must be. Now, notice I didn't say a good long hard look at 'em. The
last thing I want y'all to do is hurt your eyes durin' Christmas.

193

A Christmastime Treasure
from the High Chaparral Trailer Park

The Christmas party Anita Biggon threw in her trailer back in 2000 was one that no one in attendance will ever forget. Unfortunately I was out of town that year, so I missed the whole shebang, but it has taken its place in holiday history in these parts. Y'all might recall that in June of 2000 Anita purchased the then Three Cigarettes in the Ashtray Bar where she'd cocktail waitressed at since 1989, just after movin' back in with her momma, who in turn four years later went on to glory, leavin' Anita the trailer and everythin' else in Lot #2. Well, durin' her first year as bar owner Anita closed the Three Cigarettes in the Ashtray for Christmas Eve, 'cause even the biggest drunk wouldn't think about settin' foot in a honky tonk in our neck of the woods on the eve of our dear Savior's birth. This meant that with the night off, all the employees would be free to get together for an employee Christmas party, which she promptly announced would take place at 7 P.M. in her trailer. This announcement blew the bar staff away. As you can guess, all three of 'em was just as excited as all get out, 'cause the former owner, Darnell Fluggy, hadn't never thrown no kind of party for the employees regardless of what time of year it was. This was already sure to be a fun time that would be remembered by at least the staff and their spouses. But it wouldn't be long before the employee Christmas party would take a brand-new outlook.

After runnin' into each other at the Piggly Wiggly, Bernie D. and Melba Toast, owners of the Blue Whale Strip Club, decided to join forces with Anita and turn the gatherin' into a joint venture with both staffs havin' their Christmas parties together. Anita would provide the location, and Melba and her husband, Chef Bernie D. Toast, would take care of the food and liquor. It looked like a win-win situation at first for Anita, but that was only 'cause she had no idea of what five drunken strippers with a combined weight of well over 1,000 pounds can do to the inside of a trailer. Considerin' one of them drunks was my sister Donna Sue who resides over in Lot #6, and the shape her trailer is in, well, she should have known better. In any case, Anita's bartender Kyle Chitwood and his wife Kitty from Lot #11, and the other two employees of her bar and their dates showed up at Lot #2 right at 6 P.M. on Christmas Eve for the party. Within the next thirty minutes, Melba and her husband Bernie, the Blue Whale girls and their low-life dates, and the other five employees from the Blue Whale all arrived. As you can imagine, the booze was flowin' like Dr Pepper in a matter of no time, which helps to explain why nobody noticed Blue Whale dancer Edna Rotoweeder's ex-boyfriend Preston Sisemore peekin' through the windows, tryin' to see who Edna had brung to the party. That Preston had never been anything but trouble, and with that temper of his, well, I don't know why the state hadn't done locked him up somewhere and thrown away the key. Even though Edna had come by herself that evenin', that ex of hers was bound and determined to make sure that she didn't have fun without him. So before you could say movin' violation, Preston had hitched Anita's trailer up to the back of his beat-up 1976 white Cadillac Fleetwood Eldorado convertible and was headed down the highway. Well, it was thirty minutes before anyone inside the trailer figured out that they was movin'. If fellow Blue Whale girl Little Linda hadn't volunteered to make an ice run, and stepped out of the trailer door as they were racin' down the highway, nobody would've ever known what was goin' on. Of course the only reason folks caught on was 'cause after fifteen minutes she still hadn't returned with the much-needed ice. Fortunately Little Linda wasn't hurt. As fate would have it, her fall out the front door of the movin' trailer was broken by a tree, a couple of boulders, an unlucky bobcat, and an old rusted rundown 1934 Chevy pickup truck, which had been abandoned at the bottom of the hill where she rolled down. Since the seatbelts in Preston's Fleetwood Eldorado didn't work, and both his doors were missin', he never went over 15 miles an hour for fear of bein' sucked out, which the sheriff later admitted was a good thing. Accordin' to Sheriff Gentry, if Preston would've been drivin' just 5 miles an hour faster than he was, that tree most likely wouldn't have survived. It was also a good thing that Little Linda's red sequined halter top caught on the front doorstep when she came flyin' out of that trailer, 'cause it was the large flappin' bolt of flashy material that caught his eye when a laughin' Preston passed his parked car. Long story short, everybody at the party was just fine, and the sheriff let Anita park the trailer along the highway so they could finish their Christmas gatherin', sober up, and call somebody the followin' day to come and haul their hung-over behinds back to Lot #2. Preston was charged with theft, kidnappin', and drivin' with a whole bunch of open containers. As for Little Linda, well, she was discovered by an old widowed farmer who hooked his tractor up to her ankles and drug her back through the snow to his barn. He later said that he attempted to give her mouth-to-mouth when he first found her there, but that he had to stop 'cause he kept passin' out from the fumes. Little Linda and that old farmer did go out a few times after that, but he was a little bit country, and she was a little bit rock 'n' roll, so nothin' really came of it. Of course, my sister Donna Sue says that even now from time to time Little Linda will call her up and say she's gonna do a little drivin' down the back roads and get back to nature, which means she's off to see Farmer Lee.

CHRISTMAS CRAFTS FROM THE HEART

Jigsaw Puzzle Wreath

I can't begin to tell you how many puzzles my husband, Dew, has bought and never finished that I got settin' up in my closet. I'm sure there are some of y'all out there who have the same kind of thing tucked away somewhere. Well, pull 'em out, 'cause we're gonna kill two birds with one stone. We're gonna clear up some extra space while makin' a decoration that everyone will want. That's right, a jigsaw puzzle wreath.

SUPPLIES

Cardboard, about 2 feet × 2 feet
Scissors
Glue
Puzzle pieces
Green spray paint
Clear glitter

Hot glue gun
Handful of red pom-poms
$2^1/_2$ feet of wide ribbon to make a bow
No-nail sawtooth for hanging

1. Carefully cut out a 2-foot-diameter circle from the cardboard.

2. Next cut out a 6- × 6-inch circle from the middle of the circle and discard it.

3. Glue a layer of puzzle pieces all around the large circle. Feel free to overlap the outer edges of the circle if you like.

4. Glue a second and a third layer of puzzle pieces as well on top of the first layer. Let dry.

5. Spray paint the wreath.

6. While the spray paint is still wet, sprinkle on the glitter, then let it dry.

7. Hot glue on pom-poms throughout the wreath.

8. Take the ribbon and make a bow. Hot-glue the bow to the wreath.

9. Hot-glue the no-nail sawtooth on the back so you can hang your wreath on a nail.

TIPS FOR THE HOLIDAY HOSTESS

When it comes to food items, unless this is a dinner party or a food-themed holiday gatherin', appetizers are just fine. Now after sayin' that, let me add that you ain't got to have fifty different kinds. I personally have found that as long as you got four cold appetizers and two hot ones, you'll be just fine. Just make sure you got plenty of each. Actually you can never have too many. Even if you find that you've got two trays of appetizers still in the fridge when the party ends, you and your husband can either snack on those durin' the rest of the week or take 'em with you to the next Christmas party you attend. Or when you have guests over, serve 'em up a sweet tea and a few of them appetizers. You'll be surprised how some folks will eat just about anything, regardless of what color it might be.

Party Idea

Ornament Exchange

These are always fun. Have your guestss bring a Christmas ornament wrapped up and without a nametag on it. Then you play this like you play White Elephant. Everybody ends up with a Christmas tree ornament that they can hang up on their tree each year. Not only is this fun, but it will be somethin' that they will remember each year when they unpack it and place it on their tree. Naturally, some kind of food will be required.

Trailer Park Christmas Games

Kiss and Tell

This game is real fun for couples. You pair up into teams of two players, and yes, married or engaged couples must make up a team. Then one team member sets down in a chair with a Santa hat on. The other team member has to put on a thick coatin' of lipstick. When the hostess says "Go," the player with the lipstick has to kiss their teammate on the face as many times as possible in thirty seconds. They can reapply the lipstick as often as they wish. If they knock their teammate's Santa hat off while kissin', they have to put the hat on and change places with their teammate. That teammate now has to apply lipstick to their lips and kiss the seated player. At the end of thirty seconds, the hostess will go around and count all the kisses on each of the seated players. The seated player with the most kisses wins for their team. This can get real good when you got older couples playin'.

WHAT'S THAT SMELL?

Now you know why them little whippersnappers stick around the North Pole and make toys.

Workshop Fragrance

I don't know where this one came from, but it wouldn't be Christmas at the High Chaparral without it.

Makes a batch

3 cups fresh juniper sprigs with berries
2 cups red rosebuds
1 cup bay leaves
1/4 cup cinnamon chips
2 tablespoons cloves

3 cinnamon sticks
10 drops rose oil
3 drops pine oil
6 drops cinnamon oil
1 tablespoon orrisroot chips
20 small pinecones

Combine the first six ingredients.

In a separate bowl, combine the oils with the orrisroot. Mix the two bowls together and put in a big jar along with the pinecones. Shake well and let it set for two weeks, shakin' the jar every few days.

HOLLY JOLLY WOOHA!

* In some countries, such as Germany and the Ukraine, a spiderweb found on Christmas morning in your tree is believed to bring good luck. This is also why folks started puttin' tinsel on the trees.

* An average household in America will mail out twenty-eight Christmas cards each year and see twenty-eight cards return in their place.

✻ The world's first singing commercial aired on the radio on Christmas Eve, 1926, for Wheaties cereal.

HELPFUL HOLIDAY HINTS

✻ Cookie cutters tied with ribbons and hung up as decorations on your cabinets will make your Christmas kitchen to die for!

✻ Another fun decoratin' idea to do is to tie colorful yarn around your throw pillows to make them look like Christmas gifts.

✻ Washed-out Miracle Whip jars make wonderful potpourri containers, so save 'em all year round.

—DONNY OWENS, LOT #15
—KENNY LYNN, LOT #15

TWELVE DAYS OF YULETIME ADVICE

Dear Ruby Ann,

I am a religious person, and I do enjoy Christmas carols and carolers. However, lately there is a group from a non-Baptist church that has been comin' around right when my *Matlock* reruns are on. I do not want them to think I am being rude when they come and stand outside my door, but I do not want to miss my show. My TV is too heavy for me to carry into the other room and they can see me from the front yard. What should I do?

Matlock Rules

Dear MR,

You got three choices.

1. Foil your window, turn off all your outside lights, and don't answer the door when *Matlock* is on.

2. Videotape *Matlock* for later viewin', and enjoy the carolers.

3. When the carolers arrive, open your front door, throw 'em a box of Little Debbie Snack Cakes, and put a mannequin in the window. They'll happily think you're bein' blessed by their singin' while in fact you're actually enjoyin' your *Matlock* show.

Actually there is a fourth thing that you can do. Turn the lawn sprinklers on just before your *Matlock* show airs. This will keep your carolers at bay until *Matlock* is over, but it could also cause your pipes to burst—so be careful if you go this route.

Love, Kisses, and Trailer Park Wishes,
Ruby Ann Boxcar

PUTTIN' YOUR BEST FACE FORWARD

Powder Compact

This is a must for the holidays. Since you'll be spendin' a lot of time runnin' from party to party, you're gonna find that you can easily get overheated, especially when people got their heat cranked up. It's okay to look slightly aglow, but sweatin' like a dog is all wrong. The last thing you want is for folks to call 911 'cause they think you're havin' a heart attack. Just make sure that you give yourself a once-over with the powder puff before ringin' anyone's doorbell so that you look your best when they answer the door.

CHRISTMAS CHEER

Donna Sue suggests . . .

Santa's Pole

The North one of course.

1 shot peppermint schnapps
1 shot vodka

2 splashes Hawaiian Punch
1 full can 7-UP

Pour all ingredients in a highball glass. Mix and serve.

Elf Coffee

This explains why them little folks can produce as many toys as they do each year.

Makes 1 large or 2 smaller servin's

2 ounces unsweetened chocolate
$1/4$ cup sugar
1 cup strong coffee

$2^1/_2$ cups milk
$1^1/_2$ cups RC Cola or your
  favorite soda pop

Melt the chocolate in your microwave in a bowl and add the sugar. Mix well. Gradually add the hot coffee, then the milk, followed by the soda pop. Pour into a large mug or into two smaller cups.

TRAILER PARK CHRISTMAS GRUB

Christmas Cookie

Ollie's Baptist Butterscotch Oatmeal Cookies

All I can say is thank the good Lord above that Ollie goes to my church and always brings cookies to potluck functions and the church Christmas party.

Makes a couple dozen

$^{1}/_{2}$ cup sugar
$^{1}/_{2}$ cup margarine, softened
1 regular package butterscotch
    puddin' mix
$^{1}/_{2}$ teaspoon bakin' soda
1 teaspoon cream of tartar
$^{1}/_{4}$ teaspoon salt

1 egg
1 cup flour
1 cup dry oatmeal
$^{1}/_{4}$ cup chopped nuts
1 regular package butterscotch
    chips

Cream margarine and sugar. Add puddin' mix and stir. Add eggs.
    Sift bakin' soda, cream of tartar, salt, and flour. Add it to the mixture. Add oatmeal, nuts, and chips. Drop from teaspoon onto greased cookie sheet. Bake 12 to 15 minutes at 350 degrees F.

—OLLIE WHITE, LOT #10

Festive Fudge

Connie Kay's No Guilt Holiday Fudge

Connie managed to lose six pounds with this fudge over the holidays. Of course it was all she was eatin'.

Makes a batch

16 ounces cream cheese, softened

2 ounces unsweetened chocolate, melted and cooled

$^1/_2$ cup Splenda sugar substitute

1 teaspoon vanilla

$^1/_2$ cup chopped pecans

Put the cream cheese, cooled chocolate, Splenda, and vanilla in a bowl and beat 'em together. Add the pecans. Mix well and pour into a buttered pan. Cover and put in fridge overnight. Cut into pieces and serve. Store in refrigerator.

—CONNIE KAY, LOT #13

Pies on Earth, Goodwill Toward Men

Trailer Park Christmas Cream Pie

This pie is smoother than my daddy's head.

Makes one pie

$^3/_4$ cup light brown sugar

$^3/_4$ cup granulated sugar

3 tablespoons flour

3 cups half and half

$1^1/_2$ teaspoons vanilla

1 9-inch pie crust

Mix all your sugars together in a bowl followed by your flour. Add the half and half and vanilla and mix well, makin' sure that you ain't got no lumps or such in your mixture. Pour it into the pie crust and bake in a 400 degree F. oven for around 40 minutes. Take it out and let it cool. Then stick it in the fridge for an hour or so before servin'.

—DONNA SUE BOXCAR, LOT #6

Seasonal Supper Sensation

Good King Wenceslas' Spam Sensation

When my sister makes this for her boyfriend of the week durin' the holidays, she comes to the dinner table in nothin' but a large ribbon that she's tied around her. Did I mention that my sister don't make this a whole lot in December anymore?

Makes 4 to 6 servin's

6 ounces Spam, cubed
2 large cans chunk pineapple,
   drained
6 tablespoons flour
3/4 cups sugar

2 cups grated Cheddar cheese
1 roll Ritz crackers, crushed
2 sticks margarine, melted
A few parsley sprigs
3 maraschino cherries

Put your Spam and pineapple chunks in a 9- × 13-inch casserole dish. Set aside.

Mix the next three ingredients together. Pour it over the Spam and pineapple. Top this with the crushed crackers. Pour the melted margarine over this, and bake for 30 minutes at 350 degrees F. On the upper-left corner of the casserole, arrange your parsley and cherries out so they look like holly. Bay leaves work real good, too.

—Donna Sue Boxcar, Lot #6

CHAPTER 10

The Tenth Day of Christmas

DECEMBER 22

A vintage photo of the late Willie Dick of Lot #1 on
Christmas Day, 1957.

Traditional Gift on This Day
   Ten lords a-leaping

Trailer Park Gift on This Day
   Ten boys a-peepin' (in my bedroom window and I'm callin'
      their mommas)

ABOUT THIS DAY

Traditionally here at the High Chaparral Trailer Park this is the day
we realize that we forgot to do our Christmas cards. So we start off
the tenth day of Christmas by racin' out to the store, pickin' up our
cards, and writin' 'em out. Naturally we don't get around to puttin'
the stamps on 'em until around the eleventh or twelfth day of Christmas, but we make sure that we got 'em finished and in envelopes by
the end of this day. For the most part we will hand deliver the cards
to our closest friends since doin' it this way allows us to save a little
bit of money. Of course, I design my own card for each Christmas
and post it on my website at www.rubyannboxcar.com so y'all can
print it out and put it in your homes. I also send out my card via the
Internet to all my fans and friends who've signed up to get my cor-
respondence and online newsletter. So if you plan on givin' any of us
at the High Chaparral a call, don't do it today. We're busy gettin'
these doggone Christmas cards done.

A CHRISTMASTIME TREASURE
FROM THE HIGH CHAPARRAL TRAILER PARK

Before I start up this story, let me just throw in a few facts about the gal who lived over in Lot #1, which is where this story is set. Her name was Willie Dick, and she was somethin'. By the time I was born Willie, who was forty-nine, had already had six husbands. They'd either died on her, she'd runned 'em off, or she'd up and just plain old divorced 'em while they was off on a fishin' trip or some such thing. That was the way she was. Of course, back in December of 1957, which is when this story begins, she was up to husband number nine, and his lazy old behind was servin' a twenty-year sentence for manslaughter. It seemed that he got all hot under the collar and started screamin' at this poor fella while playin' poker, and the guy that was on the tongue lashin' went up and had a heart attack right there in the basement of the Presbyterian church. The DA blamed the untimely passin' on Willie's old man's temper, and the judge, who couldn't understand why anyone would want to be in a Presbyterian church in the first place, threw the book at him. As you can imagine, it didn't take no time for Willie to let husband number nine know that their happy weddin' bliss was blown, and that she was puttin' in for a divorce. The last thing she needed was to be workin' three jobs to feed her five babies while her "breadwinner" was in the slammer. Well, that news didn't set good with that ninth husband. He got all broken hearted and started sendin' her two or three letters a day beggin' her to change her mind and all. Why, he even managed to get his cousin Curly to drive fifty-six miles just to hand-deliver a caged canary and a note that read, "I love you, Willie." Of course Willie didn't care and she wasn't goin' to be moved. She placed the bird, which she loved and named Tweetie Pie, next to her chair in the livin' room. As for the letters, she'd read 'em and then put 'em in the bottom of her worn-out shoes to keep the snow out when she walked into town each day for work.

Well, that Christmas was gonna be a bad one for them five kids of hers, after all, she didn't have no kind of money to spend on the younguns. What she did make off them three jobs was just enough to pay her lot rent, make her trailer payment, keep the electric on, feed Tweetie Pie, and put some scraps on the table. All she could do was tell those little ones that sometimes even when you're good, Santa ain't always got time to come by everyone's home to drop off gifts. She'd go on about how Santa was gettin' up there just like their grandpa so he'd wait till next year to bring presents to the boys and girls who'd been real real good all year long, which basically described Willie's babies. Even though you could tell by lookin' in their tiny swelled-up eyes that they was disappointed, them kids gave their momma a big hug and told her that they didn't mind waitin' till next year for Santa. It was touchin'. Why even I, who was eight and a youngun myself at the time, was so moved that I almost offered to give 'em my Mr. Potato Head—which I'd asked Santa to bring for me for Christmas—after I'd unwrapped it and played with it for a few hours, naturally. Everybody knew about Willie's problems, but as I'd later learn when I got older, nobody had all that much more money themselves that year in the trailer park. Still, the ladyfolk would make it a point practically every day to bring over fudge, cookies, candy, and other homemade baked goods to Lot #1 for both Willie and her tykes in hopes that their labors of love would at least make the days leadin' up to Christmas joyful. Even today we trailer park neighbors do what we can to help out our neighbors as long as the loanin' of power tools, cars, or beer ain't involved. Willie was grateful and always offered the ladies a glass of sweet tea, even though they politely declined each offer. Willie wasn't ever known for her good housekeepin' or dish washin', if you know what I mean.

The wind whipped up on Christmas Eve day, and the snow-laden clouds rolled in over our little mobile home community. We were in for an awful storm, even a blizzard, if you could believe what that fella was predictin' on the radio. By three in the afternoon, the snow was already comin' down like blankets of white, and we'd all shoved thick socks, washcloths, and any other material we could find in the holes and cracks in the windows and along their sills. With the temperatures droppin' the way they was, we was all cuddled up together with big blankets in each trailer, enjoyin' the body heat from our loved ones along with Momma's hot water bottle as it passed around from person to person. That radio man had said that the storm should end by mornin', which was fine by all of us, 'cause regardless of how freezin' cold it might be when the sun come up on Christmas day, we was leavin' the warmth of our families to go look under the carefully decorated tree for our presents.

As night began to come upon our trailer park, our thoughts of nearly frozen-to-death sugarplums dancin' in our heads were chased out by the siren of the local sheriff's patrol car. He'd stopped by to let all seven lots, which was all we had back in 1957, know that a large grizzly bear had been seen earlier over at Old Man Sugg's place. Accordin' to the sheriff, Mr. Sugg had woke up from a nap to find a ten-foot grizzly bear standin' in his kitchen suckin' down his Kool-Aid and devourin' his Frito-Lays. Luckily Old Man Sugg was able to get out of the house and to the safety of his car with his life, a half box of Ritz crackers, and a bottle of RC Cola. The sheriff told us to keep our doors locked and be careful, 'cause this bear could be dangerous. With that, the good sheriff got back in his car and within seconds vanished out of sight into the heavy snow with the sounds of his sirens fadin' in the distance. We all returned to our trailers and regrouped into our huddles like we had been in before. Only this time we was armed with more than a hot water bottle, I can assure you.

At bedtime Willie Dick and her little ones finished their last Christmas carol. She kissed each one of 'em on the top of their heads and told them how lucky she was to have all of 'em. Willie set her caged bird on the dresser and climbed in bed with her kids. Normally they'd sleep in their own beds, but with the cold blowin' through their trailer like an old man on a harmonica, they cuddled together to stay warm. Willie threw a towel over Tweetie Pie's cage, and within no time Willie and the kids were fast asleep, which was how they remained until a little after midnight. For some reason unknown to Willie at the time, she was awakened by Tweetie Pie's high-pitched chirpin' and wild flutterin' inside her covered cage. At first she thought her bird's behavior was on account of the cold that filled the trailer, so she decided to put Tweetie Pie in a large plastic bowl with a few small holes punched in the top, and bring her to bed. By the time Willie had made it back from the kitchen with the bowl, the kids had woken up from the noise Tweetie Pie was still makin'. "Y'all kids just go back to bed," Willie instructed. She gave all her little ones a kiss and tucked 'em back under the covers. Suddenly, just as she began to open the birdcage, there was a thud on the side of their trailer. Startled to near death, the kids let out a scream and they grasped on to Willie for dear life.

"What is it, Momma?" the littlest one asked as she trembled.

"Now, y'all just hush up," Willie said in a stern but harsh tone. As the kids drew in tight, there was another thud and then another alongside the trailer. "Most likely it's just the wind makin' our pear tree smack up against the trailer," she said, not wantin' to frighten the kids. With each noise the kids would scream a little louder until finally the thuds were comin' from on top the trailer like someone was on the roof. She knew it was most likely that doggone corn-chip-lovin' bear that the sheriff had warned her about, but she didn't want to upset her kids. Still, Willie knew this would be the perfect and most likely only chance to do somethin'. So she reached under the couch and pulled out one of her ex's shotguns, which she'd kept tucked away and fully loaded. After all, a single mother can't be too careful, now can she?

"But, Momma, what if it's Santa Claus?" the baby asked in bewilderment as he saw her pull out the shotgun.

"Well, baby, then Santa better have him a good doctor." With that, Willie aimed the shotgun toward the ceilin'. Finally, as soon as she heard the next noise on the rooftop, Willie let that bear have it with both barrels.

Even with the howlin' wind, everybody in the trailer park had heard the gunfire. In no time all the menfolk had rushed over to Willie's trailer, which was easy to identify as the location of the gunfire since half the roof was blown off. Willie quickly explained what had happened while she bundled her little ones up along with her watch bird Tweetie Pie and tried to get 'em from their buckshot trailer over to a nearby one with a roof. It was durin' the trip between the mobile homes that one of the kids noticed all the red felt out in the snow. At first sight, it actually did appear that Willie Dick had shot Santa Claus. And at eight years of age, I'd have believed it myself if it weren't for one little question. Where was his reindeer and bag of toys? The sheriff was called, and even with the snow, he made it in record time. After Willie had recounted her story from the warmth of a neighbor's place, the sheriff, my daddy, and a few of the other men headed outside to try and figure out what it was that Willie had actually shot. Moments later Daddy and the sheriff made their way back to the trailer. It seemed that the sheriff had some good news and some bad news. It turned out that the bad news was that Willie had actually shot her ninth husband, who'd managed to escape from prison earlier that day. He'd secretly knocked out the Santa Claus that the Church of Christ had brought in to spread a little holiday cheer to the prisoners, stole his Santa suit, and had made his way to the trailer park in an attempt to win back her love and surprise the kids. The buckshot had caught him right in the pants, launchin' him across the trailer park and into the trees. He was in pain, but for the most part he was all right. The good news was that both the state patrol and the Church of Christ had put up a reward for the capture of Willie's soon-to-be ex (you don't mess with the Church of Christ), and since she'd actually been the one to nab him, so to speak, she was entitled to the money. It turned out to be no more than a hundred dollars, but in 1957 that was a lot of money. Needless to say, Willie was tinkled pink. She, her kids, and her canary were safe, her ninth husband was back behind bars, and, thanks to that reward money, Christmas would be able to come to Lot #1 after all. Dottie Lamb and her husband, Laverne, drove Willie Dick into town to their department store and opened it up just for her. While she picked out a few toys for her kids, which the Lambs happily offered to put down on credit with a 5 percent late-night openin' fee for her to pay off when she got her reward check, my daddy and a few of the other men of the park put up some sheetin' and tied a great big canvas onto the top of Willie's trailer. By the time Willie had made it back, her kids and Tweetie Pie were sound asleep over in our trailer, as was me and my sister Donna Sue. That next mornin' was a Christmas mornin' that I'll never forget. You should have seen Willie's kids' faces when my daddy pulled a few quickly wrapped packages out from under our humble tree.

"Why, Santa must have off and left these packages here by mistake," my daddy said as he pretended not to know who the names were on the gifts. In no time Willie's children had refreshed Daddy's memory, and he'd handed 'em first to Willie, who in turn handed 'em to her kids, as their eyes grew wide in disbelief. Could Santa have made it after all? That mornin', as she watched her babies open their presents, was the first time I'd ever seen dear sweet Willie Dick cry. The spirit of Christmas had made its way into our park that Christmas mornin' in 1957, and it had touched the hearts of all who believed and had faith that God would provide, even if it meant there'd be a man who'd never again, after that night, be able to set down like a normal person for as long as he lived.

CHRISTMAS CRAFTS FROM THE HEART

Seashell Santa

This one is as easy as my sister, but it looks a whole lot better. Even folks who hate crafts will be impressed.

SUPPLIES

1 seashell	Skin-tone paint
Red paint	Black paint
White paint	Small paintbrushes

1. What we want to do is make this shell look like Santa's head. So the first thing we need to do is paint a red hat on the top of the shell. It should only be about a third or less of the shell.

2. Now we need to paint a small face with the skin tone just below where the hat ends. This should be in the upper middle section of the shell. We want to make most of the shell Santa's beard.

3. Paint on two small black eyes.

4. Usin' your red paint, paint on a little red dot for his nose.

5. You can mix a little red with a little skin tone to make a rosy color. You can now give Santa some rosy cheeks if you'd like.

6. Take the white paint, and paint in two white eyebrows for Santa. You can also take the smallest paintbrush and put a white dot inside the black eyes to make it look like a reflection.

7. Take the white paint and paint all the rest of the shell.

8. And finally, we need to take some red paint for Santa's lips and draw 'em on. There you go.

TIPS FOR THE HOLIDAY HOSTESS

Guests always enjoy takin' somethin' home with them to remember the wonderful occasion that they enjoyed at your trailer. Mind you, food poisonin' and the flu do not count. So have somethin' for them to grab as they make their way out the door when the party's over. I usually just hand out toothpicks. Not the plain ones of course, 'cause that would be just cheap and tacky. No, I decorate 'em first with a colored highlighter.

Party Idea

North Pole Potluck Christmas Party

This Christmas gatherin' is actually a theme party where your guests have to come dressed as elves. Since your trailer is already decorated for Christmas, all you have to do is add snow. Of course, I don't mean real snow, but that fake cotton kind you use when you set out them miniature Christmas villages. Just lay some on top of your TV or entertainment center, bookshelves, over your couches and chairs like you would a blanket or quilt, on top of your coffee table, and any other place that has a flat surface. You can even put a big sign on the front door that reads, NORTH POLE POTLUCK CHRIST-MAS PARTY, NO TOY-MAKING TOOLS ALLOWED. Invite your guests to bring a canned good or unopened toy for "Santa's bag," which you can turn around and give to the homeless shelter of your choice on the followin' day. Just remember that nobody, but nobody, gets in the party unless they're in costume. And as the host, you can dress up as either an elf or Santa Claus. Don't that sound like a riot?

Trailer Park Christmas Games

Donna Sue's Boyfriend

This one is real fun! You're gonna need a big room for this game. Determine a circular area. Remove any obstacles inside the circle. You may want to rope it off to keep the players inside, or lay down a hose in a circle and be prepared to shout "out-of-bounds!" to the "One-Night Stand." The game follows the classic rules of Marco Polo. The "One-Night Stand" puts on an ugly rubber monster mask topped off with a Santa hat and a blindfold along with monster hands. Meanwhile, everyone has to stay within the circle while he/she wanders around with his arms reaching out like a zombie. When the "One-Night Stand" groans, all the players must groan back and extend their arms. This is how the zombie closes in on his/her victims. When a player gets tagged, he or she becomes the next "One-Night Stand" and gets to wear the mask. Even though a good time is had by all durin' "Donna Sue's Boyfriend," nobody, just like in real life, ends up bein' a winner.

WHAT'S THAT SMELL?

Who says pumpkins are only for Halloween and Thanksgivin'?

The Christmas Pumpkin Patch

For some strange reason, I end up cravin' pumpkin pie when I put this stuff out.

Makes a batch

2 cups pumpkin seeds, cleaned
   and dried
1 tablespoon cinnamon
$^1/_2$ tablespoon allspice
1 tablespoon oil

$^1/_2$ cup whole cloves
6 cinnamon sticks
$1^1/_2$ cups Red Hots
2 cups small pinecones

Heat up your oven to 350 degrees F.

Take a pie pan and put your seeds, cinnamon, allspice, and oil in it. Mix the seeds around to make sure that they get a coverin' of the other ingredients. Pop it in the oven and bake for about 30 to 45 minutes, stirrin' the mixture every 5 minutes. Take the mixture out of the oven and stir in the cloves. Let it set till it cools off and then add the rest of the ingredients. Put in a big jar or bowl and set out right away. Don't eat them Red Hots.

HOLLY JOLLY WOOHA!

❄ A Christmas club, a bank savings account in which a person deposits a fixed amount of money regularly to be used at Christmas for shopping, was originally offered to the public around 1905.

❄ The first British monarch to broadcast a Christmas message to his people was King George V in 1932.

❄ The earliest known collection of English Christmas carols was published in London in 1521 in Westminster.

Helpful Holiday Hints

❋ To avoid overeatin' at Christmas parties, consume eight ounces of liquid before you start chowin' down.

❋ Decorate your bathroom by tyin' ribbons around the shower-curtain rings.

—Momma Ballzak, Lot #16

❋ When you're throwin' a Christmas party, decorate your walkway and porch with plastic poinsettias decorated with white twinkle lights.

—Tina Faye Stopenblotter, Lot #17

Twelve Days of Yuletime Advice

Dear Ruby Ann,

We are all going over to my uncle's place for Christmas, but his wife is serving Chinese food instead of the traditional fare. Don't you think that will ruin Christmas for us?

Signed
Turkey and Stuffing Timmy

Dear Turkey,

Your question reminds me of the Christmas in 1997, when we all awoke to find that we didn't have no electricity. We'd gotten a real heavy ice storm, which we get in these parts from time to time, while we was all fast asleep on Christmas Eve. Needless to say, the electric lines at the High Chaparral Trailer Park hadn't made it through the storm. It was terrible. Normally we'd just run to a local restaurant for food when somethin' like this would happen, but there wasn't nothin' open on Christmas Day in our corner of the world. That was where Lois and Hubert Bunch from Lot #3 came in. They'd already braved the roads into town so they could check on their Tex-Mex restaurant / fishin' supply store, the Taco Tackle Shack. As fate would have it, neither the storm nor the electric outage had fazed their business. So they kicked up the heat and headed back to the trailer park, where they began bangin' on doors; invitin' folks to grab their gifts, pillows, and blankets; and tellin' 'em to head on over to the Taco Tackle Shack. Well, everybody took 'em up on their generosity, and we had a great big old Christmas party in what would end up to be our shelter for that night as well. The Bunches let us run tabs so we could eat, plus they gave us all a 20 percent discount on the menu items. Mind you, it was the first time I'd ever had a chimichanga for breakfast, but hey, it was good. After we gobbled up an assortment of avocado eggs, chalupas, nachos, breakfast burritos, and a whole bunch of chili con queso, all us ladies helped clean up the dishes and such. Then Lois and Hubert opened up their industrial-size kitchen sink to anyone who wanted to bathe. As you can guess, that alone took up almost an hour. The rest of the afternoon was spent singin' Christmas carols. Dottie Lamb and her dog-ugly daughter Opal of Lot #14 went over to their department store, which didn't have no electricity, and brought over a TV for all of us to enjoy. Kitty Chitwood, who used to work for the post office before she made her career change and became the night clerk at the Gas and Smokes convenience store, drove my sister Donna Sue back to her trailer so she could pick up her VCR and a few videotapes for us to watch later on. It turned out that most of the tapes couldn't be viewed in mixed company, so my niece Lulu Bell went over to the video rental store, which is located in one of the buildin's she owns, and borrowed several Christmas movies. The store owners were out of town and besides, they always let her watch anything she wants for free anyways. So our Christmas afternoon was filled with present openin', old holiday movies, and more Tex-Mex items like stuffed jalapeños, tamales, beef and cheese enchiladas, Frito chili pie, and quesadillas. We spent the rest of the holiday chattin' with each other, watchin' TV, eatin' a delicious Christmas supper (Tex-Mex–style naturally), and just enjoyin' the company of good neighbors and Sister Bertha of Lot #12. Lois and Hubert's Christian generosity had saved our holidays, even if it was the gassiest Christmas any of us can recall. Of course they got the electricity back up and runnin' by the next day, Lulu Bell returned the movies, the Lambs put the TV back on their showroom floor, and my sister made it home with her VCR even though the movies she'd brung with her had vanished. Yes, the Christmas of 1997 is one that will always be special for all of us, includin' the Bunches.

Long story short, it's not the food that will make your Christmas Day special, but the people around you. By the way, my retellin' of that story led me to call the Bunches and tell them how great that Christmas was. They agreed with me and went on to say that almost half of those tabs we ran up that Christmas were close to bein' completely paid off.

Love, Kisses, and Trailer Park Wishes,
Ruby Ann Boxcar

PUTTIN' YOUR BEST FACE FORWARD

Blush

At Christmastime lots of ladies out there love to go with a redder tone of blush than they usually use durin' the rest of the year. And I say that's wonderful. My only rule of thumb is to go a little lighter with the red stuff. After all, you want folks to think you look beautiful as well as seasonal, and not like somebody with an extreme case of rosacea.

CHRISTMAS CHEER

Donna Sue suggests . . .

The Gingerbread Man

"Run, run as fast as you can"? Heck, after a couple rounds of these he'd be lucky to walk, let alone run.

$\frac{1}{3}$ ounce Goldschlager
$\frac{1}{3}$ ounce butterscotch schnapps

$\frac{1}{3}$ ounce Bailey's Irish Cream

Put all ingredients in a shaker and mix. Pour into a shot glass. Serve.

Santa Cider

You can use this recipe to make Mrs. Claus Cider by just addin' rum.

2 cups apple cider
4 teaspoons Red Hot candies

Mix the ingredients together in a coffee mug and pop in the microwave for 3 minutes or until nice and hot. Stir.

TRAILER PARK CHRISTMAS GRUB

Christmas Cookie

Dottie's Walkin' in a Winter Wonderland Cake Mix Cookies

Now that they're married, Ben can admit that these cookies of Dottie's are better than sex. Oh, by the way, did I mention that Ben hasn't had any feelin' from the waist down since he got back from the Korean War?

Makes a couple dozen

1 package lemon cake mix	1 tablespoon water
2 eggs	$1/2$ cup nuts
$1/2$ cup vegetable shortenin'	1 cup powdered sugar

Mix all together. Chill dough for an hour. Shape in 1-inch balls and roll in powdered sugar.

   Bake at 375 degrees F. for 10 to 12 minutes. Frost with lemon frostin' if you like.

—DOTTIE LAMB-BEAVER, LOT #14

Festive Fudge

Faye Faye's Sweet Potato Fudge for Christmas

She might be a lowlife, but she sure can cook.

Makes a batch

2 cups granulated sugar	$1/2$ cup margarine, sliced into bits
$1/2$ cup whole milk	1 cup marshmallow cream
$1/4$ teaspoon pumpkin pie spice	8 ounces white chocolate chips
$1/4$ cup mashed sweet potato	$1/2$ teaspoon vanilla extract

Butter up an 8-inch pan and set it aside.

Combine the first 5 ingredients in a pan and set over a medium heat. Cook to 236 degrees F. Take off the heat and stir in the marshmallow cream, chips, and vanilla.

—Faye Faye LaRue, Lot #17

Pies on Earth, Goodwill Toward Men

We Three Kings Pumpkin Pie

Pastor Ida May Bee says after a piece of this pie she can preach for hours. Naturally nobody around these parts makes one of these on a Sunday or Wednesday.

Makes one pie

1 cup sugar
1/2 cup packed brown sugar
1/4 teaspoon salt
2 teaspoons pumpkin pie spice
1 teaspoon ground cinnamon

2 beaten eggs
1 15-ounce can canned pumpkin
1 1/4 cups milk
1 9-inch pie crust

Preheat the oven to 350 degrees F.

Combine the first five ingredients and stir well. Add the next three, again stirring well. Pour into the pie crust. Bake in preheated oven for 1 1/2 hours. Let it cool down before servin'.

—Paster Ida May Bee, Lot #7

Seasonal Supper Sensation

Better Than Snow on Christmas Chicken-Fried Steak

Your husband is cheatin' on you, your dog has made friends with your enemies, and the sheriff is lookin' for your son. Who cares, it's chicken-fried steak night! And heck, it's almost Christmas to boot.

Makes about 4 servin's

4 beef cube steaks
1 cup flour
1 teaspoon salt
1 teaspoon pepper
2 teaspoons onion powder
2 teaspoons garlic powder
1 tablespoon dried oregano

1 tablespoon dried basil
1 tablespoon dried parsley
1 cup buttermilk
1 egg
1 teaspoon chicken bouillon
2 teaspoons dry mustard
Vegetable oil for frying

Mix your flour, $1/2$ teaspoon salt, $1/2$ teaspoon pepper, and other spices together in a bowl. Set aside.

Get you a second bowl and put your remainin' salt and pepper in that bowl along with the buttermilk, egg, chicken bouillon, and mustard. Mix well. Take each steak and dip it in the flour mixture, shake off the excess, dip it in the buttermilk mixture, then once again in the flour mixture, again in the egg dip, one last time in the flour, and finally put it in a skillet that has about 3 inches of oil, which you've heated to around 360 degrees F. Let it cook for 5 minutes, flip it over, cook on the second side for about 3 minutes. Put it on a paper towel to drain.

—ELROY DASAFE, LOT #19

Opal's Pan Gravy

This goes real good on your chicken-fried steak, mashed potatoes, biscuits, bread, Twinkies, and just about anything else.

4 tablespoons skillet drippin's
4 tablespoons flour (use the
    same flour mixture you used
    for your chicken-fried steak)

2¹/₂ cups milk

Put you drippin's back in the skillet and put the skillet over a medium heat. Gradually whisk in the flour, stirrin' vigorously. Slowly mix in the milk. If you add this too fast, you'll get lumps. Stir continuously durin' this entire process. Eventually your gravy will start to thicken. Keep stirrin' until it just starts boilin'. Take it off the heat and transfer it to a dish or bowl immediately. Add salt and pepper to taste if you used fresh flour.

—OPAL LAMB-BROWN, LOT #1

Juanita's Momma's Mashed Potatoes

I'd be happy to unwrap a gift from under the tree and find a big bowl of this stuff.

Makes about 4 servin's

2 pounds potatoes, peeled and
    cut into small cubes
³/₄ cup evaporated milk

¹/₂ cup margarine
¹/₂ teaspoon salt
¹/₄ cup black pepper

Put your potatoes in a big pot and fill it up with water until the potatoes are covered.

Cook on medium high for 15 minutes. Drain. Mash potatoes. Set aside.

Put your milk in the microwave and nuke it for about 2 minutes or until hot. Add to potatoes along with the margarine, salt, and pepper. Stir well until creamy.

—JUANITA HIX, LOT #9

CHAPTER 11

The Eleventh Day of Christmas

DECEMBER 23

Not only does the local Lutheran Church have a nice nativity scene every year, but come spring, they also have one of the prettiest lawns in town.

Traditional Gift on This Day
Eleven pipers piping

Trailer Park Gift on This Day
Eleven puppies poopin' (on my livin' room carpet)

ABOUT THIS DAY

December 23 is the day that we get ready for the Christmas party at the Holier Than Most Baptist Church, which most of us belong to. Mind you, there is a difference between "belong to" and "attend on a regular basis." But still, even if you ain't been to church all year long, this is an event you don't miss. For us Baptists in these parts, it's kind of like Easter and Christmas Eve are to the Catholics—a must-see event. So we ladies spend most of the day cookin' for that night's potluck. Normally when any potluck is involved we only make up one dish, but since this is at the church, we each do at least three items. After all, we got a pastor to impress now, don't we? Speakin' of pastors, I don't know if this day is one that Pastor Ida May Bee really looks forward to or not, since she'll be forced by the church members to sample a little bit of everything before the night is over. I do know that the fella at the Piggly Wiggly says she always comes in on the twenty-third and stocks up on Pepto-Bismol and Tums. Please keep her in your prayers.

A CHRISTMASTIME TREASURE
FROM THE HIGH CHAPARRAL TRAILER PARK

It was a whole different world durin' the Christmas of 1968. It was as if the country as we knew it was on a collision course with madness. The whole year had been filled with uncertainty, that is, except at the High Chaparral Trailer Park. Sure, we got the news and all, but if there was one thing we could count on in our little neck of the world was that things would never change. My sister would always be drunk, my hair would always be teased and back-combed, and Nellie Tinkle would always be seated behind the keyboard at church on Sunday mornin'. Nellie and her husband, C.M., had been one of the first couples to move in to the trailer park, and as far back as I can remember, had laid claim to Lot #4. I grew up knowin' them as neighbors as well as close personal friends. Plus, as I've said many times, Nellie Tinkle was my music teacher when I was growin' up. So naturally Christmas music is one of the first things that come to mind when I think of Lot #4, even though it ain't the actual first thing that crosses my mind. No, that honor would have to be the event that took place on December 1 durin' that 1968 Christmas.

The folks over at Living Lake Waters Lutheran Church had run a special invitation in the local newspaper for everyone in the surroundin' area to come on out and join 'em as they marked the Christmas season with their brand-new life-size nativity scene. The thing was everyone already knew that this nativity scene was gonna be somethin', 'cause them Lutherans had been savin' up for this thing for the past two years. There wasn't a person in the park that wouldn't have given their eyeteeth to be there the night they plugged it in, but that ain't the way things are done in the Bible Belt. Sure, we'll support you in public and make you a friend, but when it comes to religious activities, if you ain't a member of our church, you might as well be one of them redneck communists. We don't attend any church that don't bear our name on its membership roster, unless of course it's for a special occasion where food is involved, and we only do those if they're held down in the church basement. And since the Living Lake Waters Lutheran Church had neglected mentionin' any kind of food item in their newspaper invite, we wasn't goin'. And besides, we have our own semi-live nativity scene, which is 100 percent Baptist approved. But since attendance had been droppin' off little by little for our Christmas season nativity presentations over the years, the then pastor of our congregation, Pastor Pickles, decided that maybe he should send over a few folks to see what kind of competition we was gonna be up against. With that in mind, he hand-picked my Me-Ma, who was only partially loony in 1968, and Nellie Tinkle to be what he called our Baptist spies for Christ. So on the afternoon of December 1, I whomped up some wigs for Nellie and my Me-Ma to wear so that folks wouldn't know who they was unless they came right up on 'em. I'm tellin' you, I had them wigs jacked up for filth, which I person- ally think always looks real nice on a woman. Of course, the hair I did for 'em was a little bit big for the rather simple outfits they was wearin' that night. I had no idea they wanted to go to this shindig lookin' as close to Mennonites as they could. Anyways, after a call from Pastor Pickles and a short prayer, C.M. and I helped guide the ladies carefully into the backseat of him and Nellie's 1958 Chevy Impala, so that they didn't mess up their bouffants. Then C.M. and I climbed in the front seat and we was off to the Lutheran church . . . with our Bibles in hand of course. You should have seen the crowd of folks who were gathered around the front of that church. I tell you, you'd have thought there were at least thirty-five Lutherans in this area. I guess I should say that the rest of the events that took place that night are just hearsay, and were not actually witnessed up close and personal by me 'cause since Pastor Pickles hadn't asked C.M. and me to actually participate in this covert operation, we just stayed in the car readin' our Bibles. With that said, let me jump back up to where we left off.

Accordin' to Nellie, that shiny new nativity scene was one of the prettiest things she'd ever seen. All the hallowed figures were life size and made out of what appeared to be a hard plastic. The crib and manger, which was big enough to house the baby Jesus and his folks, two shepherds, three wise men, and an assortment of plastic farm animals, were made of real wood. And the ground, where the nativity scene stood, was covered with piles of real hay, and not shredded-up old newspapers like we used at our semi-live nativity scene over at the Baptist church. Just the sound of Nellie describin' it was enough to give us all chills. Finally the minister came out and lead the gathered group in the Lord's Prayer, which Nellie and my Me-Ma abstained from sayin' since they didn't know if Mennonites prayed or not, and they didn't want to break their cover. They did accept the lighted candles that were passed out among the crowd even though they didn't know what kind of pagan ritual they'd be used for. Then the minister asked if Gerda Larson, who works over at the hardware store, would come up and lead 'em in a traditional song of peace and joy. With this Gerda came up, raised her candle in the air, and started off a song that Nellie Tinkle had played on the piano many times, "Let There Be Peace on Earth." Even though it was all done without a musical instrument in sight, both Nellie and Me-Ma were moved by all the love from the voices that filled that December evenin'. Why, Me-Ma was so entranced that she forgot she was holdin' a candle in her hand right next to a heavily hair-sprayed wig, and before you could say "silent night," her hair went up like a pile of dry leaves. We saw the mushroom-shaped cloud that Me-Ma's wig put off all the way back at the car. Luckily for her, the fella standin' next to her quickly yanked that burnin' thing off her head and threw it down onto the ground. Me-Ma was fine, but within seconds the few stalks of hay on the ground that had come out to where everyone was standin' from the piles in the manger lit up and quickly spread to engulf the wooden manger in flames. People were runnin' all over tryin' to find somethin' to use to put out the fire. But since it was the early part of December in Arkansas, there weren't any water hoses connected to spouts and within just minutes there was nothin' left to save. All folks could do was stand there in disbelief and watch the beautiful nativity scene burn to the ground. By the time the volunteer fire department arrived, all that was left was smolderin' wood and melted mounds of bubbling plastic. It was sad, so very very sad.

The next day word was all around town. It seemed that the Lutheran church, in the excitement of finally receivin' it, had neglected to take out insurance on their new nativity scene. Of course, seein' how this area is mostly Baptist, I found that error to be highly strange. In any case, there was no way they were gonna be able to replace it anytime soon. And then it came out that the Living Lake

Waters Lutheran Church decided to up and sue the fella who'd thrown the wig on the ground in the first place. They couldn't dare sue Me-Ma for arson, 'cause if it hadn't been for that Lutheran candle, she'd still be wearin' that wig even up to today. So instead, they sued the Good Samaritan for not throwin' the flamin' wig out into the street, but rather down on the ground among the hay. Of course once the minister and board found out that the fella they was suin' was a member of the Pentecostal Holiness Church, they dropped the suit 'cause they knew he wouldn't have any money. Later that week they decided instead to just sue the fella's church and the Baptist church that Me-Ma attended. Accordin' to the papers, they believed that the Pentecostal Holiness Church and the Baptist church had worked together in an attempt to sabotage their nativity scene. When the case came before the judge, he simply laughed and threw the whole thing out of court. After all, it don't take a rocket scientist to know that there ain't no way on earth you could ever get a Pentecostal Holiness and a Baptist to work together on anything pertainin' to religion. As for the Lutheran church, well, it eventually got another nativity scene, although it wasn't as nice. They also made amends with that fella who'd tried to do a good deed. They even invited him to come and turn on the lights that lit up the replacement nativity scene. And even though the newer set ain't as pretty as Nellie said the first one was, as you drive by it on your way to wherever you happen to be goin', it's still very movin' as well as inspirational. Of course they keep the water sprinklers on it all durin' the holiday season.

CHRISTMAS CRAFTS FROM THE HEART

Christmas Card Holder

Not only is this a great way to store your cards, but you can also empty it out and fill it with pinecones or assorted colored Christmas balls to set out for display. Regardless, this craft is truly a fine example of trailer trash Christmas, where we recycle one thing into another.

SUPPLIES

Big coffee can
Gray primer spray paint
Red spray paint
Several old Christmas cards

Scissors
Hot glue gun
A fancy medium-size bow

1. Take your coffee can and give it a good washin'.

2. Spray on the gray primer and let it dry.

3. Spray on the red spray paint. Make sure the paint is applied evenly. Let it dry.

4. Take your Christmas cards and cut the fronts off. Throw the backs away.

5. Hot-glue the front of the cards all around the can.

6. Hot-glue the bow to the top of the lid. Put the glue on the bow and let it cool for just a few seconds before puttin' it on the lid.

7. Fill can with old cards and put lid on top.

Tips for the Holiday Hostess

Unless you want your party to end real early and have guests curse you on their way home, make sure that you always have some kind of food at your event. Since folks are real busy durin' the holidays, they might not have time to set down to a full meal before racin' over to your trailer for the party. This means that once they see you ain't got no food, they'll make plans to come up with some excuse why they have to ditch your party after bein' there for thirty minutes. So at least have some finger food laid out. I still personally think that the best game plan is to make each occasion a potluck event. That way your guests are happy and you only had to make one dish.

Party Idea

Favorite Christmas Character Dress-Up Party

Why not go with a theatrical theme for your party? Have your guests come dressed up as their favorite Christmas cartoon or movie character. Tell 'em to be creative. And if you announce that you'll be awardin' a prize for best costume, you might just end up minglin' with Scrooge, Snoopy, Frosty the Snowman, Rudolph the Red-Nosed Reindeer, or even the Ghost of Christmas Past.

Trailer Park Christmas Games

The Christmas Pea

This game is real fun and simple to play. You take a handful of peas and set 'em on a chair. You scatter 'em out a bit. You hand a player an empty bowl and tell them to gently set down on the peas. The object of the game is to move the peas, with your behind only, into the bowl. You have fifteen seconds to complete this task. When the time runs out the hostess counts up the number of peas in the bowl and writes it down. The person to get the most peas in the bowl wins. Have a towel ready, 'cause somebody is gonna end up with peas stuck on their behind. If peas are too small, you can use white grapes or, with my large-bottomed family members playin', cantaloupes.

HOLLY JOLLY WOOHA!

❉ Most artificial trees are manufactured in Korea, Taiwan, or Hong Kong.

❉ Candy canes were sometimes handed out during church services to keep the children quiet. The basic confection has been around for centuries, but it wasn't until about 1900 that it was first decorated with red stripes and bent into the shape of a cane.

HELPFUL HOLIDAY HINTS

❉ Got dirty oven racks? Put a couple inches of hot water in your bathtub along with $1/2$ cup of dishwasher detergent, and mix it well with your hands. Put your oven racks in the water and let 'em set for an hour. Then simply rinse off and all the burnt-on stuff will come right off.

❉ An outdated old map makes great gift wrap for those smaller presents.

❋ If you find you got ink on your hands after writin' all them Christmas cards, simply rinse your hands with rubbin' alcohol and it'll come right off.

❋ Throw a tablecloth over an ironin' board to create more temporary counter space. With its adjustable height, it also makes for a great temporary kids' table.

—RUBY ANN BOXCAR, LOT #18

TWELVE DAYS OF YULETIME ADVICE

Dear Ruby Ann,

We just moved into a home that doesn't have a fireplace. I know my son is going to ask how Santa gets into the house without a chimney to come down. Any suggestions on what I should tell him?

Signed,
Puzzled Perry

Dear Puzzled Perry,

Don't fret, 'cause I got the answer. I was faced with this same situation back when I was just a little girl myself. It was Christmas Eve and my daddy wanted to do somethin' special for the whole family to brighten up what had turned out to be a really bad year financially. He'd bought an old Santa suit for next to nothin' off this fella who was strapped for cash on Christmas Eve, and he decided to surprise us kids on Christmas mornin' by dressin' as Santa and handin' out our lackluster gifts. Well, he sneaked the suit into the trailer without any of us kids noticin', and then with a pillow he'd grabbed from the bedroom tucked under his arm, he went into the bathroom to try the outfit on. Now, I should probably insert a little fact right about now that some of y'all might not know. You see it's very common in the South for men of all ages to go into a bathroom in the privacy of their own home and not, I repeat, not lock the door behind 'em. Now I don't know the exact reasonin' for this practice, but I'm sure one day somebody will write a whole book on men and their strange bathroom behavior. But gettin' back to the story, not knowin' that the bathroom was occupied, I put my little chubby hand on the knob and opened it. Well, you can't imagine the utter surprise and thrill that ran through my body when I found the one and only Santa Claus standin' right there in my trailer's bathroom. You'd have thought Mr. Burt Reynolds was in that bathroom with the scream of crazed zeal that I let out. God bless him, I nearly scared poor Daddy to death. I swear he jumped so far back he was in the tub when all was said and done.

"Santa Claus," I screeched, pointin' at my flounderin' daddy, "Santa Claus! Momma, Momma, Santa Claus is in the bathroom."

Daddy did what he could to regain his composure and get back on his feet. "Ho-Ho-Ho," Daddy bellowed in a deepened voice, "Merry Christmas to you. What's your name, little girl?"

With that question my face turned from gleeful to hurt, and suddenly tears were wellin' up in my eyes. He didn't know who I was. How could that be? I'd been good all year long. He should know who I was. Why, I'd even written him a letter. How could he not know who I was? Did that mean that he didn't have any gifts for me? What in the heck was all this about? "You don't know me, Santa Claus?"

Daddy, who'd managed to climb out of the tub by now, could see I was about to cry. "Well, of course I know who you are, little Ruby Ann, but I just wanted to hear you say your name." I grinned from ear to ear. He did know who I was. Somewhat ashamed that I'd doubted Santa in the first place, I quickly wiped the tears from my eyes, slightly rubbin' off part of my beauty mark that Momma put on my cheek each mornin' since I was four. "Now why don't we go into the livin' room and see everybody else," he said before lettin' out what had to be the worst attempt at a belly laugh that I'd ever heard.

"But where is your bag of gifts?" I asked as he tried to push me out of the bathroom so that I wouldn't see my daddy's clothes piled up on the floor.

"Well," Daddy said as he hem-hawed around, tryin' to think up an answer. "Well, I don't have 'em with me right now 'cause . . . 'cause . . . 'cause this is my dry run. I'm just checkin' out my travel route for tonight, that's what I'm doin'," he said while closin' the bathroom door behind us. You should have seen my sister's and brother's faces when I came walkin' into the livin' room with Santa Claus. They couldn't believe their eyes, and I couldn't have been prouder.

"But what were you doin' in our bathroom, Santa?" I asked. Daddy stopped for a second, scratched his head, and said nothin'.

"Since we ain't got no fireplace for you to slide down into," my sister Donna Sue said, "you must come into our trailer through the toilet." Her mind even back then was in the sewer.

"Is that right, Santa Claus?" I asked.

"Yes," Daddy replied, "your sister's right. I come up through the toilet, so make sure you put that toilet seat up on Christmas Eve regardless of what your mother might say." Santa then told us he had to leave and went into the bathroom. Donna Sue, my brother Jack Daniels and I waited by the bathroom door, listenin' to Santa as he told us to be good, and went on about how we should eat all our food and such. Then, after lettin' out a great big "Ho-Ho-Ho," we heard the toilet flush. And then the bathroom door opened wide. Daddy was in there, lookin' down at the toilet. "I'll make sure that they do just that, Santa Claus," he said. All this time, Daddy had been in the bathroom, and us kids hadn't even seen him. Wow, our daddy had talked to Santa Claus, too. My life was changed that night for a very long time. I will never know where my sister came up with that toilet idea, but from that day all the way up till I was fourteen years old, I left cookies and milk in the bathroom for Santa Claus and made sure the toilet seat was up on Christmas Eve as well. The last thing I wanted was to have Christmas spoiled 'cause Santa had gotten knocked out on the Boxcar toilet seat and couldn't continue his Christmas route. I can't tell you what I got on that Christmas, but it will always hold a special place in my heart 'cause it was the year that I talked to Santa Claus in our bathroom.

I hope that helps.

Love, Kisses, and Trailer Park Wishes,
Ruby Ann Boxcar

PUTTIN' YOUR BEST FACE FORWARD

Fake Eyelashes

A gal can never go wrong with fake eyelashes, just as long as they ain't them gigantic ones that can easily cool down a room every time you bat your eyes. And even though I personally think you should always wear the black ones, I guess it's all right if you want to throw on a pair that's in seasonal colors. Those ones that got the glitter on each lash are fine as well. Just make sure that come the day after Christmas them crazy lashes go back in the bottom of your under-wear drawer, only to come back out next December or if you get a job at the circus.

CHRISTMAS CHEER

Donna Sue suggests . . .

Nieve Mexicana Caliente

This will put the Feliz in your Navidad!

Makes around 6 servin's

4 cups apple cider
1 cup cranberry juice cocktail
2 teaspoons cinnamon

1 cup tequila
$^1/_2$ cup triple sec
Lime slices to garnish

Pour the cider, cranberry juice cocktail, and cinnamon into a pot and put over a medium heat. Let it get hot, but don't boil it. Take off of the stove and add tequila and trip sec. Pour in mugs, garnish with a lime slice, and serve.

Angels We Have Heard on High Punch

I've never heard an angel before, but I've seen flyin' pink elephants a lot of times.

1 cup sugar
1 pint lemon juice
1 quart strong green tea
2 quarts white grape juice

1 block ice that will fit in your
   punch bowl
2 quarts chilled club soda

Mix everything but the ice and soda together in a large bowl or pitcher and let it chill in the fridge for a few hours. When it gets close to party time, put the ice block in a punch bowl and add the mixture. Pour in the soda. Serve.

TRAILER PARK CHRISTMAS GRUB

Christmas Cookie

Daddy's French Kiss Sleigh Ride Cookies

My sister just loves these, and they really are great to eat while on a sleigh ride.

Makes several dozen

1$\frac{1}{2}$ cups powdered sugar
1 cup margarine
1 teaspoon baking soda
1 teaspoon cream of tartar
$\frac{1}{4}$ teaspoon salt

1 egg
1 teaspoon vanilla
2$\frac{1}{4}$ cups flour
6-ounce bag chocolate kisses

Combine the first seven ingredients together in a bowl. Slowly mix in the flour to make your French butter cream dough. Put in the fridge and chill for an hour. Roll the dough into balls and then flatten 'em on a greased cookie sheet. Unwrap the kisses and place one in the middle of each cookie. Wrap the dough around the bottom of the kiss. Bake at 350 degrees F. for 5 to 8 minutes or until set but not brown. Let cool for 10 minutes.

—CECIL BOXCAR, LOT #5

Festive Fudge

Nuttin' for Christmas Carrot Fudge

This is a big hit at Easter as well.

3¹/₂ cups carrots, grated
3¹/₂ cups sugar
¹/₂ cup sweetened condensed
   milk

¹/₂ cup water
¹/₂ teaspoon lemon flavorin'

Put your carrots, sugar, milk, and water in a pan and put over medium heat. Get it to the soft ball stage (238 degrees F.), and take it off the heat. Add the lemon flavorin' and stir. Let it get down to room temperature and beat it until it gets creamy. Put it in a buttered 8-inch pan. Cut into squares and serve.

—WANDA KAY, LOT #13

Pies on Earth, Goodwill Toward Men

We Wish You a Merry Christmas Peanut Butter Cup Pie

The only thing I like better than peanut butter with chocolate is peanut butter with chocolate and pie!

8-ounce package cream cheese, softened

1 bag mini peanut butter cups

1 large tub Cool Whip

1 9-inch graham cracker crust

Take an electric mixer and beat your cream cheese until it's real smooth. Unwrap the mini peanut butter cups, crumble 'em into the bowl of cream cheese, and stir by hand.

Add the Cool Whip to this mixture by foldin' it in. Pour it into the crust and even it out. Stick it in the fridge for at least 2 hours.

—LULU BELL BOXCAR-BUTTON, LOT #8

Chess Pie

Old-Time Baptist Come On, Ring Those Bells Buttermilk Chess Pie

Regardless of the name, Pastor Ida May Bee says this is an interfaith dessert.

Makes one pie

$^1/_2$ cup margarine, softened

$1^1/_2$ cups sugar

2 tablespoons flour

Pinch of salt

4 eggs

1 teaspoon vanilla

$^2/_3$ cup buttermilk

1 unbaked 9-inch pie shell

Cream the margarine and sugar until fluffy. Add the flour, salt, eggs, and vanilla; beat well. Stir in buttermilk. Pour into pastry shell. Bake at 350 degrees F. for 45 to 50 minutes or until set. Cool on a wire rack.

—BROTHER WOODY BEE, LOT #7

Seasonal Supper Sensation

Kenny Lynn's Creative Chicken Wreath

This is so pretty you almost won't want to eat it. Almost.

Makes 4 to 6 servin's

2 8-ounce cans refrigerator
   crescent rolls
$^1/_2$ cup Colby cheese, shredded
$^1/_2$ cup jack cheese, shredded
$^2/_3$ cup condensed cream of
   chicken soup

$^1/_2$ cup chopped broccoli
$^1/_2$ cup red pepper
1 5-ounce can white chicken,
   drained
2 tablespoons onion,
   chopped

Put your rolls in a ring around a pizza pan with the ends facin' the outside of the pan. Set aside.

Mix the rest of the ingredients together and pour over the rolls. Bake in a 375 degree F. oven for 25 minutes. Serve hot.

—KENNY LYNN, LOT #15

CHAPTER 12

The Twelfth Day of Christmas

DECEMBER 24

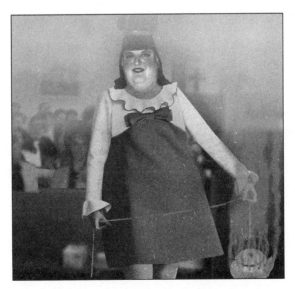

Lulu Bell pulls out all the bells and whistles for
the Christmas Eve service.

249

Traditional Gift on This Day
Twelve drummers drumming

Trailer Park Gift on This Day
Twelve drunks a-drinkin' (and y'all better get out of my
doggone yard before I call the sheriff)

ABOUT THIS DAY

There are only three days of the year that you will catch any self-respectin' trailer park dweller out at a store shoppin' for Christmas presents. And they are the day after Thanksgivin', Christmas Eve, and the day after Christmas. It's not that we don't like to spend money. Heck no! We're happy to spend money when we got it. The fact is usually these are the days when the stores really cut their prices. On the day after Thanksgivin' businesses will have a few choice items that they've slashed the prices way down just to get you in the door. On this day, Christmas Eve, they've cut their prices in hopes to get you in to buy 'cause the Christmas shoppin' season is just about over. And on the day after Christmas, they put their prices at rock bottom 'cause they don't want to have to be stuck with a bunch of stock they've got to count and carry into the next year. With that in mind, if you see me in a store on any of these days, don't try and talk to me, 'cause I'm a woman on a mission. Just wave and get the heck out of the way.

251

A CHRISTMASTIME TREASURE
FROM THE HIGH CHAPARRAL TRAILER PARK

My niece Lulu Bell, who inherited Lot #8 after my brother Jack Daniels passed several years back, will celebrate her first Christmas as a married woman this year. And just like all newlyweds, she and her husband, who are both special (as in small-school-bus special, if you know what I mean), will be creatin' new holiday memories that they'll cherish for years to come. Of course they'll never be able to top that Christmas Eve back in 2001 when I convinced the then Pastor Richard Hickey over at our church to try a little somethin' new. You see, he'd approached some of us VIP members of the church, wantin' us to see if we could come up with ways of drawin' folks in for his Christmas Eve service. Unlike most churches around the world that conduct Christmas Eve services, our attendance on that blessed night had been dwindlin' down to nearly nothin'. For some odd reason, not even the "good, all day Sunday, and Wednesday nights as well" Baptists were comin' out for church on the night before Christmas. And Pastor Hickey had tried everythin' under the sun to get folks to come in—includin' the year before, when he tried to home in on the popularity of that season's big movie *How the Grinch Stole Christmas*, by doin' the entire service dressed up like the Grinch. All that ended up doin' was frightenin' the children and confusin' the elderly. Well, after wrackin' my brain, I finally came up with an idea that I tried out first on our then Associate Pastor Ida May Bee, before takin' it on to the big dog, so to speak. I told her how one of my favorite Christmas Eve services spent outside of a Baptist church, of course, was the one me and my husband, Dew, experienced back in 1994 when we'd been in London and accidentally attended a Church of England. Mind you, the sermon was real short, they didn't have an altar call, and that stuff they was servin' at communion didn't taste a thing like Welch's, but all the pageantry was real pretty and movin'. The thing that really caught my eye though was the fella who came down the aisle swingin' this metal contraption on a chain, which put off scented smoke. He had that thing swingin' in all different directions and worked it like it was nobody's business. It was really somethin' to behold, and I personally thought that if we got somebody to swing that dilly like that fella was doin', people might just flock in to see it. After all, there ain't nothin' other than wrestlin' that excites us trailer park folks more than somethin' burnin' indoors. That of course might just be on account of how we ain't got no real wood-burnin' fireplaces in our homes to dull our sensitivity to the whole thing. Anyways, after Associate Pastor Ida May Bee had told me she thought the idea was a good one, I took the whole thing to Pastor Hickey. After runnin' the idea past the pastor, and assurin' him that he would still have plenty of time to take an offerin', an hour for his sermon, and another thirty minutes for an altar call followed by a second offerin', I quickly got a thumbs-up from the pastor. Of course, selectin' the person to actually swing that smoke machine around like that fella in London did could easily be a chore in itself, and since I'd been the one to come up with the notion, Pastor Hickey put me in charge of the hunt. Well, once the news got out as to what was goin' on, my phone rang off the wall from callers who had an idea as to who should fill that position. Most of 'em suggested our local high school's baton twirlin' captain, Donna Coon, and I could understand why. Donna does, after all, twirl fire batons durin' every scholastic half time, but she also ain't got nothin' but patches of hair left on her little singed head. Besides, twirlin' fire ain't the same as swingin' around what, after some research, I learnt was properly called a "thurible." So even though she was well liked and a good Baptist, Donna Coon would not do, which I explained as politely as I could to the callers. I did naturally end each conversation with the assurance that if Pastor Hickey ever decided to incorporate batons of fire into his sermon, Donna would surely be the first to know. As the days passed, I started to grow a little nervous. What would I do if I couldn't find somebody to work the thurible? Well, as He always does, the Lord finally hit me upside the head and reminded me that he'd already provided the answer to all my problems in the form of my niece Lulu Bell. How stupid had I been? Sure, she's as simple as a bag of dirt, but that gal's always been real talented when it comes to yo-yos and such (you should see her do one of them "Around the World" or "Walk the Dog" moves). If she can work a dollar-store yo-yo into submission, then she could easily fill the shoes of my much needed thurible swinger, a/k/a "thurifer." Since Christmas Eve was less than a week away, I put Lulu Bell into trainin' by havin' her practice her thuriferin' with buckets tied to ropes. I knew that if she could do two of them at a time, she'd have no problem workin' one little tea strainer, which we was usin' for practice until the real thurible arrived. Within days she'd mastered the buckets and was swingin' that mock incense burner like she'd been born with it in her hand. Lulu Bell had done us proud, God bless her simple little heart. With Christmas Eve just a day away, the church phone was goin' wild with folks wantin' to know what time the service would be startin'. It looked as if we had a hit on our hands. Of course the drawin' on the handouts that the kids of the church had designed and posted everywhere did play a large role in gettin' people interested in our holiday worship, even if the flames shootin' out of the thurible as the bikini-clad cartoon temptress swung it wildly over her head did most likely stretch the truth just a tad. Regardless, most folks would still be thrilled by what we were gonna be givin' 'em the followin' night. Lulu Bell was rehearsed, and we was ready— or so we thought. Then it dawned on us that the thurible kit we'd ordered hadn't arrived yet. We'd completely forgot about it. After a call to the company that sold us the package, we found out that Sister Bertha, who'd ordered the thing for us, had selected to have the items sent regular mail instead of two-day delivery like I'd suggested. There was no way our thurible would make it on time for the Christmas Eve service. I should have known better than to have let that old cow place the order, but Pastor Hickey had thought it would quench her bitterness from havin' her idea of raisin' Christmas Eve attendance turned down. Well, it wasn't my fault that no one liked her idea of havin' all of us go around town durin' the holiday season, announcin' to folks over a bullhorn that they'd be burned like a batch of fries at a bad restaurant if they didn't come to church. But regardless, she'd sabotaged my idea. Not only would it look bad on me, but our church would be the laughin' stock when there wasn't no flyin' thurible.

After talkin' with Pastor Hickey and breakin' the bad news, I decided I'd better let Lulu Bell down. I knew it'd break her heart, especially since she'd been practicin' like she had. So I set her down, gave her a plate full of Oreo cookies and a glass of ice-cold milk, and told her what had happened. To my amazement, she wasn't in the least bit upset. Instead she said that we could just use her "thurbible."

It seemed that Lulu Bell had made her own thurible by addin' a chain to the handle of an old metal teapot. She'd used a nail and a hammer to punch some holes in the sides, and had put a hinge on the lid so it wouldn't fly open. Thanks to her craftiness, our Christmas Eve service had been saved, and the show would go on. The only problem was that we still didn't have the special charcoal, which had been included in that order Sister Bertha had placed. Lulu Bell assured me that she'd take care of that part as well, so I gave her a big hug and called our pastor to let him know that we was still on.

The church was filled with people and an air of anticipation on that Christmas Eve evenin'. Outside on the church steps, Lulu Bell tipped up the bag of BBQin' charcoals and poured nine of 'em into the teapot. She then doused 'em with lighter fluid and threw in a match. Within no time she had 'em goin', as me and some of the gals from the church watched with excitement. Our excitement didn't last long, for we quickly realized that we didn't have any incense to sprinkle over the burnin' briquettes. Upon hearin' this, Sister Bertha ran to the cleanin' closet and grabbed a container of Love My Carpet carpet freshener. She assured us that she had the situation in hand and suggested that we take our seats. After bein' told by Lulu Bell that she was okay and didn't need me anymore, I went inside and took my place by my husband. Within minutes Lulu Bell had that teapot smokin' like a disco inferno and was awaitin' her entry into the services at our beloved Baptist church. As the congregation ripped into a heartfelt rendition of "Silent Night," Lulu Bell poured in a good heapin' measure of the carpet freshener and then came in swingin' that smolderin' kettle like a pro. Her "Around the World," "Walk the Dog," "The Creeper," "Rock the Baby," and other assorted yo-yo tricks, which she performed with her home-made thurible, were both inspirational and spiritual, to say the least. By the time she'd made it to the front of the sanctuary, there wasn't a dry eye in the place. Of course that was on account of the thick black toxic smoke that filled the church. No one had thought to open a window before the service. We were chokin', gaggin', and gaspin' for air, but since we weren't able see much of anythin' on account of the thick smoke blockin' out the lights that hung from the ceilin', we couldn't escape. Somethin' had gone horribly wrong. The mix of the odorless carbon monoxide and heavy smoke from the carpet freshener was quickly overtakin' the entire church. We might have all perished if it hadn't been for the quick thinkin' of two people that night. One of those people was my husband, Dew, who managed to crawl to a window and open it. The other person who we owe our lives to was my stripper sister Donna Sue. Donna Sue, who was seated at the back of the church so she could sneak out before the altar call, was able to find her way to the door, which she quickly crawled out of. Once she'd made it to fresh air, her thoughts turned to those of us who were still trapped inside. Real-izin' that we'd never find the door on our own in all that smoke, she reached into her purse and grabbed a handful of glow-in-the-dark condoms that she always keeps with her (she prefers this kind since her eyesight ain't what it use to be, especially when she's been drinkin' all day). She threw those Day-glo condoms right down what she assumed to be the middle church aisle, and then tossed a few more right by the door. Thanks to her quick thinkin', everyone was able to get out unscathed, with the exception of Sister Bertha. She made it out, but not unscathed. It seemed that, bein' the trouper that she was, Lulu Bell continued to do her twirls and spins with the smokin' teapot even after her vision was completely blocked by the smoke. Anyways, long story short, the spout got stuck in Sister Bertha's hair, causin' her bouffant to melt all around the kettle, embeddin' it. It was a mess! I've seen hair disasters in my life, but this one took the cake. Luckily for Sister Bertha, I was on hand and was able to use my beautician skills to quickly cut the teapot out before the heat caused the hairspray in her hairstyle to burst into flames. Once we'd all settled down, Pastor Hickey took up an offerin' and then sent us all home with a Christmas blessin'. After about a week of airin' out in the cold weather, and a good scrubbin', our little church was good as new. When the story got out about what all Sister Bertha had done, the blame was quickly taken off Lulu Bell and me and placed where it belonged. When the thurible, charcoal, and incense did finally arrive a week later, Pastor Hickey had it locked in the closet where it remained until the followin' year when our new pastor, Ida May Bee, took over the church. Sharin' in the vision that I'd had and told her about, Pastor Ida May Bee allowed Lulu Bell to try her hand as thurifer with the real thurible on Christmas Eve 2002. Of course Pastor Ida May Bee also has two members armed with buckets of water follow closely behind Lulu Bell durin' the service. Needless to say, not only was it beautiful and touchin', but Lulu Bell doin' her yo-yo tricks with the thurible down the aisle on Christmas Eve at the Holier Than Most Baptist Church has now become a new annual tradition. By the way, the wearin' of flame-retardant head scarves durin' this service is encouraged.

CHRISTMAS CRAFTS FROM THE HEART

A Reader's Digest Christmas Tree

Not only does this make a lovely decoration, but it helps recycle. I've told y'all for years how proud I am to be called trailer trash, since it is folks like me and my neighbors who've been reusin' old items over and over again. Regardless of where you put this paper tree, it will end up thrillin' your guests.

SUPPLIES

1 *Reader's Digest* magazine
Glue
A few paper clips or clothespins
Green spray paint

White puffy paint
Assorted items to decorate the
   tree (You can use little bulbs
   or what-have-you.)

1. Take the upper right corner of the front cover of your magazine and bend it down toward the seam so that it makes a triangle shape out of the top portion of the page.

2. Next, fold the side of the page in toward the middle of the book so that it touches the seam. This will give you a fold at the top goin' down the front of the page and a fold in the middle goin' toward the back of the page.

3. Repeat steps 1 and 2 until all pages are crisply folded.

4. Glue the front over to the back cover. You might want to hold the two pages together with a few paper clips or some clothespins. Set aside to dry.

5. Spray-paint the folded magazine green. Set aside to dry.

6. Put the white puffy paint on the top folds so that it looks like you got a flocked tree.

7. Glue on your assorted decorations. Personally I like to use hot glue for this.

8. Set out your new tree for everyone to see.

Tips for the Holiday Hostess

Make sure all your guests know how to get to your trailer. In today's world with email and all, there's no reason why you can't just shoot 'em off a hand-drawn map. And for those guests who don't have email, just take an afternoon off and run a map to their houses. Never send a map in the mail 'cause they can get lost or even discarded as junk mail by the recipient. Another big no-no is puttin' signs out around your street that help point the way to your trailer. After all, the last thing you want is a party crasher, even if it is a good friend. If you do have a party crasher, simply tell 'em that this is a private, invitation-only Christmas gatherin', but if they want to join in the merrymakin' it'll cost 'em $10. Hey, who couldn't use an extra $10 this time of the year?

Party Idea

Open Door Party

When we're in town, me and my husband, Dew, always throw a party by openin' our trailer home on Christmas Eve afternoon to all our family as well as our friends who either ain't got family to spend it with, or might otherwise be alone on that day. Of course, I pull all our Christmas gifts out from under the tree and hide 'em along with anything else of value, 'cause you never know if my drunken sister Donna Sue is gonna bring over her "temporary boyfriend" from the night before. Anyways, I'll usually make up a meat item or a casserole and have everyone else bring a side dish or dessert along with their choice of drink. Mind you, me and my husband are good Baptists, so we have strict rules when it comes to the public consumption of alcohol in our trailer, even on special occasions like Christmas Eve. We don't allow it. If you want to drink, that's fine, but when you're in our trailer home, you'll take your bottle and drink it in the closet—just like me and Dew.

Normally my little Christmas Eve get-togethers go off without a hitch. People come over, we laugh, eat, play some cards, and then everyone goes home. But last year it was a different story altogether. We opened our home up as usual, and we welcomed in a nice-size group of friends and family. The guest list included Me-Ma, who came with Momma and Daddy, Momma Ballzak, Donna Sue, who came alone thank the Lord, Little Linda from Lot #20 and her guest and dancer at the Blue Whale Strip Club Flora Delight, Anita Biggon of Lot #2, and Ollie White of Lot #10. Of course we'd invited my niece Lulu Bell and her new husband Billy Bob Button over, but she ran off to spend her first Christmas Eve as a married woman with her in-laws. She's still simple as a bag of dirt, but she's happy. We also asked the boys over in Lot #19 to come and join us, but Vance Pool, Harry Lombardi, and Elroy DaSafe had decided to close down Vance Pool's Funeral Center for the holidays so they could go their own separate ways and be with their out-of-town families. The boys were nice enough to drop off a lovely flower arrangement though, which I suspect was left over from a funeral, 'cause when I went to water it, I found a card stuck inside that read, "Rest in peace, Latisha, from the crew up at Ardelia's House of Hair." Regardless, I guess it's the thought that counts.

In the past Kenny and Donny have joined us, but this year they had some kind of event in Fort Smith they had to attend. They did stop by on their way out of town however to wish us all a Merry Christmas and drop off a cheese ball that Donny had molded into the shape of Barbra Streisand's head. It tasted real good, but it was kind of weird eatin' somebody's head on Christmas Eve.

After Kenny and Donny left, we all got to talkin' and before we knew it, it was almost time to eat. Well, as I was pullin' out the hush puppy chicken casserole I'd prepared from the oven, I heard what sounded like cries for help. I knew it wasn't my hush puppy chicken casserole, so I just set that down on the stove and hollered into the livin' room for everybody to shut up for a minute. As soon as they'd stopped laughin' and carryin' on, the pleas for assistance became clear. It was Flora Delight, and she was somewhere in the back of my modest pink two-story doublewide. All us headed toward the rear, trackin' the screams like a pack of hounds after a fox. As we got closer, it was apparent that Flora was in the bathroom.

"Flora dear," I said, "are you all right?"

"No," she replied frantically, "I need some help!" Once I'd gained her permission to open the bathroom door, I couldn't believe my eyes. There she was in tears, completely dressed, settin' on the floor with her hand wedged in the toilet. "Ruby Ann," she said, with the tears streamin' down her face, "I'm stuck in your commode." With that, everybody but my Me-Ma, who was fast asleep in the livin' room, came in to see what was goin' on. Once I calmed Flora down, she told us that she'd dribbled some of the grape Kool-Aid that she'd brung on her blouse, so she came back into the bathroom to try and clean it up before it set in. Well, I don't know how much toilet paper she'd used to try and scrub it out, but when she flushed the toilet, it clogged up. She grabbed the nearby plunger and went to town on the toilet, which in turn knocked her plastic cup full of grape Kool-Aid off the toilet tank and into the toilet itself, which I'd just cleaned before everyone had arrived. Naturally she took the cup out of what by now looked like Barney's bathwater and put it in the trashcan before again plungin' away at that clog. It was then that while Flora was lungin' down that the rubber piece on the end of our very old plunger ripped away, causin' Flora's hands to slip off the pole and down into the commode. As luck would have it, only her left hand was actually stuck down in the hole. My husband, Dew, tried everything he could think of to get her hand out, but it was to no avail. Even Little Linda tried, but the one time Flora's hand did start to move, she commenced to screamin' about her ring. It seemed that this cherished ring that one of her old boyfriends had given her was slippin' off as well, and the last thing she wanted to do was lose that keepsake down the sewer. She insisted that she just stay right there in that bathroom until we could get a plumber to come out and help, which wasn't gonna happen that day or the next. Well, I hated to tell her, but I'd seen the same dang ring in the Fingerhut catalog for $19.27. As you can imagine, I couldn't help but feel bad that poor Flora would have to spend Christmas Eve and Christmas Day in my guest bathroom with her hand in the commode, and I also couldn't help thinkin' that if that grape Kool-Aid stained my toilet bowl I was gonna have to kill her. Of course the night wasn't as much of a loss as it could've been. No, when it came time to eat, Momma Ballzak fixed up a plate and took it back to Flora. Since Flora had her right hand free, she was able to feed herself. After dinner, we played some cards. Me-Ma, who was wide awake by now, would run Flora's cards back and forth from the kitchen table where all the rest of us were.

That Flora's a really good canasta player, let me tell you. She and Little Linda, who made up a team, kicked our butts. When we moved on to charades, well, Flora wasn't really good, but she did try. And don't even get me started about her and Twister.

Anyways, about 5 P.M. that night I had an idea hit me, and since Flora was game for it, we gave it a shot. I took an old wire hanger and bent it open. Dew took out his pliers and made a small hook on one of the ends. Well, we took that wire and had Flora wiggle it around her hand until she could manage to hook it on her ring. Once she'd done that, she could start tryin' to move her hand around, in an attempt to free it without worryin' about her cheap-ass ring slippin' off and goin' down the drain. As luck would have it, in no time her hand was freed, and I could flush that doggone grape Kool-Aid out of my toilet bowl. I can't recall the last time I was that happy about my toilet durin' the holidays, but I was. By six o'clock everybody had wished us a Merry Christmas and headed on back to their trailers. It was a Christmas Eve that I'll never forget. And after I'd said my last good-bye, I paused for a moment to thank God for wonderful family and good friends. Then I grabbed the Oxi Clean and the scrub brush and I headed to the bathroom to try and salvage my toilet.

TRAILER PARK CHRISTMAS GAMES

I've Never on Christmas

Each player is given a bowl of twenty candy canes or Hershey's Kisses or M&M's. Then in a clockwise direction, the first person has to say somethin' that they've never done on Christmas. It can be as simple as "I've never put on makeup on Christmas," or as evil as "I've never been in jail on Christmas." You can play it as mean-spirited as you want. If you have done whatever that person says on Christmas, then you have to give that player one of your candies. The winner is the one person who ends up with the most candies. This can be both fun and tellin'.

WHAT'S THAT SMELL?

You can't help but have peace on earth in your trailer with the smell of this hangin' in your home.

Chimney Potpourri

Chimney not required.

Makes one batch

2 cups rose hips	$1/_2$ cup whole cloves
1 cup birch cones	$1/_2$ cup juniper berries
3 cups dried orange slices	$1/_2$ cup whole allspice
35 cinnamon sticks	20 drops cinnamon essential oil

MIx it all together and pour in a big jar. Cover and let it set for two weeks, shakin' daily.

HOLLY JOLLY WOOHA!

❄ More diamonds are purchased at Christmastime than during any other holiday or occasion during the year.

❋ In 1891, a crab pot was set down on a San Francisco street to raise money for a charity Christmas dinner, becoming the first Salvation Army collection kettle.

❋ Toys for Tots started their first toy drive in 1947.

Helpful Holiday Hints

❋ If you're cookin' in the oven, and you have a spill, toss on a mixture of 5 tablespoons of salt and one part of cinnamon on the spill. The salt will soak up the juices while the cinnamon will make the smell better. After the oven cools, you can lift the mixture up with a spatula and wipe the surface with a sponge.

❋ To get food colorin' off your fingers, take a piece of raw potato and rub it on your fingers, then run them under water.

—Vance Pool, Lot #19
—Harry Lombardi, Lot #19
—Elroy DaSafe, Lot #19

❋ Nail polish and a rag will take care of that plastic that you've accidentally burned on your toaster.

❋ Use a red or green tube sock as gift wrappin' for a small toy.

—Little Linda, Lot #20

TWELVE DAYS OF YULETIME ADVICE

Dear Ruby Ann,

I'm a big fan of yours and love your books. I hope you can help me. My aunt and uncle bought the house next to us three years ago after my father finally passed away. My mother has been gone for ten years this March. Since I'm still very close to my aunt and uncle, they always have me over for the holidays. The problem is that even though they go all out to make me feel special, it still feels wrong for me. To me this house will always be the one that I grew up in, and I will always remember the Christmastime with my family in that house. I have wonderful memories of my mother and dad in that old house, and it's hard for me to give them up. Is this wrong?

Merry Christmas,
Danny

Dear Danny,

No, it ain't wrong to feel that way. If you've read my first book, you know that we moved my husband Dew's momma, Momma Ballzak, into Lot #16 after she'd had her first heart attack back in 1994. And even though I just love her to death, in my mind Lot #16 will always be the home of my Pa-Pa and Me-Ma, even though he passed away many years ago and we put Me-Ma in the home. Maybe one of the reasons that I feel the way I do is 'cause Pa-Pa and Me-Ma's trailer still sets on Lot #16.

Momma Ballzak wouldn't let us get her a new one, so we just fumigated my grandparents' old home and then moved her in. Of course I could also feel so attached to this single-wide trailer 'cause I spent many wonderful Christmas holidays growin' up as a child visitin' Lot #16. Regardless, I know the seasonal memories that I have of Pa-Pa and Me-Ma will live on in my heart and mind. Why even now, as I take pen to paper, I can almost recall the lingerin' smells of burnt sugar cookies or scalded homemade eggnog that filled Me-Ma's Christmas kitchen (truth be told and regardless of what I've said in the past, she wasn't the best cook in the world even before, when she wasn't completely loony). And I can also see the decorations that Me-Ma would put all over the livin' room. As a matter of fact, I've included several of these easy-to-make items in this book.

As far as givin' up your memories, you don't have to go that far. I could never forget the good times I'd had at my grandparents' home. For example, there is one particular memory of Christmas that I'll never forget. The women's group that she headed up at church had given Me-Ma a gift for Christmas. No, it wasn't a Christmas box or even a brush or a chain for a pocket watch. It was a BeDazzler. Now, for those of you who don't know what a BeDazzler is, well, let me just tell y'all that if you should happen to cross its path, don't pick it up, don't touch it, heck, don't even look at it, 'cause it has a way of grabbin' the very soul out of you and not lettin' go. Basically it's a giant plastic stapler, or at least that's what it looks like. You use it to press studs or rhinestones into fabric in the same type of manner that you'd put a staple into a piece of paper. In the right hands you can create a festive handbag, a vivid hat, or even bring life back to a tired old shirt or coat. And the good part about it is that anyone can use the BeDazzler. Of course, that also happens to be the bad part about it. My Me-Ma went nuts with that thing. I'm here to tell you that if it could be BeDazzled, it was. She rhinestoned the curtains, the couch, the recliner, the throw rug, and anything else in the livin' room that didn't move, but she didn't stop there. Oh no! Come New Year's Day she'd BeDazzled the placemats, the tablecloth, the dinner napkins, the dishtowels, and a large assortment of potholders and aprons. By the middle of January Me-Ma had moved on to the bathroom, and rhinestoned both the carpeted toilet tank cover and the lid cover, the shower curtain, and had even BeDazzled the embossed HOLIDAY INN that was on most of her towels with green stones. I'm tellin' you, it was frightenin' what that woman was doin'. She'd even studded the front door welcome mat for cryin' out loud, as well as the trim on the new leisure suit we'd all chipped in on for Pa-Pa that Christmas. She'd gone mad with that thing. And the worst part was I couldn't even go over to her trailer to pay her and Pa-Pa a visit. Do you have any idea how many pairs of double-knit polyester slacks I ruined from snaggin' 'em on her demonic handy work? Why I couldn't even bend over and pet her poodle Cupcake 'cause she'd rhinestoned the poor thing's little collar with that doggone BeDazzler. I can honestly say that up until that time I'd never had the desire to strike a fellow Baptist, other than my sister of course, but I was about ready to hurt them women from church who'd turned my Me-Ma into the crafts monster that she'd become with their little gift. But the prayers of everyone in the trailer park, includin' my Pa-Pa, were finally answered when that special delivery package arrived at Lot #16 just before Valentine's Day. Thanks to Ronco Teleproducts, Inc., and their Ronco Bottle and Jar Cutter, our life was soon back to normal. It's amazin' the amount of peace of mind $7.77 plus shippin' could get you back in the 1970s. Of course it's also amazin' that the residents at the High Chaparral Trailer Park combined have the largest number of converted Mountain Dew bottle–drinkin' glasses in the entire world. Go figure.

So my advice is to hold on to those memories of your youth while makin' new ones with your aunt and uncle. Happy Holidays!

Love, Kisses, and Trailer Park Wishes,
Ruby Ann Boxcar

PUTTIN' YOUR BEST FACE FORWARD

Eyebrows

Can you imagine how bizarre it would be at Christmas to watch your Aunt Tillie's facial expression as she discovers underneath that wrappin' is a bottle of Jean Nate if she didn't have any eyebrows? That's why it's important that you draw on your eyebrows durin' this season of outward emotions. Mind you, the last thing anybody wants is to have Joan Crawford over for Christmas, so don't go nuts with that eyebrow pencil. Just fluff 'em up a bit so they show. Of course, if you're like me, and you wear glassess, use a light brown pencil or you'll end up lookin' like a clown. So arch those eyebrows with your eyebrow pencil. By the way, if you're one of those folks who are gettin' them Botox shots, instead of simply archin' your eyebrows with the pencil, do a zigzag line across your brows. That way it'll look like you're showin' emotions from the nose up.

CHRISTMAS CHEER

Donna Sue suggests . . .

Frostbite

This will make you think somethin' bit you in the behind.

³/₄ ounce blue Curaçao
2 ounces heavy cream
¹/₂ ounce white Crème de Cacao

1¹/₂ ounces tequila
¹/₂ cup ice cubes

Put everything in a shaker and shake vigorously for about ten seconds. Strain over ice into a highball glass. Serve.

Slidin' Down Your Chimney

This is really good if you're the designated sleigh driver.

6 ounces sparkling cider
¹/₄ cup fresh strawberries

¹/₂ ripe banana
2 ice cubes

Blend everything together and serve.

TRAILER PARK CHRISTMAS GRUB

Christmas Cookie

Momma Ballzak's Silent Night Whiskey Balls

When your mother-in-law is a drunk, you kind of get use to a liquor taste in her food. You should taste her tuna salad.

Makes a few dozen balls

1 cup graham cracker crumbs
1 cup powdered sugar
1 cup finely chopped walnuts
3 teaspoons cocoa powder

1$^1/_2$ tablespoons light corn syrup
$^1/_2$ cup whiskey
$^1/_2$ cup powdered sugar

Mix together the first 4 ingredients. Add the corn syrup and whiskey. Blend well. Roll the batter into small balls and then roll 'em in the $^1/_2$ cup powdered sugar. Set 'em on a cookie sheet. Cover 'em and put 'em in the fridge to set for two days. Take 'em out and serve. You can also drizzle these with chocolate if you want before you put 'em in the fridge.

—MOMMA BALLZAK, LOT #16

Festive Fudge

Opal's Jingle Bell Rockin' Oatmeal Fudge

This stuff may look as ugly as Opal, but boy will it rock your world!

Makes a batch

1 cup brown sugar
1 cup white sugar
$^1/_4$ pound margarine
$^1/_2$ cup milk
1$^1/_2$ cups oatmeal

1 cup peanut butter
$^1/_2$ cup walnuts
1 teaspoon vanilla
$^1/_2$ cup coconut

Boil the brown sugar, white sugar, margarine, and milk for 2$^1/_2$ minutes. Remove from heat and add the remaining ingredients. Mix and pour into square buttered pan.

—OPAL LAMB-BROWN, LOT #1

Chess Pie

Better Than a Glass of Milk and Some Cookies Citrus Chess Pie

It's amazin' what a fat man can do with a little orange juice and some sugar when he's tryin' to get better Christmas presents.

Makes one pie

¹/₄ cup margarine, melted
1¹/₂ cups sugar
1 tablespoon flour
3 eggs
3 tablespoons orange juice

2 tablespoons flaked
   coconut
¹/₂ cup milk, scalded
1 teaspoon vanilla
1 teaspoon lemon

Mix melted butter, sugar, and flour until well blended. Add eggs, beating well after each addition. Add other ingredients. Mix well. Bake at 350 degrees F. 35 to 40 minutes until golden brown.

—VANCE POOL, LOT #19

Seasonal Supper Sensation

Merry Christmas Macaroni Salad

The red color really brings the holidays to your dinner table.

Makes 4 to 6 servin's

1 16-ounce package macaroni,
   cooked
2 tomatoes, diced

2 cucumbers, chopped
1 onion, diced

DRESSING
1 cup vinegar
$^3/_4$ cup oil
1 cup sugar
1 tablespoon parsley

1 tablespoon dry mustard
$^1/_4$ teaspoon black pepper
$1^1/_2$ teaspoons garlic salt
$1^1/_2$ teaspoons seasonin' salt

Put the first four ingredients together in a bowl. Set aside.

In a separate bowl, mix the rest of the ingredients together. Pour over the first mixture and toss.

—LOIS BUNCH, LOT #3

Go Tell It on the Mountain Goulash Casserole

What a way to bring in Christmas.

Makes 4 to 6 servin's

16 ounces large shell noodles
2 green peppers, diced
2 onions, diced
3 pounds ground beef
1 cup oil

1 can corn
4 cans tomato soup
2 small cans mushrooms
2 cups Velveeta cheese, cubed

Cook your noodles accordin' to the instructions on the package. While you're doin' this, put the oil in a skillet on a medium flame and add the peppers, onions, and ground beef. Cook until the beef is well done. Pour into a greased casserole dish. Pour the corn, tomato soup, and mushrooms on top of this. Add the cheese and bake for 45 minutes at 350 degrees F.

—MOMMA BALLZAK, LOT #16

CHAPTER 13

Christmas Day Itself

DECEMBER 25

Santa gets his present.

When it comes to Christmas Day at the High Chaparral Trailer Park, the last thing you're gonna find are early risers. Heck, the kids don't spring up out of bed to rush and see what Santa left 'em until well after 11 A.M. on this glorious day. No, we like to play it pretty simple and laid back. We don't make up any wonderful potpourri, construct any special crafts, play any fun-filled games, or do much of anything on the twenty-fifth of December. Instead, we simply rest and eat. Boy do we eat! As a matter of fact, we practically eat near all day long. Why it's just like Thanksgivin', but with the parade switched out for cheap gifts you'll be returnin' to the stores on the twenty-sixth. Of course we also don't usually do turkey for Christmas. The reason for this is 'cause we just finished all the leftover turkey from Thanksgivin', and we won't want to see another piece of that stuff until next November, thank you very much. Normally it's either beef, chicken, ham, or Spam on our dinner tables. Actually Donny and Kenny over in Lot #15 do up a Christmas goose real good, but when it comes to preparin' Christmas food, they've always been a little uppity. Mind you, I don't mean that in a bad way. I simply mean that they're always in the mood to try somethin' different. Naturally they still have the old standbys, but they'll be the first to pull out the Crisco and grease up a pan to try out a new recipe regardless of how exotic it might sound to the rest of us here in the trailer park. Personally I've always made it a habit not to eat anythin' that flies ('cept for chickens, which have wings but don't do no real flyin'). Don't ask me why, but I don't eat nothin' that flies or anything with mincemeat in it. Still, since my way ain't always the High Chaparral Trailer Park way, you're gonna find in this section along with the traditional Boxcar family Christmas favorites what I'm assured are some of the tastiest recipes for Christmas goose and mincemeat pie. So it's a win-win Christmas for everybody. Just remember that you'll only be havin' to cook two meals on Christmas. You start off with breakfast, regardless of what time you get up, and then you cook up what would be called your dinner or midday meal. When it comes time for supper at night, you just keep on eatin' what you got leftover from dinner that afternoon. Trust me, you'll have plenty of food, and it don't get much better than this. With that in mind, y'all kick up the oven, grab them pots and pans, and let us show you how to have the best Christmas you've ever tasted.

Now, I do have one top secret regardin' Christmas cookin' that we Boxcars have kept to ourselves for years. We've each passed it on only to our children for well over 100 years. Seein' how I ain't got no kids, and my dogs really can't use this information, I'm gonna share it with you. The secret to a successful Christmas meal is cinnamon. That's right, I said cinnamon! Regardless of what you're cookin', always add a dash of cinnamon regardless if the recipe calls for it or not. Not only will it add just a hint of exotic flavor, but it will fill your trailer with the most beautiful aroma that'll be sure to please all who smell it, includin' you. But now keep that to yourselves. As a matter of fact, since most folks who taste these recipes I'm about to lay on you will want them, I'm not gonna include our Boxcar family secret in them. You'll just know to add a dash of cinnamon. That way even though you give 'em the recipe, they'll still never be able to get it quite as good as yours comes out to be.

CHRISTMAS DAY MENU

Breakfast

Kris Kringle's Casserole

Old Santa Claus just might come back to your place after deliverin' all his presents if he peeks in your fridge and sees you're gonna be makin' this on Christmas Day.

Makes one casserole

2 pounds bulk sausage, browned, crumbled, and drained

8 slices bread, torn up into quarter-size pieces

3/4 pound grated sharp Cheddar cheese

8 large eggs, beaten

3 cups milk

1 1/2 teaspoons salt

1 1/2 teaspoons dry mustard

A day before you plan to serve this, grease you up a 9- × 13-inch casserole dish, and cover the bottom with the bread pieces. Carefully put your sausage on top of this. Add your cheese to the top of that. Set aside.

In a bowl mix the eggs, milk, salt, and mustard up real good. Pour it over the stuff in the casserole dish. Cover it up, put it in the fridge, and forget about it until Christmas Day. Pull it out, uncover it, and pop it into a 350 degree F. preheated oven. Let it bake for 45 minutes. Take it out and let it set for about 10 minutes. Serve.

—TINA STOPENBLOTTER, LOT #17

Red Ribbons and Silver Bells Beaver Tails

To be honest, there really ain't no red ribbons or silver bells in this wonderfully quick breakfast pastry. For that matter, there ain't no beaver tails in 'em either. Oh well, after one bite of these tasty treats you really won't care that they don't live up to their name.

Makes 24 tails

3 regular cans of refrigerator
    biscuits
1 cup sugar
3 tablespoons ground cinnamon

5 tablespoons margarine,
    melted
Juice of 1 lemon
1 bottle red sugar for decoratin'

Pop open your cans of biscuits. Take each piece of biscuit dough and flatten it out with your hand so it looks like a beaver's tail. Place two of these in about 4 inches of hot grease, and fry 'em on both sides till they're golden brown. Drain 'em on a paper towel. Put the sugar and cinnamon in a plastic bag. Shake it up to mix it. Once it's well mixed, set aside.

In a small bowl, combine the margarine and the lemon juice. Make sure you mix it up real good. Take each tail and put a light coatin' of lemon margarine on it. Drop it into the plastic bag and gently shake until the tail has been completely covered. Place the beaver tails on a plate, sprinkle on some red sugar for appearance, and serve. If you ain't got no red sugar, don't worry about it. But whatever you do, don't decorate with green sugar. People will think you've got a moldy tail, and that's the last thing you want.

—LULU BELL BOXCAR, LOT #8

Snackin' Around the Trailer

Born in a Manger Butterscotch Dip

If it wasn't for dippin' apples or bananas or even Twinkies in this stuff while us ladies labor over a hot Christmas stove, we most likely wouldn't have the strength to go on.

Makes about 26 servin's

4 cups butterscotch-flavored chips
$2/3$ cup evaporated milk
2 teaspoons rum extract (Momma Ballzak and Donna Sue like to use 2 tablespoons of rum instead, which is just fine.)

A mix of apple wedges, banana pieces, Twinkies, or whatever you want to use for dippin'

Pour your butterscotch chips in the Crock-Pot. Add your milk and then cover. Let it cook on low for about an hour. Stir until you get a smooth mixture. Add your rum extract. Stir. This will keep its consistency for about 2 hours (even though none of us at the High Chaparral Trailer Park have ever had a batch last long enough to see how well it does after 2 hours).

—HARRY LOMBARDI, LOT #19

The Real Meal Deal for the Day

Native American Christmas Corn Puddin'

Legend has it that a Native American first presented this recipe to the folks at a trailer park many Christmases ago. The legend also says that the trailer folks accidentally melted the plastic bowl it came in while heatin' it up in the microwave, tried to pick up the Native American's wife, and borrowed some tools they never returned. I think it's closer to truth than to legend.

Makes 6 to 8 servin's

1 regular can creamed corn
1 regular can whole-kernel corn
1/4 pound margarine, softened

1 (8½ ounce) package corn bread mix

Put your margarine in a 2-quart casserole dish, and stick it in the microwave. Nuke it for about 2 minutes or until the margarine is melted. Add both your corns as well as your corn bread mix. Mix well. Preheat your oven to 350 degrees F., slap it in, and let it go to town for 30 minutes.

—BEN BEAVER, LOT #14

Gloria in Excelsis Easy Glazed Carrots

I don't know anybody that wouldn't lift up their voices for a great big scoop of these.

Makes 4 servin's

3 cups sliced baby carrots
1 cup water

1/4 cup orange juice
1 tablespoon brown sugar

Combine the carrots and the water and place in the microwave. Cook on high for about 8 minutes. Drain and then set aside.

Put your juice and brown sugar in a bowl and mix. Put it in the microwave for about a minute. Stir until the sugar melts. (You might have to zap it again in the microwave.) Pour over the carrots. Serve or cover and place in the fridge for an hour. Reheat in the microwave and serve.

—SISTER BERTHA, LOT #12

O Tanenbaum Taters

One of the best things about this dish is that you ain't got to water it on a daily basis, and it won't drop pine needles on your floor.

Makes 6 servin's

3 cups instant mashed potatoes
3 cups water
$^{1}/_{4}$ cup milk
8 ounces Velveeta cheese, cubed

$^{1}/_{4}$ cup sour cream
1 regular can cream of chicken soup
1 regular can corn, drained

Put your water and milk in the microwave. Heat 'em up for 5 minutes. Add the Velveeta and stir. Let as much of it melt as will melt. After that, put it all in the microwave and heat it up for another 2 to 3 minutes. Once it's all melted and mixed together, add the potato flakes. Follow directions on the box for how much time to cook.

Combine the corn and soup together. Heat up. Combine the corn mixture with the potato mixture. Add the sour cream. Stir. Serve.

—MOMMA BALLZAK, LOT #16

God Rest Ye Merry Gentlemen's Green Bean Casserole

This one will set you free!

Makes about 6 servin's

2 regular cans green beans
1 regular can condensed cream of mushroom soup
1 teaspoon garlic powder
$^{1}/_{2}$ teaspoon onion powder

Pinch salt
Pinch pepper
9-ounce can French-fried onions
$1^{1}/_{2}$ cups Cheddar cheese

Preheat your oven up to 350 degrees F. Drain your green beans. Pour them and your soup into a large bowl. Add your powders, salt, and pepper. Mix well and microwave the mixture on high for 5 minutes. Add half the cheese and stir. Microwave again for 3 minutes. Pour it into a 9- × 13-inch casserole dish. Pour on $^3/_4$ of the French-fried onions and the rest of the cheese. Bake at 350 degrees F. for 5 minutes. Sprinkle on the rest of the French-fried onions and bake for another 3 to 5 minutes or until the onions start to brown.

—WANDA KAY, LOT #13

I'll Be Ham for Christmas

Heck, I'd actually skip the annual Christmas Eve Midnight Madness Bingo Bash I hit every year over at the VFW for a big ol' helpin' of this here ham.

1 10–20-pound ham	1 cup brown sugar, packed
1 20-ounce can sliced pineapple	$^1/_2$ teaspoon mustard
1 can premium beer	1 tablespoon balsamic vinegar

Preheat your oven to 325 degrees F. Put your ham with the fat side up in an 18-quart roastin' pan. Take toothpicks and pin your pineapple rings all over the ham. Pour your beer over the ham, cover it, and cook for as long as the directions suggest. Baste every half hour. Durin' the last 15 minutes, mix together the remainin' ingredients and pour over the ham. Don't worry, you won't taste the beer, which is why I make sure and drink one can before I baste the ham.

—DONNA SUE BOXCAR, LOT #6

Christmas Day Pork Chops

A Christmas at Momma and Daddy's without these would be like a Hooters without at least one Baptist hidin' at the corner table.

Makes 8 chops

8 pork chops, browned and
    drained
1 cup ketchup

$1/2$ cup onions, diced
1 tablespoon Worcestershire
    sauce

In a bowl combine the ketchup, onions, and Worcestershire sauce. Place the pork chops in a casserole dish and pour the mixture over them. Cover and bake at 375 degrees F. for 2 hours.

—MOMMA BOXCAR, LOT #5

Kenny and Donny's Easiest Goose in Town Christmas Goose

Donny says Kenny will pick up his goose a week or so before the holidays roll around on account of how he "likes to get his Christmas goose early."

Makes 8 good-size servin's

10-pound goose, cleaned and
    washed
1 pound prunes, soaked in water
    overnight
2 pounds apples, peeled and
    diced
2 cups burgundy wine

1 cup hot water
1 cup zwieback crumbs
$1/3$ cup sugar
$1/8$ teaspoon salt
Dash pepper
Dash flour

Pour 1 cup of the wine in a saucepan and add your prunes. Cook until your prunes get tender. Add the apples, zwieback crumbs, sugar, and salt. Mix well. Set aside.

Take your goose and rub the inside and the outside with salt. Spoon in your prune stuffin'. Close the openin' with skewers. Tie the legs together. Prick the skin in several places so the fat can run out when it cooks. Make sure you do this before placing in the roastin' pan or you might end up with a pierced roaster and a kitchen floor full of grease. Now place your goose breast side down in a large roastin' pan. Cover and cook at 400 degrees F. for 1 hour. If the pan fills up with fat, use your baster to remove the excess. Mix the rest of the wine and the water together and baste frequently with this durin' your entire cookin' time.

After that first hour, turn your goose so that it's now breast side up and cook uncovered at 325 degrees F. for 25 minutes per pound, or about 4 hours.

Skim fat from liquid in bottom of pan. Measure liquid: add enough water to make 3 cups. Thicken with flour as desired. Season with salt and pepper and now you got your gravy as well.

—Donny Owens and Kenny Lynn, Lot #15

Mincemeat Pie

Word is that this here pie is one of the best, but I'll just have to trust 'em on this one.

Makes one pie

 2 9-inch pie crusts
28-ounce jar mincemeat
1¹/₂ cups chopped apple

¹/₃ cup chopped nuts
2 teaspoons grated orange
   peel

Preheat your oven to 425 degrees F. Put one of the pie crusts in a pie pan. Set aside.

Combine your mincemeat, apple, nuts, and orange peel, and pour it into the pie-crust–lined pan. Put your second pie crust over top this. Seal and flute the edges, and then cut a few slits in the top so the steam can escape. Bake at 425 degrees F. for around 30 minutes or until the crust is golden brown. Serve as is or with ice cream.

—WENDY BOTTOM, LOT #4

Happy Birthday Jesus Cake

Instead of waitin' for the birthday boy to blow the candles out himself, y'all might want to help out a little. That or you can just wait until they melt themselves all the way down.

Makes one cake

4 cups cake flour
1 tablespoon bakin' powder
$^1/_2$ teaspoon salt
$^1/_2$ pound margarine, softened

$1^1/_2$ cups sugar
4 eggs plus 2 yolks, well beaten
2 teaspoons vanilla extract
$1^1/_2$ cups milk

Preheat your oven to 350 degrees F.

Use the wrappers off your sticks of margarine if you got 'em to grease up two 9-inch round cake pans. Put parchment paper in the bottom of each pan and grease and flour the pans up. Set aside.

Sift the flour, bakin' powder, and salt together. Set aside.

Cream the margarine in a mixin' bowl, addin' the sugar gradually. Beat until light and fluffy. Beat in your eggs a little at a time. Blend in the vanilla. Gradually add the sifted ingredients, alternatin' with the milk. Make sure you beat for a minute in between each added portion. Finally mix until it's nice and smooth. Pour the batter $^2/_3$ full in each pan. Bake for 25 minutes. When the cakes are done take 'em out and let 'em cool for 10 minutes in the pan, then turn 'em out on a wire rack. Peel off the paper and leave for an hour.

To make the frostin', simply combine the followin' ingredients.

1 cup margarine

1 cup shortenin'

3 cups confectioners sugar

$\frac{1}{2}$ cup cocoa powder

3 tablespoons hot water

$\frac{1}{3}$ cup milk

2 teaspoons orange extract

$\frac{3}{4}$ cup semisweet mini chocolate chips

Use an electric mixer to blend the first three ingredients together until they're creamy. Set aside.

In a small bowl, combine the cocoa powder and hot water by whiskin' until smooth. Add this and the milk to the first mixture. Pour in the orange extract and mix well. Fold in your chocolate chips. Let it get firm and then spread it on one of the layers. Add the second layer on top of that and spread the frostin' on that one, too. Let it set for 15 to 20 minutes before cuttin' into it or addin' birthday candles.

—THE LATE WILLIE DICK, LOT #1

Well, dear readers, that about wraps up Christmas for us here at the High Chaparral Trailer Park. Why, all we have left to do to bring this wonderful joyous time of the year where we share our love for one another and join hands in peace is return the crappy gifts we got just as soon as the stores open in the mornin'. So to all of you from all of us, Merry Christmas and a Happy New Year.

Love, Kisses, and Trailer Park Wishes,
Ruby Ann Boxcar

Acknowledgments

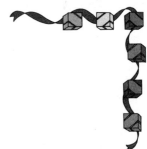

Don't quote me on this, but I got a feelin' that Santa Claus and Danny the Dreidel are gonna be passin' out a lot more gifts this holiday season to all them wonderful folks up at Citadel Press/Kensington Publishing. Not only have all of 'em been real good this year, but look at the wonderful work they did puttin' this here book together. All I can say is I'm sure proud to have 'em on my team, and even though it took me a while to find Danny the Dreidel's mailin' address (he winters in Florida, you know), I sent off letters to both him and Santa Claus tellin' him how great all them folks at the publishin' company have been. Thanks to Margaret, Bruce, Steven, Walter, Joan, Mary, Frank, Laurie, Doug, John, and everybody else who's had a hand with this feel-good holiday collection.

I also have to thank my much older sister, Donna Sue. I can't begin to tell y'all how many times when I was down and life seemed to be goin' all wrong that I simply looked to my dear sister and realized that regardless of how bad it might seem, it could be worse, 'cause I could be her. Your failures and really bad choices in life, dear sister, have been the best Christmas gifts I could ever have been given. I know that I speak for all losers everywhere when I say thank you and thank the good Lord above for makin' your trials and tribulations so painfully public.

And I got to thank my assistant Kevin for always bein' just a phone call away when I need him to help me look pretty. It just amazes me what all he can do with a little lipstick, blush, foundation, blue eye shadow, and plaster of Paris.

Index

All I Want for Christmas Is My Chocolate Chess Pie, 89
Angel hair, 14–15
Angels We Have Heard on High Punch, 245
Anita's Bar and Grill up on the Housetop Chocolate Buttermilk Pie, 45
Appetizers, 198, 238
Arkansas State Police, 184
Artificial trees, 5, 8–9, 239
Auto mechanics, holiday tip for, 123
Away in the Manger Breakfast Rolls, 43

Baby-sitters, holiday tip for, 122
Barbed wire garland, 13
Bathroom decoratin' tips, 18, 84, 221
Beatles, the, 73–74
Beauty Barge, 173–74
Beauty marks, 165
Beef Bourguignon, Christmas Is Comin' Trailer Park, 189–90
Beer Batter Dip, Donna Sue's, 118
Beer Bottle Reindeer, Donna Sue's, 55–57
Better Than a Glass of Milk and Some Cookies Citrus Chess Pie, 273
Better Than Snow on Christmas Chicken-Fried Steak, 227
Bisquick Puddin' Cookies, Lulu Bell's God Bless Everyone, 87
"Blow It Out for Santa" (game), 33–34
Blue Christmas Cookies, Sweat Scarves of Elvis Fan Club, 105
Blue eye shadow, 64
Blue Whale Strip Club, ix–x, 18, 127, 166, 184, 194
    Christmas party, 193, 194–95
Blush, 224
Booze, 141, 261. *See also* Drinks

Born in a Manger Butterscotch Dip, 281
Breakfast Rolls, Away in the Manger, 43
Bring a Can Party, 141–42
Brown Sugar Pie, Heard the Bells on Christmas Day, 147–48
Bumblebee Christmas Fudge, Wanda's Traditional Trailer Park, 88
Butterscotch Dip, Born in a Manger, 281
Butterscotch Oatmeal Cookies, Ollie's Baptist, 204

Cake Mix Cookies, Dottie's Walkin' in a Winter Wonderland, 225
Candy canes, 239
Carols. *See* Christmas carols
CB radio, 174–79
"Check Is in the Mail" (game), 100
Cheesecake Cookie Bars, Connie Kay's Attention-Christmas-Shoppers, 186–87
Chess Pie
    All I Want for Christmas Is My Chocolate, 89
    Better Than a Glass of Milk and Some Cookies Citrus, 273
    Lamb's I Saw Momma Kissin' Santa Claus's Assistant at the Mall Lemon, 189
    Nellie's Jolly Old Saint Nicholas Apple, 167–68
    Old-Time Baptist Come On, Ring Those Bells Buttermilk, 247
Chicken Casserole, Here We Come A-Wassailin', 107–8
Chicken-Fried Steak, Better Than Snow on Christmas, 227

Chicken Wreath, Kenny Lynn's Creative, 248
Child care providers, holiday tip for, 122
Chimney Potpourri, 265
Chocolate Buttermilk Pie, Anita's Bar and Grill up on the Housetop, 45
Chocolate Pecan Pie, 188
Christmas Apple Pie (potpourri), 162
Christmas books, xi–xii
Christmas Cake (drink), 165
Christmas Card Holder, 237
Christmas Card Placemats, 77–78
Christmas cards, xiv, 82, 200, 209
Christmas carols, 34, 143, 163, 201–2, 220
    Singin' Party, 161
Christmas club, 220
Christmas Day, 275–88
    menu for, 279–88
Christmas Day Pork Chops, 285
Christmas decoratin' tips. *See* Craft projects; Decoratin' for Christmas
Christmas drinks. *See* Drinks
Christmas Eve services, 252–58
Christmas gifts, 181, 251, 265
    wrap for, 143, 239, 266
Christmas goose, 277–78, 285–86
Christmas Grasshopper Fudge, 147
Christmas in Florida (potpourri), 81
Christmas Is Comin' Trailer Park Beef Bourguignon, 189–90
Christmas lights, 11–12, 19, 35, 143, 151–58
Christmas Mimosas, 145
Christmas Mouse, 179–81
Christmas music, 17, 36, 117
"Christmas Pea, The" (game), 238–39
Christmas Pumpkin Patch, 220
Christmas Shot, 104
Christmas talent contest, 133–34
Christmas Tree (drink), 125
Christmas trees, 3–16
    bracin' the, 10
    craft projects, 97–98
    decoratin' party, 99
    decoratin' the, 11–15
    fake versus real, 5, 8–9

findin' right spot for, 5–7
fun facts about, 62, 81–82, 101, 120
game, 61
helpful hints, 121
pickin' out, 4–9
skirt, 15–16
stand for, 9–10
takin' it down, 16, 163
topper for, 7–8
Christmas Tree Water (drink), 145
Christmas wreaths, 35, 143
    Jigsaw Puzzle Wreath, 197–98
Cinnamon, 278
Citrus Chess Pie, Better Than a Glass of Milk and Some Cookies, 273
Clay Pot Christmas Tree, 97–98
Clothespin Santa, 139–40
Cocktails. *See* Drinks
Color Party, 181
Color scheme, for Christmas trees, 12
Connie Kay's Attention-Christmas-Shoppers Cheesecake Cookie Bars, 186–87
Connie Kay's No Guilt Holiday Fudge, 204–5
Connie Kay's No Time to Cook 'Cause I'm Christmas Shoppin' Hawaiian Sandwiches, 68
Cookie exchange, 31–32
Cookies
    about, 41
    Connie Kay's Attention-Christmas-Shoppers Cheesecake Cookie Bars, 186–87
    Daddy's French Kiss Sleigh Ride Cookies, 245–46
    Dottie's Walkin' in a Winter Wonderland Cake Mix Cookies, 225
    Hark! The Herald Angels Eat No-Sugar Raisin Cookies, 146
    Holly Jolly Eggnog Cookies, 43–44
    Lulu Bell's God Bless Everyone Bisquick Puddin' Cookies, 87
    M&M Bisquick Cookies, 166
    Momma Ballzak's Silent Night Whiskey Balls, 271–72

Ollie's Baptist Butterscotch Oatmeal
Cookies, 204
Quickie Kris Kringle Cookies, 66
Sweat Scarves of Elvis Fan Club Blue
Christmas Cookies, 105
Trailer Park Christmas Mouse, 179–81
Wendy's Old-Time Let It Snow Sour
Cream Cookies, 126
Corn Puddin', Native American
Christmas, 281–82
Counter space, ironin' board for, 240
Craft projects, 17
Christmas Card Holder, 237
Christmas Card Placemats, 77–78
Clay Pot Christmas Tree, 97–98
Clothespin Santa, 139–40
Donna Sue's Beer Bottle Reindeer,
55–57
Jigsaw Puzzle Wreath, 197–98
Mrs. Claus Tissue Box Cover, 115–16
Reader's Digest Christmas Tree,
259–60
Seashell Santa, 217–18
Shotgun Shell Santa, 158–60
Traditional Potpourri, 35
Trailer Park Christmas Mouse, 179
Wooden Spoon Reindeer, 26–30
Cream Pie
Half and Half, 128
Trailer Park Christmas, 205

Daddy's French Kiss Sleigh Ride Cookies,
245–46
Dear Ruby Ann, 36–37
"Decorate the Christmas Tree Game," 61
Decoratin' for Christmas, 16–19, 51. *See
also* Craft projects
Delight, Flora, 1, 58, 127, 261, 262–64
Demolition derby, 134–39
Diet soda, 141
Directions, to party, 260
"Dirty Santa" (game), 33, 182
Dirty Snowman (drink), 186
Dish washin' tips, 143
*Donna Sue's Down Home Trailer Park
Bartending Guide*, 80
Donna Sue's Beer Batter Dip, 118

Donna Sue's Beer Bottle Reindeer, 55–57
"Donna Sue's Boyfriend" (game), 80,
219
Dottie's Walkin' in a Winter Wonderland
Cake Mix Cookies, 225
Drinks, 141, 163
Angels We Have Heard on High
Punch, 245
Christmas Cake, 165
Christmas Mimosas, 145
Christmas Shot, 104
Christmas Tree, 125
Christmas Tree Water, 145
Dirty Snowman, 186
Elf Coffee, 203
Frostbite, 271
Gingerbread Man, 224
Happy Elves Punch, 104
Hot Buttered Apple, 125–26
Jingle Bell Punch, 86
Little Drummer Boy Beverage, 166
Nieve Mexicana Caliente, 244
Orange Eggnog Float, 40
Reindeer Power Punch, 65
Rudolph the Red-Nosed Reindeer, 40
Santa Cider, 224
Santa Shot, 185
Santa's Pole, 203
Slidin' Down Your Chimney, 271
Sugar-Free Holiday Nog, 86–87
White Russian Winter, 65
Dr Pepper, 141
Drunken guests, 160–61

Eggnog
helpful hints, 183
Holly Jolly Eggnog Cookies, 43–44
Orange Eggnog Float, 40
Eggnog Pie, 106–7
Elf Coffee, 203
Eyebrows, 85, 270
Eyelashes, fake, 244
Eyeliner, 144–45
Eye shadow, 64

Fake eyelashes, 244
Fake trees, 5, 8–9, 239

Family doctor/vet/dog groomer, holiday tip for, 122–23
Family troubles, advice for, 164, 267–70
Favorite Christmas Character Dress-Up Party, 238
Faye Faye's Fried Christmas Corn Dish Delight, 47
Faye Faye's Sweet Potato Fudge for Christmas, 225–26
Finger foods, 198, 238
Fireplace, 240–43
Flatland Baptist Bible Academy, xvi, xvii
Flora Delight's Winter Wonderland Rum and Butter Fudge, 127
Fondue party, 24–25, 117–18
    recipes, 118–19
French Kiss Sleigh Ride Cookies, Daddy's, 245–46
Fried Christmas Corn Dish Delight, Faye Faye's, 47
Frostbite, 271
Fudge, 41
    Christmas Grasshopper Fudge, 147
    Connie Kay's No Guilt Holiday Fudge, 204–5
    Faye Faye's Sweet Potato Fudge for Christmas, 225–26
    Flora Delight's Winter Wonderland Rum and Butter Fudge, 127
    Kenny and Donny's White Chocolate Carol of the Bells Fudge, 167
    Nuttin' for Christmas Carrot Fudge, 246
    Opal's Jingle Bell Rockin' Oatmeal Fudge, 272
    Opal's Snow Fudge, 44
    Pastor's First Noel Pumpkin Fudge, 106
    Sister Bertha's O Holy Night Sanctified Sour Cream Fudge, 187
    Velveeta Cheese Fudge, 66–67
    Wanda's Traditional Trailer Park Bumblebee Christmas Fudge, 88

Games, 33
    Blow It Out for Santa, 33–34
    Check Is in the Mail, 100
    The Christmas Pea, 238–39
    Decorate the Christmas Tree Game, 61
    Dirty Santa, 33, 182
    Donna Sue's Boyfriend, 80, 219
    Hey, What's My Sock, 161–62
    I've Never on Christmas, 264–65
    Kiss And Tell, 199
    Pass the Aqua Net, 80–81
    White Elephant, 33, 181, 182
Garbage man, holiday tip for, 123
Garland, 13–14
General Grant Tree, 183
Gift wrap, 143, 239, 266
Gingerbread Man, 224
Girl Scout Cookies, 93
Glitter, 124
Gloria in Excelsis Easy Glazed Carrots, 282
God Rest Ye Merry Gentlemen's Green Bean Casserole, 283–84
Good King Wenceslas' Spam Sensation, 206
Go Tell It on the Mountain Goulash Casserole, 274
Goulash Casserole, Go Tell It on the Mountain, 274
Green Bean Casserole, God Rest Ye Merry Gentlemen's, 283–84
Guests
    bringin' food, 98–99
    drunken, 160–61
    gifts for, 181
    invitin', 57–58, 79

Half and Half Cream Pie, 128
Ham for Christmas, I'll Be, 284
Happy Birthday Jesus Cake, 287–88
Happy Elves Punch, 104
Hark! The Herald Angels Eat No-Sugar Raisin Cookies, 146
Heard the Bells on Christmas Day Brown Sugar Pie, 147–48
Here We Come A-Wassailin' Chicken Casserole, 107–8
"Hey, What's in My Sock" (game), 161–62
Hickey, Pastor Richard, 252–58

High Chaparral Trailer Park. *See specific lots*
Holiday tips (tipping), 121–24
Holiday troubles, advice for, 82–85
Holier Than Thou Most Baptist Church, 173, 231, 252–58
Holy Bible, xvi–xix
Holly Jolly Eggnog Cookies, 43–44
Honey Buttermilk Bread, Momma Boxcar's I'll Be Home for Christmas, 47–48
Hot Buttered Apple, 125–26
House cleaner, holiday tip for, 122
How the Grinch Stole Christmas (movie), 252
Human Christmas Light Display, 152–58

I'll Be Ham for Christmas, 284
Inspirational Holiday Thought (Pastor Ida May Bee), xv–xix
Invitations, 57–58, 79
It's Beginnin' to Smell a Lot Like Christmas, 101
"I've Never on Christmas" (game), 264–65

Janssen, Jeannie and Jimmy, 24–25
Jewelry cleanin' tip, 101
Jigsaw Puzzle Wreath, 197–98
Jingle Bell Punch, 86
Juanita's Momma's Mashed Potatoes, 228

Kenny and Donny's Easiest Goose in Town Christmas Goose, 285–86
Kenny and Donny's White Chocolate Carol of the Bells Fudge, 167
Kenny Lynn's Creative Chicken Wreath, 248
"Kiss And Tell" (game), 199
Kissin' cousins, 102–3
Kitchen smells, getting rid of, 82
Kris Kringle's Casserole, 279

Lamb's I Saw Momma Kissin' Santa Claus's Assistant at the Mall Lemon Chess Pie, 189
Lamb Super Center, 30–31, 96, 151
Landlord, holiday tip for, 122

Last Stop Nursin' Home, 111
Lawn decoratin' tips, 18–19
Lemon Cheesecake Pie, Taco Tackle Shack's North Pole, 67
Lights, 11–12, 19, 35, 143, 151–58
Lingerie Christmas party, 58–61
Lip balm, 183
Lip gloss, 185
Lipstick, 38–39
Liquor, 141, 261. *See also* Drinks
Little Drummer Boy Beverage, 166
Living Lake Waters Lutheran Church, 232–36
Lot #1 (Opal Lamb-Brown), 18, 222
  helpful hints, 36
Lot #1 (Willie Dick), 210–16
Lot #2 (Anita Biggon), 194–97
  helpful hints, 36
Lot #3 (Faye Faye LaRue), 74–77
Lot #3 (Hubert and Lois Bunch), 134–39, 222–23
  helpful hints, 62–63
Lot #4 (Nellie Tinkle and Wendy Bottom), x, 232–36
  helpful hints, 63
Lot #5 (Momma and Daddy Boxcar), 30–31, 31, 74–77, 75, 95, 112, 175, 240–43
  helpful hints, 82
Lot #6 (Donna Sue Boxcar), 18, 23, 36, 39, 58, 74–76, 80, 257
  as "Boozy Beaver" on CB, 174–79
  helpful hints, 82
Lot #7 (Pastor Ida May Bee), 231, 252–53
  helpful hints, 101–2
  Inspirational Holiday Thought, xv–xix
Lot #8 (Lulu Bell Button), 12, 111, 223, 252–58
  helpful hints, 120
Lot #9 (Harland and Juanita Hix), 134–39
  helpful hints, 121
Lot #10 (Ollie White), 94–97
  helpful hints, 143
Lot #11 (Kyle and Kitty Chitwood), 112–15, 156–57, 195
  helpful hints, 143

Lot #11 (the Janssens), 95–97
Lot #12 (Sister Bertha Fay Bluemoker),
 x–xi, 39, 84, 134–39, 193, 222–23,
 257–58
 helpful hints, 163
Lot #13 (Connie Kay and Mickey Ray
 and Wanda Ray Kay), 59, 83–85, 84,
 113–15, 135–39, 153, 155
 helpful hints, 163
Lot #14 (Ben Beaver and Dottie Lamb),
 151–58, 222
 helpful hints, 183
Lot #15 (Kenny and Donny), 51–54, 262,
 277–78
 helpful hints, 201
Lot #16 (Me-Ma and Pa-Pa), 77, 111,
 233–36, 267–70
Lot #16 (Momma Ballzak), 263, 267–70
 helpful hints, 221
Lot #17 (Divina Lee LaRue), 74–77
Lot #17 (Tina Faye Stopenblotter),
 helpful hints, 221
Lot #18 (Ruby Ann and Dew), 53, 57, 59,
 60, 80, 93, 112–13
Lot #19 (Vance Pool and the Boys), 24,
 261
 helpful hints, 266
Lot #20 (Little Linda), 30, 173, 193,
 195–97
 helpful hints, 266
 lingerie party, 58–61
Lulu Bell's God Bless Everyone Bisquick
 Puddin' Cookies, 87
Lutherans, the, 232–36

Macaroni Salad, Merry Christmas,
 273–74
Mail carrier, holiday tip for, 123
Maple Ham, Vance Pool's 'Tis the Season,
 46
Marco Polo, 219
Margarine versus butter, 42
Mascara, 103
Mashed Potatoes, Juanita's Momma's,
 228
Matlock (TV show), 201–2
Melba Toast, 194–95

Merry Christmas Macaroni Salad,
 273–74
Mickey Ray's Here Comes Santa Claus
 Sandwich, 169
Mimosas, Christmas, 145
Mincemeat Pie, 286–87
Mistletoe, 18, 185
M&M Bisquick Cookies, 166
Momma Ballzak's Silent Night Whiskey
 Balls, 271–72
Momma Boxcar's I'll Be Home for
 Christmas Honey Buttermilk Bread,
 47–48
Mrs. Claus's Favorite potpourri, 62
Music, 17, 36, 117. *See also* Christmas
 carols

National Rifle Association (NRA), 158
Native American Christmas Corn
 Puddin', 281–82
Nativity scene, 18, 232–36
"Naughty Girl Lingerie" party, 58–61
Nellie's Jolly Old Saint Nicholas Apple
 Chess Pie, 167–68
Newspaper delivery boy, holiday tip for,
 123
Nieve Mexicana Caliente, 244
No Guilt Holiday Fudge, Connie Kay's,
 204–5
North Pole Potluck Christmas Party,
 218–19
No-Sugar Raisin Cookies, Hark! The
 Herald Angels Eat, 146
Nutcracker, 38
Nuttin' for Christmas Carrot Fudge, 246

O Come, All Ye Faithful Pot Roast
 Supper, 129
Office parties, advice for, 37–38, 63–64
Old-Time Baptist Come On, Ring Those
 Bells Buttermilk Chess Pie, 247
Ollie's Baptist Butterscotch Oatmeal
 Cookies, 204
Ollie's Old St. Nick Spam Stuffin', 45–46
Opal's Jingle Bell Rockin' Oatmeal
 Fudge, 272
Opal's Pan Gravy, 228

Opal's Snow Fudge, 44
Open Door Party, 260–64
Orange Eggnog Float, 40
Ornament Exchange, 199
Ornaments, 12, 14, 16
O Tanenbaum Taters, 283
Oven cleanin' tips, 239, 266
Overeatin' at Christmas parties, 221

Pan Gravy, Opal's, 228
Party games. *See* Games
Passover, 42
"Pass the Aqua Net" (game), 80–81
Pastor, holiday tip for, 123
Pastor Ida May Bee's White Chocolate
    Fondue Dip, 119
Pastor's First Noel Pumpkin Fudge,
    106
Peanut Butter Cup Pie, We Wish You a
    Merry Christmas, 246–47
Pentecostal Holiness Church, 236
Peppermint Stick, 142
Personal care professionals, holiday tip
    for, 121–22
Pies. *See also* Chess Pie; Cream Pie
    about, 41–42
    Anita's Bar and Grill up on the
        Housetop Chocolate Buttermilk Pie,
        45
    Chocolate Pecan Pie, 188
    Eggnog Pie, 106–7
    Heard the Bells on Christmas Day
        Brown Sugar Pie, 147–48
    Santa's Soda Cracker Pie, 88–89
    Taco Tackle Shack's North Pole Lemon
        Cheesecake Pie, 67
    We Three Kings Pumpkin Pie, 226
    We Wish You a Merry Christmas
        Peanut Butter Cup Pie, 246–47
Placemats, Christmas Card, 77–78
Poinsettias, 81, 120, 221
Popcorn garland, 13, 36
Pork Chops
    Christmas Day, 285
    Preacher's Peace on Earth, 148
Potato Chips, Ruby Ann's Homemade Joy
    to the World, 69

Potluck, 32, 77, 98, 102, 164
    Bring a Can Party, 141–42
    North Pole Potluck Christmas Party,
        218–19
Potpourri, 34, 201
    Chimney Potpourri, 265
    Christmas Apple Pie, 162
    Christmas in Florida, 81
    Christmas Pumpkin Patch, 220
    helpful hints, 62–63
    It's Beginnin' to Smell a Lot Like
        Christmas, 101
    Mrs. Claus's Favorite, 62
    Peppermint Stick, 142
    Santa's Smell, 120
    Three Wise Men's Stovetop Potpourri,
        182
    Traditional Potpourri, 35
    Workshop Fragrance, 200
Pot Roast Supper, O Come, All Ye
    Faithful, 129
Powder compact, 202–3
Preacher's Peace on Earth Pork Chops,
    148
Prizes, for games, 33
Pumpkin Fudge, Pastor's First Noel, 106
Pumpkin Pie, We Three Kings, 226
Puritans, 143, 163

Quickie Kris Kringle Cookies, 66

Reader's Digest Christmas Tree, 259–60
Real trees, 5, 8–10, 16, 163
Recipes
    about, 41–42
    All I Want for Christmas Is My
        Chocolate Chess Pie, 89
    Anita's Bar and Grill up on the
        Housetop Chocolate Buttermilk Pie,
        45
    Away in the Manger Breakfast Rolls, 43
    Better Than Snow on Christmas
        Chicken-Fried Steak, 227
    Better Than a Glass of Milk and Some
        Cookies Citrus Chess Pie, 273
    Born in a Manger Butterscotch Dip,
        281

Recipes *(cont.)*
  Chocolate Pecan Pie, 188
  Christmas Day Pork Chops, 285
  Christmas Grasshopper Fudge, 147
  Christmas Is Comin' Trailer Park Beef
    Bourguignon, 189–90
  Connie Kay's Attention-Christmas-
    Shoppers Cheesecake Cookie Bars,
    186–87
  Connie Kay's No Guilt Holiday Fudge,
    204–5
  Connie Kay's No Time to Cook 'Cause
    I'm Christmas Shoppin' Hawaiian
    Sandwiches, 68
  Daddy's French Kiss Sleigh Ride
    Cookies, 245–46
  Donna Sue 's Beer Batter Dip, 118
  Dottie's Walkin' in a Winter
    Wonderland Cake Mix Cookies,
    225
  Eggnog Pie, 106–7
  Faye Faye's Fried Christmas Corn Dish
    Delight, 47
  Faye Faye's Sweet Potato Fudge for
    Christmas, 225–26
  Flora Delight's Winter Wonderland
    Rum and Butter Fudge, 127
  Gloria in Excelsis Easy Glazed
    Carrots, 282
  God Rest Ye Merry Gentlemen's Green
    Bean Casserole, 283–84
  Good King Wenceslas' Spam
    Sensation, 206
  Go Tell It on the Mountain Goulash
    Casserole, 274
  Half and Half Cream Pie, 128
  Happy Birthday Jesus Cake, 287–88
  Hark! The Herald Angels Eat No-
    Sugar Raisin Cookies, 146
  Heard the Bells on Christmas Day
    Brown Sugar Pie, 147–48
  Here We Come A-Wassailin' Chicken
    Casserole, 107–8
  Holly Jolly Eggnog Cookies, 43
  I'll Be Ham for Christmas, 284
  Juanita's Momma's Mashed Potatoes,
    228

Kenny and Donny's Easiest Goose in
    Town Christmas Goose, 285–86
  Kenny and Donny's White Chocolate
    Carol of the Bells Fudge, 167
  Kenny Lynn's Creative Chicken
    Wreath, 248
  Kris Kringle's Casserole, 279
  Lamb's I Saw Momma Kissin' Santa
    Claus's Assistant at the Mall Lemon
    Chess Pie, 189
  Lulu Bell's God Bless Everyone
    Bisquick Puddin' Cookies, 87
  Merry Christmas Macaroni Salad,
    273–74
  Mickey Ray's Here Comes Santa Claus
    Sandwich, 169
  Mincemeat Pie, 286–87
  Momma Ballzak's Silent Night
    Whiskey Balls, 271–72
  Momma Boxcar's I'll Be Home for
    Christmas Honey Buttermilk Bread,
    47–48
  Native American Christmas Corn
    Puddin', 281–82
  Nellie's Jolly Old Saint Nicholas Apple
    Chess Pie, 167–68
  Nuttin' for Christmas Carrot Fudge,
    246
  O Come, All Ye Faithful Pot Roast
    Supper, 129
  Old-Time Baptist Come On, Ring Those
    Bells Buttermilk Chess Pie, 247
  Ollie's Baptist Butterscotch Oatmeal
    Cookies, 204
  Ollie's Old St. Nick Spam Stuffin',
    45–46
  Opal's Jingle Bell Rockin' Oatmeal
    Fudge, 272
  Opal's Pan Gravy, 228
  Opal's Snow Fudge, 44
  O Tanenbaum Taters, 283
  Pastor Ida May Bee's White Chocolate
    Fondue Dip, 119
  Pastor's First Noel Pumpkin Fudge,
    106
  Preacher's Peace on Earth Pork Chops,
    148

Quickie Kris Kringle Cookies, 66
Red Ribbons and Silver Bells Beaver Tails, 280
Ruby Ann's Homemade Joy to the World Potato Chips, 69
Santa's Soda Cracker Pie, 88–89
Sister Bertha's O Holy Night Sanctified Sour Cream Fudge, 187
Sweat Scarves of Elvis Fan Club Blue Christmas Cookies, 105
Taco Tackle Shack's North Pole Lemon Cheesecake Pie, 67
Trailer Park Bubble and Squeak, 90
Trailer Park Christmas Cream Pie, 205
Vance Pool's 'Tis the Season Maple Ham, 46
Velveeta Cheese Fudge, 66–67
Wanda's Traditional Trailer Park Bumblebee Christmas Fudge, 88
Wendy's Mistletoe and Holly Rooster Taters, 168
Wendy's Old-Time Let It Snow Sour Cream Cookies, 126
We Three Kings Pumpkin Pie, 226
We Wish You a Merry Christmas Peanut Butter Cup Pie, 246–47
Red Ribbons and Silver Bells Beaver Tails, 280
Reindeer Power Punch, 65
Ruby Ann's Down Home Trailer Park Guide to Livin' Real Good, 64, 80
Ruby Ann's Homemade Joy to the World Potato Chips, 69
Rudolph the Red-Nosed Reindeer, 40
Rum and Butter Fudge, Flora Delight's Winter Wonderland, 127

St. Jude's Ranch for Children, xiv
Salvation Army, 266
Sanka, 141
Santa Cider, 224
Santa Shot, 185
Santa's Pole, 203
Santa's Smell, 120
Santa's Soda Cracker Pie, 88–89
School Christmas parties, 93–94

Seashell Santa, 217–18
Shopping days, busiest, 183
Shotgun Shell Santa, 158–60
Singin' Party, 161
Sister Bertha's O Holy Night Sanctified Sour Cream Fudge, 187
Sledding, 112–15
Slidin' Down Your Chimney, 271
Soda Cracker Pie, Santa's, 88–89
Soda pop bottles, 102
Sour Cream Cookies, Wendy's Old-Time Let It Snow, 126
Sour Cream Fudge, Sister Bertha's O Holy Night Sanctified, 187
Spam Sensation, Good King Wenceslas', 206
Spam Stuffin', Ollie's Old St. Nick, 45–46
Sugar-Free Holiday Nog, 86–87
Sweat Scarves of Elvis Fan Club Blue Christmas Cookies, 105
Sweet Potato Fudge for Christmas, Faye Faye's, 225–26

Taco Tackle Shack, 79, 134–36, 222
Taco Tackle Shack's North Pole Lemon Cheesecake Pie, 67
Thanksgiving Day, 163
Three Cigarettes in the Ashtray Bar, 194
Three Wise Men's Stovetop Potpourri, 182
Tinsel, 14–15
Tips (tipping), 121–24
Tissue Box Cover, Mrs. Claus, 115–16
Toothpicks, 218
Towelettes, alcohol, 183
Toys for Tots, 93, 266
Traditional Potpourri, 35
Trailer Park Bubble and Squeak, 90
Trailer Park Christmas Cream Pie, 205
Trailer Park Christmas Mouse, 179–81
Trailer Park Christmas party, 79–80
Trailer park manager, holiday tip for, 122
Trees. See Christmas trees
Tupperware, 31, 58
Turkey, 74–77
Tweetie Pie, 211, 213–15

Vance Pool's Funeral Center, 261
Vance Pool's 'Tis the Season Maple Ham,
    46
Velveeta Cheese Fudge, 66–67

Wanda's Traditional Trailer Park
    Bumblebee Christmas Fudge,
    88
Wendy's Mistletoe and Holly Rooster
    Taters, 168
Wendy's Old-Time Let It Snow Sour
    Cream Cookies, 126
We Three Kings Pumpkin Pie, 226
We Wish You a Merry Christmas Peanut
    Butter Cup Pie, 246–47

Whiskey Balls, Momma Ballzak's Silent
    Night, 271–72
White Chocolate Fondue Dip, Pastor Ida
    May Bee's, 119
White Christmas (movie), 163
"White Elephant" (game), 33, 181, 182,
    199
White Russian Winter, 65
Whitman samplers, 143–44
Wooden Spoon Reindeer, 26–30
Workshop Fragrance, 200
Wreaths, 35, 143
    Jigsaw Puzzle Wreath, 197–98

Yard decoratin' tips, 18–19